D0209276

Unlock Congress

UNLOCK CONGRESS

REFORM THE RULES • RESTORE THE SYSTEM

Michael Golden

WHY NOT BOOKS

Pacific Grove, California

Why Not Books
831 Spruce Avenue
Pacific Grove, CA 93950
www.WhyNotBooks.com

Grateful acknowledgment is made to Fairvote.org
for permission to reprint Figures 7.1 – 7.4.

Cover and interior design by Tessa Avila
Copy edited by John Deever

FIRST EDITION

10 9 8 7 6 5 4 3 2 1

Library of Congress Control Number 2014959208

ISBN 978-0-984-99198-3

While the author has made every effort to provide accurate Internet addresses at the time of publication, neither the author nor the publisher is responsible for errors or for changes that occur after publication. Further, the publisher does not have any control over and does not assume any responsibility for author or third-party websites or their content.

Join the movement to reform the rules, restore the system, and unlock the U.S. Congress. Please visit **www.unlockcongress.com** for more information.

Printed with soy inks
Printed in the United States of America

Dedicated to the memory of Fred Cohen, dear friend and authentic hero. You always took an active interest, and you were always interested in seeing me become more active.

Contents

Note to Readers

As the Table of Contents demonstrates, this book consists of two major parts. Readers who already feel like they have a firm grasp on Congress's powers and purpose, as well as the damage being wrought by the faulty congressional *product,* have the option of jumping straight ahead to Part II, where a breakdown of the *problem* begins. Chapters 5 and 6 present a discussion of various causes and effects at the heart of our congressional mess, and then Chapter 7 follows with a *platform* of corresponding solutions.

If, however, you're one of the many Americans who hasn't been following politics quite so closely and can't remember all that civics stuff they tried to cram into our brains during middle school, Part I is the perfect entry point. Take a brief trip through U.S. political history, starting with public opinion over the years about Congress, then tracing back further to the legendary debates and decisions that set up our legislative branch, and then back again to the present and beyond—a big picture of the relative state of our nation on the issues that Americans say matter most.

Preamble

Instead of being the world's greatest example of
representative government, we seem to have become
the nation's largest kindergarten—only with control
of the nation's checkbook and nuclear arsenal.

U.S. Rep. Mark Pocan (D-WI)[1]

We're talking about building roads and bridges for
Christ's sake. We're not talking about big Democratic
and Republican initiatives ... But more than being an
embarrassment to the House of Representatives, it was
indicative of the fact that people are more interested in
fighting with each other than they are in getting the
no-brainers done and governing.

Former U.S. Rep. Steven LaTourette (R-OH)[2]

I t was a split-second decision. It was also the last one U.S. Army Captain Jennifer Moreno would ever make. A trained nurse from San Diego, Moreno had volunteered for a particularly dangerous assignment in Afghanistan. On October 5, 2013, she and dozens of special operators approached a bomb-making compound in Kandahar. The Army later revealed that its mission was to thwart an attack that "would have resulted in the deaths of unknown multitudes of innocent civilians." What the soldiers encountered was a compound that was booby-trapped and occupied by insurgents who were determined not to be taken alive.

Moments after being told to surrender, an Afghan woman walked out wearing a suicide vest. She detonated the explosive, killing herself and setting off a second blast nearby. Six U.S. soldiers were wounded. When two more soldiers rushed to help them, they inadvertently set off a third bomb. Seconds later, another Afghan insurgent detonated a fourth device.

It was then that Moreno heard two conflicting orders. One came from a staff sergeant, directing her to assist her injured comrades. The other was from the ground commander, who ordered all members of the unit to wait in their positions. The language in Moreno's Bronze Star commendation reveals what happened next: "Disregarding her own well-being, Moreno unhesitatingly moved to assist (the soldiers) upon realizing the severity of the wounds sustained by her fellow teammates."

Tragically, the Bronze Star was a posthumous honor. As she was rushing in to provide aid, Moreno detonated a fifth bomb. The explosion killed her.

In all, twelve blasts would rock the compound that day. More than two dozen soldiers were wounded; four of them lost their lives. The sixth and seventh bombs delivered fatal wounds to Sergeant Patrick Hawkins and Specialist Cody Patterson. The eighth and ninth explosions killed Special Agent Joseph Peters. It took an arriving force of twenty soldiers—several of whom were injured by subsequent blasts, one of them even crawling forward and sweeping the earth for mines with his hands—to retrieve the bodies of the fallen. It was a scene of tragedy and courage, one that brought out the best in America's bravest.

In a eulogy for Moreno, Captain Amanda King, the commander of her Special Operations support team, marveled at how the 25-year-old ran "into hell to save your wounded brothers, knowing full well you probably wouldn't make it back." Moreno refused to leave her comrades behind, just as her fellow soldiers refused to leave her. They brought her body home.[3]

But back home, Americans were watching their elected representatives engage in a pitiful display not worthy of our courageous warriors. A congressional squabble was, in a very real way, leaving the families of the soldiers behind. Earlier in the week, the U.S. Congress had failed to pass legislation to continue funding the operation of our government. So in the days following the soldiers' deaths, the families were told that they would not receive $100,000 "death benefits" dictated by U.S. law. These funds are meant to cover funeral expenses and families' travel to Dover Air Force Base, where their loved ones' coffins were unloaded.

According to Moreno's Bronze Star commendation, she "sacrificed her life so others could live." But the sacrifices of Moreno and her comrades were sullied by Congress's inability to compromise. The shutdown meant that a private foundation had to voluntarily swoop in and provide funds to the families—with the hope of the U.S. paying back the loan when the government reopened its doors.[4] "The government is hurting the wrong people," said Shannon Collins, mother of a fifth soldier who died in a separate incident that fateful weekend, Marine Lance Corporal Jeremiah Collins Jr. "Families shouldn't have to worry about how they're going to bury their child."[5]

U.S. Senator John McCain (R–AZ), who endured more than five years as a prisoner of war in Vietnam, agreed. In a speech on the Senate floor, McCain railed: "Shouldn't we as a body—Republican or Democrat—shouldn't we be embarrassed? Ashamed? What do American people think when they see that death benefit for those who served and sacrifice—they're not eligible? I'm ashamed! I'm embarrassed. All of us should be."[6]

And most of us are. A record number of Americans have come to believe that Congress is a disgrace—worse than it has ever been, a Washington version of the Bermuda Triangle where good ideas and best intentions go to die. Gallup began its polling on the U.S. Congress in 1973. That year, one year before Richard Nixon resigned the presidency, Congress registered its highest ever rating of public confidence at 42 percent. On

June 4, 2013, forty years later, the same Gallup question pinpointed Americans' confidence at *10 percent.* This was the lowest favorable rating ever recorded on this question by Gallup, landing it dead last out of sixteen institutions graded in the survey.[7] One year later, during the summer of 2014, Congress tallied yet another record low in the Gallup poll: 7 percent.[8] Mathematically, there is very little downward space left to explore.

These numbers represent far more than simply a snapshot of national disappointment in Congress. Huge challenges confront the country, and relying on our legislative branch to help solve them feels like the equivalent of asking WWE wrestlers to ratify international peace accords.

This is not because we don't have good men and women serving in Congress. A great many representatives from both political parties work hard every day in honest efforts to strengthen America. But in recent years, members of Congress have found themselves increasingly handcuffed. Their shackles? Glaring flaws in the process. The ever-expanding obstacles in the system make it incredibly difficult for our leaders to achieve the kind of consensus that leads to meaningful results. Politics has always been a messy business in our country, but the "means to an end" argument no longer holds up—because the *end product* has become impossible to justify.

Of course, criticizing Congress is the easy part. Bashing the performance of our elected representatives has become a national pastime. The crucible lies in answering the hard questions that hold the keys to unlocking the U.S. Congress and resolving our current crisis of government:

- Does Congress still matter enough for us to care about it?
- As Americans, are we reasonably entitled to expect a better *product* from our legislative branch?
- In what specific ways is Congress failing? Can we identify the causes?
- Once we understand the defects that are driving the poor product, what concrete changes can we push for as a citizenry to improve the system?

The importance of answering these questions cannot be underestimated. Yes, Congress still matters—enormously. But in the grand scheme, it is we as Americans who matter far more. So many of us in recent years have become used to watching Congress fail. But we should not feebly accept such failure as the new normal. A public pact exists in our country between our elected leaders and we the people. Our nation's founders set forth Congress's powers and purpose in the Constitution, and these powers have been repeatedly confirmed and further defined throughout our history. That pact will be the theme that drives this book: As taxpaying American citizens governed by the rule of law, we are owed a reasonable level of effectiveness from the U.S. Congress—*a worthy product.* We all know we are not receiving one. Congress's inability to uphold its end of the contract is hurting our country. We must take action to stop the bleeding.

To accomplish our goal—to make it possible for Congress to offer us a worthy product—we will first need to grasp exactly how that legislative body's failures are negatively affecting our daily lives, and why. We'll need to dig deeper to see the ways in which the United States is falling behind and what that means for Americans. A shared understanding of how Congress's problems contribute to our national pain will ultimately motivate and empower us to steer the system back onto the rails.

The legislators quoted atop this chapter are far from lone voices in their criticisms. They are members of a growing chorus of both incumbent and former lawmakers who firmly believe that the House and Senate have crossed a line. For years now, Americans have grown accustomed to using words like "gridlocked" and "dysfunctional" to describe the constant brinksmanship and ridiculously slow pace of progress in Congress. But we have reached a new threshold, where people both inside and outside the system know that it is deteriorating. The results are blunt inaction on some issues and counterproductive legislation on others, as well as careless oversight. Such poor performance is diminishing the quality of our everyday lives. It is causing the U.S. to regress in the world. It is simply unsustainable.

Congress's substandard work product makes Americans feel even more cynical about their representatives—and that disdain is becoming ingrained. A poll conducted toward the end of the 112th Congressional session by the nonpartisan Center on Congress broke down the negative opinion. Survey participants were asked: "What do you think is the main thing that influences what members of Congress do in office?" The largest group, at 49 percent, chose the answer "special interests," followed by 36 percent who selected "personal self-interest." Only 14 percent believed that their representative was influenced by what would be best for the people in their state, district, or the country.[9]

Political scholars agree about the depressed state that we have reached, and they speak from decades of close observation. Norman Ornstein and Thomas Mann have been studying and writing about the U.S. Congress since the 1960s. In their 2012 book *It's Even Worse Than It Looks*, they described a new level of acrimony and dysfunction in Congress, as well as what it means for Americans:

> The single-minded focus on scoring political points over solving problems, escalating over the last several decades, has reached a level of such intensity and bitterness that the government seems incapable of taking and sustaining public decisions responsive to the existential challenges facing the country ... the country is squandering its economic future and putting itself at risk because of an inability to govern effectively.[10]

Former U.S. Representative Mickey Edwards (R) has a similar view and speaks from sixteen years representing Oklahoma inside the belly of the beast. Edwards left the House in 1993. Twenty years after his retirement, he described a different Congress than the one in which he had served:

> What we thought was a democratic government made up of leaders committed to the national good has turned into a new form of contact sport, an attempt to score more points than the other team by any means possible. Meanwhile, our bridges grow old and collapse, our banks and investment houses pursue policies that cripple our economy, and we become ever more dependent on Chinese money.[11]

Across the aisle, in early 2010, U.S. Senator Evan Bayh (D-IN) announced he would not run for another term. A former governor, Bayh could no longer stomach being part of a Congress where inaction was the norm. Explaining his decision to put Washington in the rearview mirror, Bayh said:

> For some time, I have had a growing conviction that Congress is not operating as it should. There is too much partisanship and not enough progress—too much narrow ideology and not enough practical problem solving. Even at a time of enormous challenge, the people's business is not being done.[12]

These are just a few witnesses testifying to the backwards process that plays out daily in the nation's capital. We will hear from many more. But the consensus is indisputable. The American people, congressional scholars, even many elected representatives inside the beltway know full well that a malignancy has taken root in Congress.

This shared opinion—nearly unanimous—is the first reason that we should be concerned. When only one in ten Americans has a favorable view of our government, that belief has an inverse impact on our participation: the worse we feel about Congress, the less power we feel we have to change it. And when we think of ourselves as helpless individuals instead of parts of a greater whole, we become apathetic. Indifference is truly the greatest threat to democracy. Every private and public effort to advance collective goals throughout our history has been sparked and fueled by individual citizens first caring, then coming together, then working together. Common endeavor will never be obsolete in our country—unless we allow it to be.

The second and equally important reason why every American should still care about the state of Congress may seem obvious, but it is something we often lose sight of. Among the federal government's three branches, Congress has the most power vested in it by our Constitution. Beyond the fact that only Congress can remove a president or Supreme Court justice, it is the place where our laws are written and passed. Congress is the sole branch with the power to tax and appropriate; to collect and spend our money. It is also responsible for the oversight of a huge portion of our government.

Still, to most Americans, the federal government seems like a massive bureaucracy that doesn't work properly. The U.S. Congress looks like an exclusive insiders' club where childish arguments are the order of the day, every day. So why should we pay close attention to all of this endless negotiation that seems to lead nowhere? Why should we take precious time out of our days to learn about Congress and its problems? Why bother?

The reason is that the laws that Congress enacts matter far more in our everyday lives than we sometimes realize. As an increasingly interconnected world keeps changing at what seems like light speed, the laws passed by our legislators arguably become even more meaningful. Is our nation's infrastructure solid? Are our children receiving a quality education? Is college affordable? Will a degree lead to a job? Are we safe as a nation? Are we taking care of the U.S. veterans who sacrifice on our behalf? Do we have an efficient health care system? What about our privacy? Taxes? Retirement security? National debt? Congress's inbox is an ever-changing list of complex challenges that never gets shorter. These issues affect us all.

We need not look far to find examples writ large of pain inflicted on the country caused in part by Congress's inability to negotiate and pass effective public policy. In December 2014, six years after the economic crash and bank bailouts, financial experts and leaders from both parties in the U.S. Senate insisted that "too big to fail" still exists and that taxpayers are still at risk.[13] Even before the crash, between 2001 and 2007, 98 percent of all income gains in our country accrued to the wealthiest 10 percent.[14] Three months prior to the 2014 midterm elections, a *Wall Street Journal* poll revealed that 71 percent of Americans blamed the country's economic problems "more on Washington leaders than on any deeper economic trends."[15]

Social Security and Medicare have traditionally provided a cushion for our senior citizens, but the trust funds in those federal programs are projected to face shortages in less than twenty-five years.[16] Meanwhile, the Pew Research Center and the U.S. Bureau of Labor tell us that the more than *85 million* "Millennials," those born between 1982 and 2000, are "the first in the modern era to have higher levels of student loan debt, poverty, and unemployment, and lower levels of wealth and personal income than their two immediate predecessor generations (Gen Xers and Boomers) had at the same stage of their life cycles."[17] The Great Recession and protracted recovery that followed produced punishing effects on an already squeezed middle class. Even as employers increased hiring toward the end of 2014, wage growth remained historically low—just enough to keep pace with inflation.[18]

Despite increased access to insurance, the health care system in America is exorbitantly priced and riddled with inefficiencies. An average hospital stay in the United States costs nearly three times that of one in other developed nations. We also lead the pack with the highest annual health care cost per person. And even as we spend far more, we actually trail many of those same countries in life expectancy. The U.S. carries the highest rate of preventable deaths.[19]

Certainly the executive branch shoulders a large share of the federal government's responsibility to function productively. And of course Congress requires the President's signature to pass any piece of legislation. But paralysis, and in some cases incompetence, is perceived to be far more prevalent in Congress. Amid the shutdowns of the federal government in 1995 and 2013, Americans blamed the failure on the opposition party in Congress versus the President—by more than 20 percent.[20] Many pin the blame for the disgraceful performance of our representatives on whichever political party is in control. But Congress receives a terrible grade from its constituents no matter who is in charge of the chambers, and that includes one-party rule, as we will examine. Americans have made up their minds.

It is easy to become somewhat numb to these consistent letdowns. But there is a critically important fact in this picture that is often forgotten: Congress actually owes us better. Our representatives are obligated to deliberate, negotiate, and pass public policies that are designed to "promote the general welfare." Many members of Congress want to work in a constructive fashion toward this goal—but they can't. Not anymore. And one big reason is because we have a set of counterproductive *rules* in Congress that have fostered a *defective system.*

BREAKDOWN

It's a word that is now used so often to describe Congress that it has become a tired cliché: "broken." But it sure is broken.

When parents have a suspicion that one of their children has broken something, they will sometimes offer a "Get Out of Jail Free" card. "Tell us what you did, and we promise we won't be angry or punish you. We just want to know what happened." Without having any scary consequences to worry about, the child can now tell the real tale.

The same bargaining also happens in criminal prosecutions. A suspect has broken the law, but because that person is not the main target of the investigation, he will receive a grant of immunity in exchange for telling the whole story. "Tell us what you know, and we'll cut you a break. You're just a guppy in this crooked scheme, and we want to net the big fish."

Well, it's actually a similar case in national politics. In the U.S. Congress and in our nation's capital, people inside the warped system are well aware of what is going on, but there's little chance of them voluntarily calling a penalty on themselves and *changing the rules*—right in the middle of the game. Not when the consequences would conflict with their ambitions, or for that matter, their survival. But once they've exited the system? That's when the truth starts to spill—not to mention a curiously sudden sense of urgency.

It all starts with the absurd amounts of money politicians must chase down to get into the game—and stay in it. A record high sum was spent on congressional elections in 2014: more than $3.7 billion.[21] Just how serious a problem is all that cash? Tim Wirth (D-CO) will tell you. Wirth served in the U.S. House and Senate from 1975 to 1993. His throat is very clear as he describes the ka-chinging in Congress:

> A lot of people up on Capitol Hill know that it's very poisonous, very corruptive to your system. So I left, that was twenty years ago, that was kids' play compared to what goes on now ... Extortion's one part of it. Bankruptcy is another part of it. Getting paid for political outcomes is a way of describing it. It's basically corrupt.

It is legalized corruption. And people aren't going to say that. They will recoil when you say it, but it's true.[22]

Next we have the obstacle of two-year terms in the U.S. House of Representatives—tiny time windows within which members of Congress must juggle greatly increased responsibilities, always with the specter of the next election lurking around the corner. In 1789, congressional districts housed roughly 30,000 constituents. Today: more than 700,000. Five decades ago, both President Dwight D. Eisenhower and President Lyndon B. Johnson lamented the anachronism of the two-year House term. In his memoirs, Eisenhower explained:

Through the years, government has grown in size and has proliferated into many activities that were undreamed of when the nation was young. Sessions of Congress grow longer. If a congressman is to do his job well these days, he simply cannot be forever running for re-election. Yet this is what the two-year terms compel him to do.[23]

Then there are the rules that permit the rigging of House elections, reducing fair and effective representation in Congress. This problem starts, but by no means ends, with the runaway political practice of "gerrymandering" congressional districts. Rahm Emanuel, former U.S. Representative (D-IL) and former chair of the Democratic Congressional Campaign Committee, describes how it works:

The House of Representatives is set up for the voters to pick their representatives. Through redistricting, and through technology, representatives now pick their voters! So the system is now turned upside down ... And I say this as a person who practiced those dark arts. It's wrong ... And that does skew the system.[24]

Emanuel is right that the manipulation of district boundaries distorts the number of seats "won" by each party—which does not accurately reflect the choices we make on the ballot. We should find that revolting in a democracy where we are told "one person equals one vote." But our election format also largely operates on rules that advance one candidate from each party in the primaries, leaving voters with a narrow, left–right choice in the general election. Because our House races are winner-take-all contests in single-member congressional districts, a ton of our votes go unrepresented. U.S. Rep. James Clyburn (D–SC), a twenty-year House veteran, explains why this rules system is way past its time:

> I sincerely believe it to be the primary cause for voter apathy. By giving all the power to a candidate who may only receive a plurality of the votes depresses voter participation and increases voter disenchantment ... Winner-take-all means candidates can get less than 40 percent of the vote and their supporters still get 100 percent of the representation.[25]

In a country that has become far more politically polarized along geographical lines, the rigged nature of our winner-take-all elections weakens the political center and makes a mockery of fair representation in the U.S. House.

And finally we have the filibuster rule, which has allowed a minority of senators to consistently lock down the U.S. Senate. Former Senator Robert Dole (R–KS) is a good person to ask about it. As Senate minority leader, Dole used the filibuster all the time to hold up bills, even those supported by majorities in both chambers. In 1993–1994, he used a record-high number of blocking tactics—more than had been used in total between 1917 and 1970. But after watching both parties shatter his record in recent years to freeze the government, Dole changed his tune. On his 90th birthday, he announced: "There are things that should be stopped, but at least there ought to be a vote. It can't continue, this constant holding up bills."[26] Ah, the wisdom of experience.

The collective use and abuse of these wrongheaded rules have spawned an unprecedented degree of paralysis in Congress that now inflicts damage on our country. The Senate has not operated on the principle of majority rule for decades. House members are caged in a constant reelection campaign, leaving little time or latitude for effective governing. They are forced to make nearly every decision from the short-term perspective of how it will affect their chances of hanging onto their jobs. Our nation's founders originally created two-year terms in order to keep members of Congress close to the concerns of the people. But that rule was created more than two centuries ago, and over time our country has changed immensely. The demographics have changed. The media landscape has changed. The whopping financial cost of running campaigns has changed, both in the Senate and in "The People's House." It all adds up to a skewed system that spits out a faulty product.

Of course, it should be self-evident that our government is not single-handedly responsible for solving all of the country's problems. But using the guidelines passed down from our nation's founders, combined with a wealth of experience from our shared history as Americans, we know that most of our current and future challenges *can be positively impacted* by the laws Congress passes. The argument for a better government is nonpartisan and nonideological. No matter where one falls on the political spectrum or whether one favors a larger or smaller government, it is only logical for each of us to want a reasonably mature and effective U.S. Congress. We don't have it.

RECOURSE

It was not always thus. The U.S. Constitution, ratified in 1788, still stands out as an extraordinary historical achievement. It is easy to be awestruck by what our country's prescient founders created when they set up our system of government. The fact that our Constitution has served us well for more than two centuries, and that we have felt it necessary to add only 27 amendments, is impressive by any measure. But we must never forget that these leaders did not have all the answers. They had proudly pronounced in the Declaration of Independence that "all men are created equal" with "certain unalienable rights, that among these are life, liberty and the pursuit of happiness." Yet that "equality" was unmistakably denied to black Americans and to women by the Constitution. The authors of the Constitution may have been great thinkers, but they were far from perfect. They were not divine seers, and they knew it.

The irony is that the founders cautioned their contemporaries as well as future generations about the very perils of factionalism, runaway political parties, and the growing scourge of undue influence that we have been witnessing for years. They wanted elected leaders of good will to be able to disagree, but to not allow their divisions or personal ambitions to negate their capacity to negotiate in good faith and achieve progress for the nation.

James Madison, known as the "father" of the Constitution, wrote in 1788: "The aim of every political constitution is, or ought to be, first to obtain for rulers men who possess most wisdom to discern, and most virtue to pursue, the common good of the society; and in the next place, to take the most effectual precautions for keeping them virtuous whilst they continue to hold their public trust."[27] The rules in today's system do not encourage virtue.

The framers had assiduously studied the history of the world's governments and knew there would be challenges far into the future that they could not possibly foresee. But that is the good news. Because of their concerns, they intentionally created procedural options to remedy major drawbacks in our system when they arose. As citizens, if we determine that our system of government is no longer equipped to provide us a quality product—to effectively promote our general welfare—we have recourse available to us. We can exercise our citizen warranty and push to change the rules. Our founders foresaw these scenarios.

And there is more good news. A growing political middle in America is starting to voice its discontent with political extremism, as well as its support for practical solutions. Such a development may seem at odds with the screechy partisan divide we hear in the Capitol and the highly visible, nasty election campaigns that draw most of the media attention. But a huge percentage of Americans are sick of the shouting and the stubbornness—and their minds are somewhat open when it comes to politics and reform.

In 2013, the opposing lead pollsters who had worked for President Barack Obama and former Governor Mitt Romney teamed up with NBC News and *Esquire* to do a broad survey about politics in America. One of those pollsters, Daniel Franklin of the Benenson Group, summarized their findings: "All you hear in Washington is that there's nothing in the middle of the aisle ... but it turns out that's not true. We have a massive American center, and it's probably been there for years, just waiting to be found."[28]

Specifically, polling about the "New American Center" found that 58 percent of voters often agree with ideas from both Republicans and Democrats alike. At the same time, 49 percent agree that our two-party system is broken and obsolete. An equal percentage acknowledged having no faith in politicians due to constantly being disappointed by them. Perhaps most interesting in the survey, 54 percent of Americans agreed with the statement: "After 230 years, the Constitution can't provide guidance for many of the problems we face now."[29]

These opinions matter a great deal, but unless backed up by action, the "New American Center" will not get very far. And generally the most fervent political passions in our electoral landscape lie mostly on the fringes. Even if the center could agree on what changes we need to make, it is currently too passive to be a real force for reform.

This lack of intensity is terribly important, and it's the first big challenge that will be undertaken on the following pages. Ironically, Americans who at first blush may be unlikely to read this book are also an important part of the constituency that will be essential to achieving the reforms proposed here. Political extremists and their purchasers have been holding onto the power for too long, but that should not, and does not, have to last forever. Not if we can energize the "New American Center."

In order to jolt the system, we'll need to lock in on a common motivator. We begin with a clear understanding of Congress's responsibilities and obligations under our constitutional system, and the specific ways in which its failures are harming the country—the congressional **product.** Once this basis has been established, we will then be ready to take the second step of understanding the **problems** that plague our defective system. Analysis of the breakdown will lead directly to a **platform** of solutions designed to unlock Congress—a platform that every American will have the opportunity to support.

We must reform the rules to restore the system. There are options available to us. Our country's founders provided them for an express purpose. We have exercised them many times before. It is time for us to exercise them once again.

Part One

1 The Passion

Passion rebuilds the world for the youth. It makes all things alive and significant.

Ralph Waldo Emerson

We speak not strictly and philosophically when we talk of the combat of passion and of reason. Reason is, and ought only to be the slave of the passions, and can never pretend to any other office than to serve and obey them.

David Hume

T hrough the votes we cast and the tax dollars we pay, we elect and compensate members of the U.S. Congress. Because the law actually requires the majority of us to pay for our government, what Congress delivers in return is akin to a product. And Americans can't stand that product.

The poor quality of the performance we see in Congress is not for lack of time spent trying. In 2011–2012, the Republican-controlled House and Democrat-controlled Senate were in session for more days than they had been in any congressional session over the previous thirty years.[1] Yet, that 112th Congress enacted 283 public laws, the fewest passed since the birth of the statistic back in 1947. In 2013–14, the 113th Congress managed to nudge that figure up to 296—the second lowest total.[2] By comparison, the "Do-Nothing Congress" of 1948, infamously nicknamed by President Harry Truman, passed 906 bills into law.[3]

Of course, the total number of laws enacted is hardly the only measure of legislative effectiveness. In fact, many Americans actually prefer that even fewer laws be passed. But either way, we are collectively disgusted with the work of our representatives. Recent polls have revealed the lowest levels of public confidence in Congress in four decades. And in 2014, 74 percent of Americans believed that Congress was "unproductive"—with 50 percent labeling its work as "very unproductive."[4]

So the broad answer to our first important question—"Why should we still care about the state of the U.S. Congress?"—is that we should because it is not delivering the kind of quality product we are paying for. Rather, it is providing a product that is defective and harmful.

It is true that our founding fathers did not set up our system of government, and especially Congress, to run efficiently and arrive at big decisions quickly. On the contrary, they purposely created a system that would foster measured deliberation and steer clear of any sudden, dangerous moves. In this way, the founders sought a legislative branch that would operate in a manner rational and responsible enough to serve the people well. In making the case for creating Congress, and advocating for passage of the Constitution, James Madison wrote in 1788, "No government, any more than an individual, will long be respected without being truly respectable; nor be truly respectable, without possessing a certain portion of order and stability."[5]

Today, though, we see a childish Congress bickering on a daily basis, governing by crisis, and holding very little "respectability" at all in the eyes of Americans—including many of our very own incumbent representatives. The epic level of failure in the House and the Senate is not just about conservatism or liberalism—it is about a lack of pragmatism. Concepts like negotiation and compromise, upon which our legislative process has historically been based, now seem nearly extinct.

It is often observed that our country is politically divided. We will investigate this fact as we move deeper into our analysis. But the problem we are facing stretches beyond the battle between red states and blue states. Structural defects within the system play a major role in the constipation of our Congress. Thankfully, we have political and constitutional avenues available to us through which we can repair these breaches, if we care enough to do so. We *should* care, as the stakes could not be much higher. It will take time, effort, and education. It will also take passion.

GET A LITTLE MAD

In 1976, the searing satire *Network* hit American movie screens, and it would go on to win four Academy Awards. One went to screenwriter Paddy Chayefsky—his third Oscar in the category. Another was awarded to Peter Finch for his best actor portrayal of a fictional network television anchor named Howard Beale.

Beale is fed up with the news business and even more irritated by the problems gripping the country. He is so outraged that he no longer cares about network protocol. The anchorman lets loose in a series of improvised on-air rants—first putting him in a vice with his corporate bosses, then, ironically, turning him into a national sensation. In the movie's classic scene, Beale scowls from behind his anchor desk, lamenting the sorry state of the nation—the busted banks, the gun-toting shopkeepers, the violent crime, the recession, the inflation, the Russians. And then his voice rises menacingly as he stalks toward the newsroom camera:

All I know is that first you've got to get mad. You've got to say, "I'm a *human being,* God damn it! My life has *value!*" So I want you to get up now. I want all of you to get up out of your chairs. I want you to get up right now and go to the window. Open it, and stick your head out, and yell, *"I'm as mad as hell, and I'm not going to take this any more!"* I want you to get up right now, sit up, go to your windows, open them, and stick your head out and yell—"I'm as mad as hell and I'm not going to take this any more!" Things have got to change. But first, you've gotta get mad![6]

As soon as Beale is done, we see people opening up their windows across American cities and yelling out the complaint exactly as he instructed them to. Chayefsky's words touched something deep in popular culture in that moment, and four decades later we can still hear the catchphrase being recited from time to time by pols, protesters, and people who are just plain exasperated. After all, each of us knows what it feels like to be at our wit's end watching what seems like a world spinning out of control.

Of course, we can all agree that screaming our anger aimlessly in public is not a very effective way of dealing with life's daily frustrations. But when a great number of voices come together to express collective anguish, the sound becomes powerful. Throughout American history, many of our most consequential political movements for justice and change have been born out of a deeply felt sense of righteous indignation.

Organized, passionate outrage is how our country was founded in the first place. Were it not for the bravery and sacrifice of the Revolutionary War generation, discussions about our rights and the government's responsibility to its citizens might never have been possible. That same passion, balanced by a great deal of reason and collaboration, led to the ratification of the U.S. Constitution. Great intellectual debates continued in the years following ratification, but modern historians now take note of the fervently held beliefs that powered political life in the 1790s. In one of his many books and articles about the American Revolution, historian Marshall Smelser dubbed this decade "The Age of Passion."[7]

From that starting point, we can clearly look back at the battles that Americans waged and won by pressuring the government to act during the most turbulent times in our country's history. Some of these victories took far too long in hindsight, but still the United States achieved the abolition of slavery, women's suffrage, civil rights, workers' rights, and other milestones that promoted enormous civic advances. They all began with groups of individuals feeling collectively ignored, abused, oppressed—often all of the above. Pain has the power to generate passion, and passion becomes high-octane fuel for action.

Decades later, many of the observations in Howard Beale's rant still ring true. When we remove a couple of historical references, many of the same challenges still resonate today—and some seem even more formidable.

During that same year, 1976, Jimmy Carter was elected to his only term as president. In 1979 Carter delivered his "Crisis of Confidence" speech. The national television address also came to be known as the "malaise" speech, although that word was never actually spoken. In it, among other things, Carter bemoaned inflation, recession, the decline of American workers' productivity, and the urgent crisis of that time: the energy shortage. Speaking directly to the issue, the president criticized Washington and specifically the Democratic-controlled Congress:

> Looking for a way out of this crisis, our people have turned to the federal government and found it isolated from the mainstream of our nation's life. Washington, D.C., has become an island. The gap between our citizens and our government has never been so wide. The people are looking for honest answers, not easy answers; clear leadership, not false claims and evasiveness and politics as usual ... What you see too often in Washington and elsewhere around the country is a system of government that seems incapable of action. You see a Congress twisted and pulled in every direction by hundreds of well-financed and powerful special interests ... You see every extreme position defended to the last vote, almost to the last breath by one unyielding group or another.[8]

Throughout his presidency, Carter's party controlled Congress with strong majorities in both the House and Senate. The year he gave this speech, Gallup tracked public confidence in Congress at 34 percent.[9] Surely this was an awful number, *but it was still almost five times higher than the 2014 rating of 7 percent.* We have traveled a humiliating distance downward. Some may point to leadership in the executive branch or the controlling political party of the moment as the culprit, but as the voice of the people will demonstrate in the next chapter, Congress gets a failing grade regardless.

In late 2012, during one of the recent doomsday debates in D.C. over our nation's debt limit, *New York Times* columnist David Brooks summed up the state of affairs:

> What's happening in Washington right now is pathetic. When you think about what the Revolutionary generation did, what the Civil War generation did, what the World War generation did—we're asking not to bankrupt our children and we've got a shambolic, dysfunctional process.[10]

So if this "dysfunctional process" is at an all-time low, why doesn't our dissatisfaction drive the same kind of passionately focused movement for change as the ones described above? If our own Congress fills us with distrust and disgust, why don't we care enough to band together and do something about it?

It may very well be because the kind of fights Brooks cites are far more personal and straightforward in nature. Movements to defend a nation, or to struggle for fair treatment and equal rights, are directly related to definitive parts of a person's life or a community's identity. These missions are often based on an easily understood sense of personal injustice. The stakeholders have a common stake. Civil rights and suffrage are among the most high-profile examples of this point. When persecution or undue hardship is experienced personally, it can be a rallying cry that activates great collective strength.

Hilbert Bradley was someone who knew this kind of persecution. As a young African-American growing up in the 1920s in the tiny town of Repton, Alabama, Bradley saw it all around him: "It was very segregated during those times and I would go to the movies and watched those court-room lawyers. Watching them in the movies sparked a fire."[11]

During World War II, Bradley put his college studies on hold to enlist in the Army. But following the war, he kept after his dream and in 1950 broke a barrier by becoming the first African-American law school graduate at Valparaiso University. Then he put his degree to work.

Bradley served as counsel in landmark civil rights cases, and in 1957 he lobbied Congress to pass the Civil Rights Act. In 1963, Hilbert Bradley led a delegation from his adopted home city of Gary, Indiana, to join Rev. Martin Luther King Jr. and more than 200,000 other Americans in the March on Washington.

But Bradley didn't slow down after civil rights legislation was passed. He kept fighting, and in 1987 he founded the Indiana Coalition for Black Judicial Officials. The coalition achieved its first victory three years later, with the election of Bernard Carter to the Superior Court bench. Later, Bradley himself became a judge.

Hilbert Bradley never stopped standing up for what he believed in and stayed active until the day of his passing on October 13, 2013. He was 93 years old. The next day a *Chicago Sun-Times* headline proclaimed: "Civil Rights Advocate Bradley Had Passion For Justice."[12] Although not a famous or hallowed name like others we recognize from the civil rights era, Brad-ley's story reinforces the age-old lesson that one person truly can make a difference. And when a very large number of people get on board—all rowing in the same direction—there is virtually no limit to how far the movement can travel.

At the same time, issue-specific personal passion for change is dif-ferent from mustering up the motivation to push for broad reforms in a system of government. American disappointment with Congress is far more sprawling and impersonal in nature compared with a scenario in which a great number of us are feeling aggrieved about a single, high-pro-file problem.

Congress itself is a large and complicated entity that has the respon-sibility of overseeing even larger bureaucracies. Our complaints about it are varied and vast. We dislike so much about the institution that it can be overwhelming. Without a common and focused passion, it is hard to reform any established organization, and particularly one as entrenched as our nation's legislative branch.

But this is precisely the point. Because in this case we are not relying on the power of a single-issue grievance to bind us together, we must arrive at a common understanding of just how profoundly Congress is failing us across the board—and how much it hurts. Later, in Part II of this book, we will be investigating the problems that directly contribute to the congressional mess, followed by recommendations on how to fix it. *But our first big goal in this process is to establish a shared and definitive understanding that the product we are paying for is substandard—and harmful.* We need to know just what we are entitled to expect from Congress, and just what we are receiving.

The next three chapters will define and explain the two major ways that the U.S. Congress is failing the American people:

1. Americans have an overwhelming lack of confidence in Congress, which erodes our civic participation and, in turn, our ability to repair the problem.
2. The defective product that Congress delivers is damaging the quality of life for the American people.

We all have ample reason to feel a real sense of Howard Beale's outrage. This is *our* country. And the colossal failings of the Congress should make us mad as hell and unwilling to take it any more. If we can take that disappointment and more specifically define it, we will then be equipped to passionately coalesce around it. We will have the power to speak with one voice about why and how we are going to resuscitate the system.

Finally, it bears pointing out that our founding fathers warned us of the dangers that passion can lead to when not balanced by thoughtfulness and common sense. It is a wise observation, and it is exactly why we must have a solid understanding of the situation. When a protest is backed up by a factual, reasoned narrative about the problem, as well as proposed solutions, a mass complaint can morph into a potent movement.

2 The Public Opinion

Americans are reading their papers and watching their televisions and what they see drives them nuts, and it should. Because all they find are talking heads yelling at each other on cable news and cynical reckless partisanship paralyzing their government.

U.S. Senator Michael Bennet (D-CO), March 3, 2010[1]

Who are the seven percent of people who actually think we do a great job?

Former U.S. Senator Tom Coburn (R-OK),
December 21, 2014[2]

Three years before Senator Tom Coburn marveled at how *anyone* could possibly approve of Congress's performance, one of his colleagues took to the Senate floor to denounce that legislative body in a way that would seem hilarious if the subject weren't so serious. Senator Michael Bennet presented a chart (Figure 2.1) that contrasted Congress's approval rating with 11 other people and institutions that traditionally attract negative responses. In a tone of bewilderment, he exclaimed, "My goodness, the Internal Revenue Service has a 40 percent approval rating compared to our 9 percent! BP had a 16 percent approval rating at the height of the oil spill! And we're at 9 percent ... More people support the United States becoming communist—I don't, for the record—at 11 percent, than approve of the job that we're doing!" He added dryly, "I guess we can take some comfort that Fidel Castro is at 5 percent."

Figure 2.1 Congressional Approval Ratings Compared with Other Ratings[3]

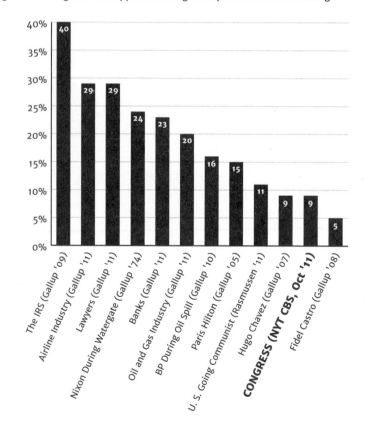

Bennet took the liberty of using different years for the responses and also used two polls that were from different sources than the other nine figures recorded by Gallup. He did so most certainly for dramatic effect, and it worked. But his point is reflected in poll after poll, including the annual survey released by Gallup on June 13, 2013 (see Figure 2.2). In it, Congress ranked dead last in public confidence when measured against fifteen other American institutions. Our elected leaders sat in the basement at 10 percent, with the next closest choice being HMOs at nearly double that approval rate. Congress ranked in the cellar on this same question in 2012, but in 2013 it actually dropped three points to a forty-year low.

Figure 2.2 Americans' Confidence in Congress and Other Institutions, 2012 and 2013.[4]

"I am going to read you a list of institutions in American Society. Please tell me how much confidence you, yourself, have in each one—a great deal, quite a lot, some, or very little?"

% Great deal / Quite a lot. Sorted by most to least confidence in 2013.

	2012 %	2013 %	Change Pct. pts
The military	75	76	+1
Small business	63	65	+2
The police	56	57	+1
The church or organized religion	44	48	+4
The presidency	37	36	−1
The medical system	41	35	−6
The U. S. Supreme Court	37	34	−3
The public schools	29	32	+3
The criminal justice system	29	28	−1
Banks	21	26	+5
Television news	21	23	+2
Newspapers	25	23	−2
Big business	21	22	+1
Organized labor	21	20	−1
Health Maintenance Organizations (HMOs)	19	19	0
Congress	13	10	−3

Just four months later, on October 1, 2013, the House and Senate came to a standstill over voting to continue funding the government. As the clock ticked down toward a midnight government shutdown, CNN released a new poll that afternoon. The news organization's numbers had finally matched its colleagues at Gallup and *The Wall Street Journal*, registering a historic low approval rating for Congress—10 percent.[5] Nine hours later, the government shut down for the first time in seventeen years. More than 780,000 workers were furloughed the following day. (Meanwhile, by law, members of Congress continued to receive their salaries.)[6]

Clearly, public confidence in Congress over the last few years is swimming in the shallowest end of the pool. Now, for some context, let's get a glimpse of public perception over the last four decades. When we analyze a similar question from Gallup on Americans' confidence in Congress, we see plenty of fluctuations. But over the last ten years we see a sustained drop, swooning to a new record low of 7 percent in July of 2014 (see Figure 2.3).

Figure 2.3 Confidence in Congress[7]

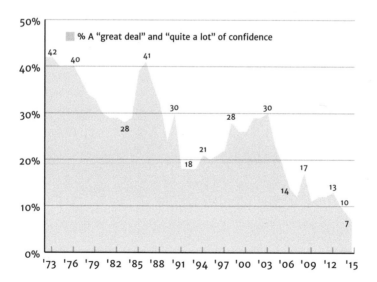

It is also revealing to look at Americans' opinions about how Congress has handled a specific national issue that has attracted huge attention in recent years—negotiations over the budget and the debt ceiling. Although there are disparate ideas regarding the best course of action, it is the responsibility of Congress to come to majority agreements on these issues and make decisions. This is not to say that it is always easy, or that the job itself is easy. But sometimes agreeing is part of the job.

During the first high-profile standoff over the debt ceiling in the summer of 2011, Americans were asked in a CNN/ORC poll, "In general, do you think elected officials in Washington who have dealt with the debt ceiling in the past few days have behaved mostly like responsible adults or mostly like spoiled children?" A total of 17 percent answered "responsible adults" versus 77 percent who selected "spoiled children."[8]

Just over a year later, after the 2012 elections kept Republicans in charge of the House, Democrats in charge of the Senate, and President Barack Obama in the White House, a CNN/ORC poll asked Americans a similar question about the upcoming budget negotiations: "What's your best guess—do you think in the upcoming discussions on this matter, elected officials in Washington will behave mostly like responsible adults or mostly like spoiled children?" This time, with a newly elected government in place, the "responsible adults" option climbed a mere nine points to 28 percent, while "spoiled children" came in at 67 percent.[9]

The blame game in politics is usually a Rorschach test. Many Americans who identify with a specific political party or ideology are likely to believe that the opposing party of the moment is responsible for congressional failure. But it is important to point out that these depressing numbers and perceptions have been registering for decades—and during separate points in time when each party has had control of the White House and one or both chambers of Congress.

It is often observed that we have more gridlock when our government is divided, and that conversely far more legislative consensus exists when we have one-party rule. But Americans abhor the product in both circumstances. It is only a matter of degree.

In the 2013–2014 congressional session, the Democrats controlled the White House and the Senate while the Republicans had the House. Finger-pointing was at a fever pitch. Both chambers are dysfunctional, to be sure, but the public heaped a great deal of blame on the House during the

112th and 113th Congresses. That sentiment is likely because the House majority came to power in 2010 on the strength of the Tea Party, whose members vigorously exercised their will during their first two legislative sessions.[10]

Many on the left argue that accusations of poor performance are well-deserved and that the House majority's path has been irrational and counterproductive. On the other side of the battle lines, backers of the newer conservative grassroots movement argue that new members' actions are principled and long overdue. Whether one side or the other is correct or can even be proven correct *is not the issue here.* The larger point is that focusing on the latest political faction or ideological trend that is "causing gridlock" makes it easy to take aim and target opponents. But this trend has been building for many years and for a variety of reasons. It is easy to forget that in 2010, the year *before* control of the House changed hands from the Democrats to the Republicans, Americans already believed that Congress was pathetic. During a time when our government had one-party control, although far more bills were becoming laws, the product and process were still not passing public muster.

On the evening of February 26, 2010, in the midst of that congressional session where Democrats were holding the reins, CNN broadcast "Broken Government: A Special Report." The one-hour program led with the words, "Almost nine out of ten Americans think our government's broken. Seventy-five percent think that our government officials are dishonest." The coverage then went on to mostly critique the failings of Congress.[11]

That same month, in 2010, the cover of *Time* magazine blared the headline "Why Washington Is Frozen." The subhead of Peter Beinart's cover story asserted: "Discontent with government is at its highest level in more than a decade—making it harder to solve the country's biggest problems. A breakdown of how Washington stopped working, and what to do about it." Beinart then went further and zeroed in on the legislative branch: "Sixty-two percent of Americans say most members of Congress do not deserve re-election, up ten points from 2006. Public skepticism about the federal government and its ability to solve problems is nothing new, but the discontent is greater today than it has been in more than a decade and a half."[12]

Also that month, *Atlantic* magazine's national correspondent, James Fallows, wrote a cover story titled, "After the Crash: How America Can Rise Again." In a wide-ranging analysis from a journalist who has been reporting on Washington for forty years, it wasn't hard to find his focus on Congress:

> We could correct all these problems—and that is the heart of the problem ... That is the American tragedy of the early twenty-first century: a vital and self-renewing culture that attracts the world's talent, and a governing system that increasingly looks like a joke. One thing I've never heard in my time overseas is "I wish we had a Senate like yours."[13]

This sampling of negative numbers, headlines, and commentary adds up to just a glimpse. A comprehensive statistical analysis could fill an entire book, but it isn't necessary. It is easy to see and feel the pattern, and it has been building for many years. We loathe Congress.

Obviously such a negative perspective is embarrassing for our country, and it does not inspire much hope for our democracy. Even worse though, our opinion of the Congress has a practical effect: apathy. Here is where it truly matters. Too many of us don't vote and won't get involved, which makes the challenge of reforming and repairing the system all the more difficult. As the saying goes, "We in America do not have government by the majority. We have government by the majority who participate."

We can see our frustration with Congress affecting our attitudes about elections and voting participation—or lack thereof. The American National Election Studies has been tracking voting patterns since 1964. That year, when Americans were asked to decide whether "having elections makes government pay attention to what the people think," 65 percent answered "a good deal." That was the high point over the next 44 years. By 2002 it was down to 51 percent, and by 2008 it had dropped to 47 percent.[14]

This attitude is reflected in America's disappointing voter turnout levels—and it especially applies to midterm congressional elections versus presidential elections. U.S. voter turnout hovers around 60 percent in presidential years (20 percent below democracies in countries such as Austria, Italy, and Sweden), and the turnout figure plummets to 40 percent in our midterm cycles.[15]

Let's dig a little deeper into voter participation numbers. In the 2010 midterm congressional elections, 217 million Americans were eligible to register to vote.[16] Of those, 59.8 percent reported that they had registered,[17] and 41.8 percent actually turned out for the election.[18] When we extrapolate the math on these percentages, the numbers look even uglier. We find that approximately 87 million Americans were not registered to vote. And of the 129.7 million who were registered, nearly 40 million didn't punch a ballot. A grand total of 127 million potential voters chose to stay away.

People cite many reasons for not exercising this right, but our skepticism about Congress and our government is one of the main deterrents to voting. In 2006 the Pew Research Center did a survey on voter participation before the midterm congressional elections. Of the Americans who voted "rarely," 30 percent agreed with the statement "Voting doesn't change things." Among unregistered voters, 33 percent agreed with the same statement. These percentages were more than double the proportion of "regular" or "intermittent" voters who agreed with it. Millions of Americans don't think it matters whom we send to represent us in Washington.[19]

In the 2012 cycle, a presidential election year, there were eight million more eligible voters than in 2008. But voter turnout *still fell* by more than four percentage points.[20] A *USA Today*/Suffolk University poll three months before the election accurately predicted the drop-off. Registered voters in the survey were asked to agree or disagree with statements about why they don't "pay much attention to politics." The top two answers were: 1) "Nothing ever gets done / it's a bunch of empty promises" at 59 percent; and, 2) "It is so corrupt" at 54 percent. And when it came to evaluating the political parties, 42 percent agreed that "there's not a dime's worth of difference between Democrats and Republicans."[21]

Between 1974 and 1990, lower approval of Congress meant lower turnout in midterm elections. But even when voter turnout has ticked up slightly alongside lower ratings for Congress, the participation number has still been dire. In the five midterms between 2002 and 2010 where disapproval coincided with more voting, national turnout only ranged from 38.1 percent to 41.1 percent.[22] And in 2014, a year where approval of Congress hit a forty-year low of 7 percent, the midterm turnout fell to 36.4 percent—the worst in 72 years (or, as *Time* magazine noted, the worst since newly minted Senate Majority Leader Mitch McConnell was nine months old.)[23]

Long-term correlations on voter participation can be hard to pinpoint. But we can safely assume that the totality of Americans' negative feelings about Congress and our government are not having a positive impact on their exercise of the franchise. And although voter apathy does not fall directly into the main group of structural problems in Congress that will be laid out in Chapter 5, it is true that an effort to increase political participation will be a critical ingredient to reforming and improving Congress. We need Americans to engage.

THE EXCEPTION

There is certainly no shortage of bad news on the subject of how we view Congress. However, we should keep in mind one distinction, a fact that actually offers a glimmer of hope against this darker picture: As Americans, we perceive our individual senators and representatives differently than we view Congress overall. This book focuses on the ineffectiveness of Congress as a systemic whole as opposed to that of its individual members—a point that bears repeating. The two are not the same.

In a May 2013 survey, Gallup reported, "Although Americans overwhelmingly disapprove of the job Congress in general is doing, voters re-elect most members of Congress in every election. This phenomenon is partly explained by the finding that Americans have significantly more positive opinions about their own representative than they do of Congress overall." The numbers in that Gallup poll drove the point home: Only 16 percent of Americans approved of Congress, but 46 percent approved of the way *their own representatives* were handling the job.[24] This is most definitely still a weak approval figure, and it slid even further after the October 2013 debt ceiling fiasco, but it has generally remained well above the stunning depths when Congress is judged as an institution.

This contrast is so important because effectively unlocking Congress is not about "throwing all the bums out." True, we will always have some members in Congress who need to be replaced. Perhaps plenty. But the real problems that require reform are the counterproductive rules in the system that create unnecessary blockages and distort the lawmaking process. These same obstacles also rob our legislators of the valuable time they need to execute proper oversight over how the executive branch is carrying out legislation and running our government.

So although we know the institution is in trouble, we have not totally given up on the individual legislator. Nor should we. Even with all of our disappointment in our representatives, Americans still have a general awareness of how important lawmaking is. In late 2012, 88 percent of Americans said they believe Congress has an impact on our lives, with 50 percent saying "a great deal."[25] In big ways, we need Congress to work.

In our own congressional districts, many of us have had positive experiences with our representatives and senators. Often we can see them for the people they are and with the good intentions that they have. So many of them are putting in hard work. The sad part is that they are putting it into a skewed system that pulls them down with it.

———

So now we've set the baseline. We are sickened by our Congress. It is a depressing fact, to be sure, but it definitely has not been enough to ignite a passionate, national effort to pull the wreck back up onto the road. In fact, we have seen how this overarching disapproval may actually *decrease* our civic participation—a right and responsibility upon which our country was founded. Therefore, beyond our general disappointment, we need to clearly understand how our legislative branch's dreadful performance is actually reducing the quality of our lives. Dramatically. We must see the big picture that surrounds each of our smaller personal frames, and soon we will go over it piece by piece.

But to fairly judge the outcomes of Congress's performance—the *product*—first we must agree on just what it owes us. We know that we are paying for it with our tax dollars, and we know our overall opinion of it. Now we need to define both the stated and implied obligations that Congress is meant to live up to. What are we entitled to expect? Ninety percent of us agree that the U.S. Congress owes us better. Much better. But why? How do we determine what the benchmarks are in this public pact? How do we evaluate Congress in the kind of meaningful way that will form a reasonable basis and national passion for reforming it?

To accomplish this goal, we need to have a clear understanding of just what our legislature has been obligated and empowered to produce on our behalf.

3 The Promises and the Powers

war·ran·ty   *noun* \ wòr–n–t, wär–\ a usually written

guarantee of the integrity of a product and of the maker's

responsibility for the repair or replacement of defective

parts.

Merriam–Webster Dictionary

A good number of the consequential issues we face as a nation tend to change in scope or severity over the years. Few get completely solved. Many actually grow in their potential to make life harder for Americans. We do not expect our elected representatives to confront every single challenge we face, but sometimes there is a clear need for the government to be involved. And Congress is the linchpin in our federal system. It was not random when James Madison referred to Congress as our "first branch" of government, a designation further confirmed by its positioning as Article I of our Constitution.[1]

The statistics in the preceding chapter might tempt us to jump straight ahead and start specifying exactly how Congress is falling down on the job. But that's not enough. It is far too easy to just start launching darts at a caricature on the wall. In addition, because we have such a diversity of opinion in our country about our government and its purpose, we also have a pretty broad spectrum of expectations for Congress. Still, no matter what one person's preferences are with regard to how limited or robust we want our government to be, when it comes to basic effectiveness, many objective standards exist, ones on which most of us can agree.

As American citizens, by definition we are constituents of our respective representatives. But one could argue that we also have a relationship with our government as its customers. Informal contracts exist between all of us and the officeholders we elect to Congress. So although we may not be engaged in a traditionally commercial arrangement with our government, we do pay for and vote for its operation—a relationship that can be viewed as transactional, because it is.

The customer analogy is not meant to be absorbed literally, but metaphorically—and logically. Think of all the products we purchase in our economy that come with warranties promising that the product will perform as advertised. Shouldn't we also be able to expect a reasonably effective performance from the branches of government we subsidize? Aren't we as patrons entitled to a *"guarantee of the integrity of (the) product"* being provided?

Certainly any law professors worth their teaching positions will quickly point out that business law and constitutional law are quite separate realms. Anyone trying to file suit against the government for doing a generally awful job would of course have zero chance of winning monetary damages. But our system does afford us another type of recourse as citizen consumers of our government's product. Thomas Jefferson articulated our democratic right to peacefully alter the rules in 1787, a year before our Constitution was ratified, when he wrote: "Happy for us, that when we find our constitutions defective and insufficient to secure the happiness of our people, we can assemble with all the coolness of philosophers, and set it to rights, while every other nation on earth must have recourse to arms to amend or restore their constitutions."[2]

Along with the powers granted to our federal government's first branch come obligations to each one of us within its constituency. The enduring public pact set out and affirmed in our Constitution contains a civic warranty outlined on the very same pages. There are powers that have been assigned to Congress and there are purposes for these powers. There are promises and pledges that have been made, and we all have a right to expect that they be kept.

OUR END OF THE BARGAIN

It is axiomatic that U.S. citizenship is a privilege, even if we are fed up with our government. But that privilege comes with requirements, and it all starts with following the rules. As Americans, we are obligated to adhere to the laws passed by our government. Most of us do this without too much difficulty, and when we don't, we face the prospect of paying the price or serving the sentence meted out by the justice system.

We are also aware that a big part of our citizenship consists of paying taxes according to the rates passed by Congress and signed into law by the president. Among these are income taxes, payroll taxes, gift taxes, and estate taxes. This includes our contributions to Social Security and Medicare. We may not always be thrilled about forking over a substantial share of our hard-earned income to the government, but most of us do so aware of our collective identity as a nation of laws—as well as the penalties for not complying with them.

Our abiding citizenship, including our tax dollars, drives our government and guides our country. Our voting choices determine who will serve as our public leaders, and our money pays for those elected officeholders' salaries, benefits, and operational expenditures. And, of course, our tax base also pays for all of the laws, structures, and systems that Congress creates and is responsible for monitoring.

Drilling down a bit further, in the 113th Congress our U.S. senators and representatives earned an annual salary of $174,000 (members of leadership earn higher salaries). Members and their staff are also provided health care benefits. Additionally, according to the Congressional Research Service, U.S. representatives receive a "members' representational allowance" which "may be used for official expenses including, for example, staff, travel, mail, office equipment, district office rental, stationery, and other office supplies." U.S. senators receive a similar allowance to cover their "official and representational duties."[3] Many other costs are associated with the legislative branch, and in 2014 the price tag for running Congress was $4.2 billion—about $200 million more than in 2013.[4]

These numbers are not reported to pass judgment on whether members of Congress are underpaid or overpaid. Or, for that matter, whether its operational costs are too low or too high. A great many members of Congress, as well as staff, work incredibly hard for their salaries and benefits. No shortage of sacrifice and effort is being exerted in offices across Capitol Hill. Indeed, congressional scholars point out that most members of Congress would easily make more money in the private sector.[5]

However, we, the American people, are voting and then paying for that $4 billion to run the House and Senate. And this amount is a barely visible slice of the entire pie. We are also paying for the bulk of the overall federal budget that Congress decides how to spend on our behalf—*three and a half trillion dollars.*[6] These are our tax dollars. This is part of our citizenship. They constitute a substantial piece of how we are keeping up our end of the bargain.

All of these contributions we make to our democracy raise a terribly important question: What has our government, and specifically our lawmakers, promised to deliver to us in exchange for our citizenship? What's *their* end of the bargain? What type of quality product are we legitimately entitled to?

The answer is tricky, because it necessarily combines general parameters that our Constitution lays out as to Congress's powers and purpose, as well as the individual promises our candidates for office are perpetually making to us. One the one hand, we have the founders' constitutional language, which has wisely guided us for centuries, but which is also intentionally ambiguous in certain areas. And on the other hand, we have campaign pledges that twist and turn over time, due in good measure to the changing nature of our country's challenges, as well as the political climate of the day.

Nevertheless, we can ascertain the answers to these questions through a logical review of relevant historical sources, combined with our own powers of reason. Moreover, we absolutely must define what we are entitled to demand before we can really be prepared to grade Congress on its work. Warranty remedies are available to all of us as the recipients of our government's product—but establishing the presence of an effective *breach of contract* is imperative in this scenario. What should Congress be producing and achieving for us?

SPOKEN WARRANTY

Let's return to the movies for a moment. In 1972, the political film *The Candidate* was released to critical acclaim. Like *Network*, it satirized one of American society's most powerful institutions—in this case national politics. The movie also earned a best screenplay Oscar, which went to former presidential campaign speechwriter Jeremy Larner.

In *The Candidate,* protagonist Bill McKay, played by Robert Redford, is an idealistic young lawyer living in California. McKay is recruited by the Democrats to run as a sacrificial lamb against the seemingly unbeatable incumbent, Republican Senator Crocker Jarman. McKay decides to risk taking a long shot run, thinking that he will at least get to publicly voice his thoughts and ideas about what kind of change the country needs.

Then comes the twist: after McKay sees that he's losing by a humiliating margin in the general election, he decides to play ball. He starts speaking in political platitudes and offering the kinds of promises that would have turned his stomach only weeks earlier. The climax arrives when

McKay ends up edging out his opponent by a thread, shocking the experts and becoming the Golden State's next U.S. senator.

In the movie's final sequence, campaign manager Marvin Lucas implores his candidate to go celebrate with the throng of exhilarated campaign supporters who are waiting to hear from their new senator-elect. But McKay just sits there, looking terribly unsettled. It seems as though he cannot move, or doesn't want to. After a long pause comes the last line of the film; McKay looks at his manager and says: "Marvin, what do we do now?"

Incumbent lawmakers and challenger candidates alike have been talking big about what they're going to "get done" since the dawn of election campaigns. A paper factory churning out blank pages 365 days a year might not provide enough space to scribble down all of the promises congressional candidates have made to American voters over the decades. It seems as if these claims are running on a continuous broadcast loop, and they vary little from election to election. We've heard them over and over. Promises to lower unemployment. Promises to insure retirement security. To lead the world in clean energy. To repeal this law or that law. To correct the imperfections in our voting systems. On and on. And then beyond the guarantees we receive on specific issues, we hear the perennial promises from those candidates who vow to "work with colleagues from across the aisle, to compromise, forge consensus on issues of common concern, and together move the country forward."

As voters, we might categorize these campaign pledges as the "spoken warranties" we have been given. That phrase can immediately conjure up the sounds of shady guarantees from hard-charging salesmen that are usually too good to be true. In fact, according to consumer guidance from our very own Federal Trade Commission, which Congress itself helped to establish in 1914, Americans are cautioned: "If a salesperson makes a promise orally ... get it in writing. Otherwise, you may not be able to get the service that was promised."[7]

Here is the first place where we must apply our common sense. Does any American really believe that one representative or senator out of 535 members of Congress can independently deliver on all or even most of the individual campaign promises when it comes to specific issues? Of course not. But that is not how the legislative branch was intended to work in the first place. The founders designed Congress for deliberation and debate, for measured discussion and then collective construction of solutions to address public policy concerns.

Intuitively, we know this. It is one of the reasons the satirical tone in *The Candidate* hits home. Americans are by now very much accustomed to the political process, so when we hear candidates spouting hackneyed campaign pledges about solving problems, we take it with a full shaker of salt. A great many of us have been cynical about this stuff for some time now, and for good reason.

But that second promise about "compromise" is more relevant in this warranty equation, because it applies not only to individual candidates or lawmakers, but to the institution as a whole. Our constitutional system, and particularly Congress, was purposely designed to allow competing interests in the country to balance each other out and for our representatives to build consensus around national questions.

It is easy to forget—and in fact many Americans do not know—that a titanic struggle and debate took place before our Constitution was finally ratified by all thirteen states. On May 5, 1787, delegates from twelve states convened to address the shortcomings of the Articles of Confederation. Ultimately, they decided to draft a new Constitution intended to formally unite and guide a new country. Just over three years later, on May 29, 1790, Rhode Island became the final state to vote for ratification and join the union.[8]

But it was not easy. Over those three years, a sustained and historic intellectual battle was waged between the Federalists and Anti-Federalists over nearly every conceivable nuance and potential consequence of the draft Constitution. In 1788, a series of essays titled *The Federalist Papers* were published to promote ratification of the Constitution. Written anonymously at first by James Madison, Alexander Hamilton, and John Jay, the eighty-five essays sought to answer all of the Anti-Federalists' questions and criticisms over whether the newly proposed system would place too much power in the hands of a centralized national government.

In making the case for ratification, *The Federalist Papers* also necessarily laid out how and why the new system of government would work.

Two hundred years later, eminent U.S. historian Richard B. Morris described them as "an incomparable exposition of the Constitution, a classic in political science unsurpassed in both breadth and depth by the product of any later American writer."[9]

We will turn to *The Federalist Papers* repeatedly in this discussion on Congress. They appear here to specifically address that oft-spoken promise of "compromise," which is precisely what the framers of the Constitution wanted our legislative branch to be able to accomplish.

Over the course of U.S. history, *Federalist 10* has come to be thought of as one of the most relevant documents in the study of how and why the framers designed our republican system of government. Written by Madison, *Federalist 10* was a continuation of *Federalist 9,* which had been titled, *"The Union as a Safeguard against Domestic Faction and Insurrection."* Early on, Madison explains the challenge:

> Complaints are everywhere heard from our most considerate and virtuous citizens, equally the friends of public and private faith, and of public and personal liberty, that our governments are too unstable, that the public good is disregarded in the conflicts of rival parties, and that measures are too often decided, not according to the rules of justice and the rights of the minor party, but by the superior force of an interested and overbearing majority.[10]

Madison soon became more specific about the danger of "factions," which could amount "to a majority or a minority of the whole, who are united," and whose objectives could be in opposition "to the rights of other citizens, or to the permanent and aggregate interests of the community."[11]

Acknowledging that factionalism is often a natural state of human affairs, Madison explained that instead of trying to eliminate its causes, the new Constitution must find a way to manage its effects. Mistrustful of the uninformed masses, he therefore opposed the idea of direct democracy, where the aggregate votes of the people decided every issue. Instead, Madison favored a republican form of government, where decisions and laws for the country would be agreed upon by representatives whom Americans would elect to Congress. The founders believed that elected legislators would be more inclined to favor the national interest over any smaller factional interest. Having studied many forms of government that had perished, they weighed those failures very carefully when they designed the Constitution.

Our system has always placed a high value on pluralism, which embraces the presence of a wide variety of interests in American society. Because of this broad spectrum of opinion, Americans, and therefore our legislators, have always had to deal with our differences through constructive negotiation. Congress was designed to allow our leaders to thoughtfully consider what is in the best interest of the American people and to arrive at decisions to advance the common good. Through this republican system, Madison believed it would be "less probable that a majority of the whole will have a common motive to invade the rights of other citizens."[12]

Former Congressman Lee Hamilton (D-IN) served in the House from 1965 to 1999 and took very seriously the responsibility of directly representing his constituents. At the same time, he knew full well the meaning of *Federalist 10* and the importance of always considering what's best for the country. Hamilton wrote about this not long after leaving office, quoting Madison in his interpretation: "The founders didn't believe that Congress should simply mirror the will of the people. They believed it ought to 'refine and enlarge the public view.' They thought that members should favor the *national interest* in their deliberations."[13]

Negotiating for the common good necessarily involves compromise. From the very beginning, the authors of the Constitution knew that Congress would have to compromise to achieve significant progress for the people. Not to say the process would be neat, efficient, or quick, it nevertheless would be requisite, indeed critical, for the United States to exist as a peaceful and prosperous nation governed by the rule of law.

The framers also wanted majority rule within Congress to activate decisions and pass laws. Once we elect our leaders, and then those leaders reach a majority consensus on an issue, they are to move on to the next order of business. In *Federalist 22*, Alexander Hamilton warned specifically about how the violation of this precept could gum up the works to the detriment of the people:

In those emergencies of a nation, in which the goodness or bad-
ness, the weakness or strength of its government, is of the greatest
importance, there is commonly a necessity for action. The public
business must, in some way or other, go forward. If a pertinacious
minority can control the opinion of a majority, respecting the best
mode of conducting it, the majority, in order that something may
be done, must conform to the views of the minority; and thus the
sense of the smaller number will overrule that of the greater, and
give a tone to the national proceedings. Hence, tedious delays;
continual negotiation and intrigue; contemptible compromises of
the public good.[14]

Establishing this historical basis is absolutely essential in determining
what our system has promised us in terms of the process. Two hundred
twenty-five years after Madison and Hamilton penned those expository
papers, Americans still have a right to a legislative system that is based on
constructive negotiation. In 2009, Lee Hamilton reaffirmed its importance:
"In a nation as big and diverse as ours, in which so many people hold so
many differing opinions, that means finding solutions to issues that allow
us to work peaceably and productively together; and that, in turn, means
finding compromises."[15]

At this point, some readers may reasonably point out that at least one
compromise was made during our nation's founding of precisely the kind
Federalist 22 had warned against. Delegates to the Constitutional Convention who wanted to abolish slavery ultimately permitted the terrible
scourge to continue in order to secure the requisite number of states needed
to ratify the Constitution. On July 12, 1787, the "three-fifths compromise"
was enacted, keeping black Americans in bondage and actually valuing
them as fractions of a person for the purposes of apportioning House representatives, presidential electors, and direct taxation. The Constitution
disallowed any future law regarding the slave trade from being passed in
the United States until 1808.

In today's world, it would be an understatement to describe this agreement as "contemptible," to use Alexander Hamilton's adjective. Although

the compromise may have been deemed necessary to hold our union together, it will never dilute the fact that slavery remains an indelible stain on American history.

Certainly much has changed in our country over the decades. But we must acknowledge that even today, even if only occasionally, compromise can at times lead to wildly immoral or counterproductive outcomes. We should be aware of this fact and not fool ourselves into thinking that bad deals will never occur. Yet such moments are no basis for condemning the art of compromise and its importance to a well-functioning Congress. The goal is to get to a place where our representatives can actually negotiate in good faith to make the best possible decisions.

To be sure, big disagreements on massive challenges in our country do exist, and many issues have only become more complicated as our population has grown from three million to more than three hundred million. But that growth only emphasizes the essential need for a legislature capable of analyzing national challenges and producing legislation to meet those challenges. Moreover, members of Congress must be able to work well enough together to ensure that the government programs over which they have oversight power are actually operating as intended.

In Chapter 2, we observed Americans' terribly negative opinion of the product. In the next chapter we will investigate this product—the actual consequences of the legislation being passed (and not passed) through the process as it plays out today. Here, though, we have taken note of the spoken warranties from our officeholders for building coalitions and consensus, as well as our founders' intent for the legislative branch to manage to achieve rational compromise. Naturally we expect our representatives to disagree, haggle, and engage in all of the hardball that is raw politics. But if they cannot ultimately come together in a timely fashion to make decisions, we are not receiving the legislative process we have been promised. One that we vote for. One that we pay for.

We hear one more "spoken warranty" from our members of Congress: the Oath of Office. In a tradition that began with the first Congress in 1789, every January of every odd-numbered year, each member of the House, and one-third of Senate, rises to make the following pledge:

I do solemnly swear (or affirm) that I will support and defend the Constitution of the United States against all enemies, foreign and domestic; that I will bear true faith and allegiance to the same; that I take this obligation freely, without any mental reservation or purpose of evasion; and that I will well and faithfully discharge the duties of the office on which I am about to enter: So help me God.[16]

Note that in this pledge, this spoken promise, members of Congress swear no allegiance to a political party. They make no vow tied to an ideology, nor to their own state or congressional district. Nor even to the voters who just elected them. They pledge fidelity to one entity: the Constitution. They pledge to "support and defend" it. The Constitution. A document that, while certainly imperfect, still serves as the guiding charter for the United States. It is the oldest written constitution in the world that is still in use.[17] Passed down from one American generation to the next, to the next, to the next.

WRITTEN WARRANTY

Think for a minute about the huge role that rules play in our lives. We create rule systems, sometimes for ourselves, sometimes for our families, sometimes for our businesses or for social organizations. Rules abound, and these rule systems usually change over time due to how well they're working, which is always a matter of interpretation. There are times in life when each of us is, in a sense, a legislator.

In a household, the parent or parents set up most of the rules. They have the power, after all, and they're the ones who determine how they want their family to benefit. The rule system is geared toward maintaining order and safety and keeping the family on track toward having the kind of quality life they want to live.

In a general sense, it's not very different in more formal organizations. Entities such as businesses, social clubs, schools, and nonprofits all have boards of directors or some council of decision makers who set the goals, make the rules, and then oversee their execution and enforcement. These same councils get together to review their organizations' processes and results. If they are unhappy with the status quo, or foresee the potential to achieve better outcomes, they make course corrections that will guide them accordingly. They change the rules.

We all know from experience that setting up such rule systems can be difficult, and the larger the organism being governed, the trickier the challenge. This is one reason the U.S. Constitution has been revered for more than two centuries. A relatively small group of patriotic minds put great thought and much debate into how to build a system that would sustain a nation through the rule of law—and a system that would last.

In fact, the task was so fraught with challenges that it had to be undertaken twice. The first attempt led to the adoption of the Articles of Confederation in 1777. The Articles were deemed to have too weak a central government, so a Constitutional Convention played out ten years later to confront its drawbacks. Out of that convention, a historic new rule system was born and still survives.[18]

The Constitution sets out the powers for the three branches of government. Through the exercise of Congress's legislative powers, as well as related questions that are often adjudicated in our court system, we are continually learning about the purview of lawmakers. The Constitution's malleability is part of its brilliance. The framers knew they could not predict all future issues and predicaments, so they created a set of rules that would enable our government to lawfully modify the system when unforeseen challenges or circumstances required us to do so.

The same applies to our individual state constitutions. We have avenues to redress our government and insist on systemic changes within it. Specified paths to correcting large-scale problems in the system comprise an important part of our warranty as citizens.

The Preamble of the Constitution immediately introduces the reason for its creation and for the rule system within it:

> We the people of the United States, in order to form a more perfect union, establish justice, insure domestic tranquility, provide for the common defense, promote the general welfare, and secure the blessings of liberty to ourselves and our posterity, do ordain and establish this Constitution for the United States of America.[19]

The words of the Preamble must never be given short shrift. They lay out the purpose for our Constitution—which members of Congress pledge to "support and defend" when they are sworn in. In his book *Framed,* constitutional law professor Sanford Levinson makes the case that although not often cited by the Supreme Court, the Preamble is the most important part of the entire Constitution:

> The reason is simple: It announces the *point* of the entire enterprise. The 4,500 or so words that followed the Preamble in the original, unamended Constitution were all in effect merely means that were thought to be useful to achieving the great aims set out above. It is indeed the ends articulated in the Preamble that justify the means of our political institutions. And to the extent that the means turn out to be counterproductive, then we should revise them.[20]

The first three Articles of the Constitution set out the duties and the powers of the legislative, executive, and judicial branches, respectively. Sections 2 through 7 of Article I lay out the rules for electing our representatives, how they are compensated, and how laws are to be passed. In Section 8 the Constitution grants Congress a set of "enumerated powers" and first explains the general purpose for these powers: "to lay and collect taxes, duties, imposts, and excises, to pay the debts and provide for the common defense and general welfare of the United States; but all duties, imposts and excises shall be uniform throughout the United States."[21]

Congress's additional powers are:

- To borrow money on the credit of the United States;
- To regulate commerce with foreign nations, and among the several states, and with the Indian tribes;
- To establish a uniform rule of naturalization, and uniform laws on the subject of bankruptcies throughout the United States;
- To coin money, regulate the value thereof, and of foreign coin, and fix the standard of weights and measures;

- To provide for the punishment of counterfeiting the securities and current coin of the United States;
- To establish post offices and post roads;
- To promote the progress of science and useful arts, by securing for limited times to authors and inventors the exclusive right to their respective writings and discoveries;
- To constitute tribunals inferior to the Supreme Court;
- To define and punish piracies and felonies committed on the high seas, and offenses against the law of nations;
- To declare war, grant letters of marque and reprisal, and make rules concerning captures on land and water;
- To raise and support armies, but no appropriation of money to that use shall be for a longer term than two years;
- To provide and maintain a navy;
- To make rules for the government and regulation of the land and naval forces;
- To provide for calling forth the militia to execute the laws of the union, suppress insurrections and repel invasions;
- To provide for organizing, arming, and disciplining, the militia, and for governing such part of them as may be employed in the service of the United States, reserving to the states respectively, the appointment of the officers, and the authority of training the militia according to the discipline prescribed by Congress;
- To exercise exclusive legislation in all cases whatsoever, over such District (not exceeding ten miles square) as may, by cession of particular states, and the acceptance of Congress, become the seat of the government of the United States, and to exercise like authority over all places purchased by the consent of the legislature of the state in which the same shall be, for the erection of forts, magazines, arsenals, dockyards, and other needful buildings;—And
- To make all laws which shall be necessary and proper for carrying into execution the foregoing powers, and all other powers vested by this Constitution in the government of the United States, or in any department or officer thereof.

The first sentence and the last sentence in Section 8 have been the subject of much debate over the course of U.S. history. Specifically, the phrases "general welfare" and "all laws which shall be necessary and proper for carrying into execution the foregoing powers," have a history all their own. It makes sense, because both expressions are so general in nature and because their meaning has such great consequence when it comes to which powers our strongest branch of government has the right to assert.

Significantly, we have now seen the words "general welfare" twice—both in the Preamble and in Article I. The debate over the meaning of this phrase goes all the way back to our nation's inception. In fact, "general welfare" is still categorized as an "essentially contested concept" within the context of political analysis; the term is continually being defined and interpreted.

These words are particularly relevant to the scope of Congress's power to tax and spend. Each year, our federal budget is not only large but also the primary method through which our government maps out the country's priorities.[22]

In a comprehensive volume covering U.S. Supreme Court case history titled *"The Constitution of the United States of America—Analysis and Interpretation,"* congressional scholar Johnny Killian explains the early dilemma:

> With respect to the meaning of "the general welfare" the pages of
> *The Federalist* itself disclose a sharp divergence of views between
> its two principal authors. Hamilton adopted the literal, broad
> meaning of the clause; Madison contended that the powers of
> taxation and appropriation of the proposed government should
> be regarded as merely instrumental to its remaining powers, in
> other words, as little more than a power of self-support. From an
> early date Congress has acted upon the interpretation espoused by
> Hamilton. Appropriations for subsidies ... had their beginnings in
> the administrations of Washington and Jefferson. Since 1914, fed-
> eral grants-in-aid, sums of money apportioned among the states
> for particular uses ... have become commonplace.[23]

The Supreme Court heard several cases during the nineteenth and early twentieth centuries regarding the scope of Congress's spending power. Some will point to the 1905 case of *Jacobsen v. Massachusetts* in which the Court noted that the Preamble had not previously been held "as the source of any substantive power conferred on the government of the United States or on any of its departments."[24]

But three decades later in *United States v. Butler,* Killian writes, the Court "gave its unqualified endorsement to Hamilton's views on the taxing power."[25] In that opinion, Justice Owen Roberts wrote:

> While, therefore, the power to tax is not unlimited, its confines are set in the clause which confers it, and not in those of § 8 which bestow and define the legislative powers of the Congress. It results that the power of Congress to authorize expenditure of public moneys for public purposes is not limited by the direct grants of legislative power found in the Constitution.[26]

One year later, in 1937, the Court cemented the principle in *Helvering v. Davis.* The case further established that Congress has the power to define what amounts to the "general welfare," and it gave Congress considerable latitude in deciding what spending will advance that cause.[27] Additional cases have only further empowered Congress in this capacity, and to this day, it is the Hamiltonian understanding of "general welfare" that prevails in our federal government structure.

From the above case law we can draw the conclusion that the enumerated powers written into the Constitution give the U.S. Congress broad latitude to make laws that it sees as being in the interest of our welfare. We are entitled to expect this from Congress as the recipients of its product. Americans most certainly have sharply differing opinions about how and why our tax money should be spent. Political debate about these opinions forms a natural and often controversial part of our national political dialogue. But we do know that the power is considerable. Congress has a great deal of discretion on spending and investment. Its decisions are to be made in the context of *promoting the general welfare.* And as we will see in upcoming chapters, these decisions touch our lives in countless ways every day.

IMPLIED WARRANTY

While Article I actually enumerates the powers and purpose of the legislative branch, assisted frequently by interpretation from our court system, Congress may also exercise what have come to be known as "implied powers."

Just as the Federal Trade Commission provides guidance about what we are promised in spoken and written warranties, it also offers us guidance about things that are not specifically guaranteed: "If problems arise that are not covered by the written warranty, you should investigate the protection given by your implied warranty."[28]

The authors of the Constitution actually anticipated this scenario, and so in the final clause of Section 8 they expressly permitted Congress "to make all laws which shall be necessary and proper for carrying into execution the foregoing powers, and all other powers vested by this Constitution in the government of the United States, or in any department or officer thereof."

This blanket grant of power sounds extremely far-reaching, and it was the subject of much debate even before the Constitution was ratified—especially between Thomas Jefferson and Alexander Hamilton. The issue first came to a head for the U.S. government in 1791 when Hamilton endeavored to create a national bank. Ultimately, President Washington sided with Hamilton, and the question was resolved through legislative compromise. But a precedent was set that gave Congress considerable discretion under the "necessary and proper" clause.[29]

In 1819, the legitimacy of the federal bank, and Congress's power to create it, was legally challenged and heard by the Supreme Court. In *McCulloch v. Maryland,* the Court affirmed the implied power of the federal government and its lawmakers. Writing for the majority, Chief Justice John Marshall spoke to the issue of federal power:

> We admit, as all must admit, that the powers of the Government are limited, and that its limits are not to be transcended. But we

think the sound construction of the Constitution must allow to the national legislature that discretion with respect to the means by which the powers it confers are to be carried into execution which will enable that body to perform the high duties assigned to it in the manner most beneficial to the people. Let the end be legitimate, let it be within the scope of the Constitution, and all means which are appropriate, which are plainly adapted to that end, which are not prohibited, but consistent with the letter and spirit of the Constitution, are constitutional.[30]

In the *McCulloch* case, the Court basically found the "necessary and proper" clause as holding powers that belonged to Congress, as opposed to being limitations on Congress. At the same time, the Court reaffirmed the principle of "judicial review" established in *Marbury v. Madison.* The *Marbury* case held that the Court could at any time void legislation if it deemed Congress had gone too far and violated limits within the Constitution.[31] In *McCulloch,* Justice Marshall explained this concept:

Should Congress, in the execution of its powers, adopt measures which are prohibited by the Constitution, or should Congress, under the pretext of executing its powers, pass laws for the accomplishment of objects not intrusted to the Government, it would become the painful duty of this tribunal, should a case requiring such a decision come before it, to say that such an act was not the law of the land.[32]

These early decisions define the way our federal government works. Congress passes laws it deems to be "necessary and proper," and if the constitutionality of those laws is questioned, the Supreme Court has the final word. We are then governed by the Court's interpretation of the law, unless the decision is overridden through constitutional amendment, or Congress passes new laws within Court-imposed boundaries.

Beyond its effect on the power to legislate, the "necessary and proper" clause is critically important for another reason. Through these "implied powers," as well as public laws, Congress derives its authority to *conduct oversight.* This is no small task in a country as large as the United States. According to the Congressional Research Service, congressional oversight "serves a number of overlapping objectives and purposes:

- improve the efficiency, economy, and effectiveness of governmental operations;
- evaluate programs and performance;
- detect and prevent poor administration, waste, abuse, arbitrary and capricious behavior, or illegal and unconstitutional conduct;
- protect civil liberties and constitutional rights;
- inform the general public and ensure that executive policies reflect the public interest;
- gather information to develop new legislative proposals or to amend existing statutes;
- ensure administrative compliance with legislative intent; and
- prevent executive encroachment on legislative authority and prerogatives."[33]

Congress's powers and responsibilities in oversight are broad and challenging. Over time, the Supreme Court has either granted or upheld Congress's power to: conduct investigations in the national interest, regulate corruption, protect civil rights, protect labor rights, regulate foreign commerce, regulate land transportation, and a number of other functions geared toward promoting our general welfare.[34]

THE UPSHOT

Congress was created and designed as our government's strongest branch, and over the years its powers have only grown. Throughout U.S. history, debates and disagreements about the balance between our three branches of government have been litigated time and time again. The few cases above provide just a glimpse into the complex and ongoing interpretation of what Congress is charged with producing in its service to the people. Defining Congress's powers is an unending process, as our world and the challenges we confront continually change. We can reasonably interpret, though, based on the above brief legislative and judicial history, that Congress has been granted a considerable amount of authority in its directive to promote the general welfare.

To be clear, Congress's possession of these muscular powers does not suggest they should always be flexed. In his book *Why Government Fails So Often: And How It Can Do Better,* Yale Law Professor Peter Schuck argues that a "cautious, incremental approach" is often the more prudent and effective method for government to practice in meeting the nation's domestic policy challenges.[35] Many Americans who believe firmly in limited government will agree with Schuck's conclusions. But no matter where we as individuals fall philosophically on that question, our constitutional system and judicial review define what Congress is permitted to do on our behalf. Having this knowledge, as voters and as taxpayers, we may then judge the product of our lawmakers based on our own understanding and beliefs of what is in the best interests of our general welfare.

For many years, the argument could be made that the lawmaking and oversight process in Congress actually did work more or less as it was intended to. Along those same lines, a great many Americans would also argue that Congress has produced a substantial amount of legislation that has made a positive difference in our lives.

Not long after Lee Hamilton retired from his congressional seat in 1999, he became the director of the Center on Congress at Indiana University. Acutely aware that many Americans are ever leery of the federal government's scope, he nevertheless makes a powerful case for the essential need for an effective Congress: "America rightly emphasizes individual values and independence, but when epidemic disease threatens our health, when dangers lurk at our borders, when energy shortages develop, when foreign trade barriers harm our exports, or when business irregularities undermine investor confidence, part of the way to cope with these problems more effectively is through actions in Congress."[36]

And it is true that over the years Congress has passed meaningful legislation that influences our everyday lives in ways we hardly ever think about—from bringing electricity to rural areas in the 1930s, to setting standards for safe drinking water in the 1970s, to funding research that has prevented disease and ensured the safety of our medications, to requiring food inspections, to mandating seat belts and airbags, to increasing fuel efficiency, to shaping the roads we drive on and the mass transit we ride on, to prohibiting job discrimination, to creating the land grant college system and the federal student aid that powers enrollment, and so on.[37]

We do know that Congress has been capable of passing laws that make our nation stronger. But as public opinion and even the perspectives of our incumbent lawmakers have indicated, that brand of meaningful progress seems to be a thing of the past.

So just how bad is it? That is the question we are about to explore. And now we have a rationale for grading Congress's work product. Through both the enumerated and implied powers our Constitution grants to the legislative branch, as American citizens we possess both written and implied warranty language regarding the promises, the powers, and the purpose of the U.S. Congress. The Constitution tells us how Congress is supposed to work, and why. A large part of its intended purpose is to "promote the general welfare." Our founders emphasized the practices of negotiation and compromise to legislate solutions that would serve the greater good of the nation.

Are those solutions what our Congress is delivering to us? Is the process operating as it was intended? Beyond the preening and posturing and acrid atmosphere in the nation's capital, to what degree is our country being set back by congressional failure? The only way to know the answer to this question is to investigate the individual components of the product, one at a time.

4 The Product

To form a safe and satisfactory judgment of the proper remedy, it is absolutely necessary that we should be well acquainted with the extent and malignity of the disease.

Alexander Hamilton, *Federalist 21*[1]

Something has gone terribly wrong when the biggest threat to the American economy is our American Congress.

U.S. Senator Joe Manchin (D-WV)[2]

S o at this point in our analysis, we know a few things. We know of Americans' overwhelmingly negative opinion of the job Congress is doing. We know what our nation's founding fathers intended Congress to be. We know of its given powers, as well as the purpose for these powers. We know that our government is tasked in large part with *promoting our general welfare,* and that our legislative branch was designated and designed to lead this charge.

We are also aware of our lack of passion regarding the poor state of Congress. In this chapter, we will attempt to tackle that apathy head-on. We will see what kind of grade Congress actually deserves regarding the product it delivers. And we will see just how much it matters to us.

The one final term we must further define as we begin this evaluation of Congress is "general welfare," which comprises a large part of the product that our representatives take an oath to "promote." We see this objective set out both in the Preamble and in Article I of the U.S. Constitution.

The laws that Congress passes are akin to parts along an assembly line. They are the inputs. These laws should not be confused with the ultimate product in this exchange—Americans' general welfare in the areas where Congress has great capacity to affect it. The United States is still a wealthy and prosperous country in many ways, but millions of Americans have serious concerns about how the state of the nation intersects with their daily lives. In fifty public polls jointly conducted by NBC and *The Wall Street Journal* between 2009 and 2014, at least 50 percent of citizens in every survey believed that the nation was "on the wrong track." In the four polls taken in 2014 alone, the average wrong track number was 66 percent.[3]

So how exactly do we define the term "general welfare"? As we saw in Chapter 3, this phrase has been ambiguous from the very beginning. And although our common American history, including judicial review, has helped to clarify what powers Congress is obligated to exercise on our behalf, something is still missing in this transactional equation: us.

WHAT WE WANT

As American consumers, when we purchase a product or service, we have a good idea of what we're paying for and why. And going back to the definition of "warranty," we are also entitled to the expectation that the "integrity of the product" and its features will live up to their promise. Our expectations may include some combination of the following: functionality, durability, design, efficiency, reliability, and safety.

When we shop for a car, for instance, we begin the process knowing at least some of the things we want. Once we select a model and shell out the purchase price, we are given an inventory of all of the vehicle's relevant features, as well as assurances of quality regarding its operation and performance. If the total mileage per gallon doesn't measure up to the advertised fuel efficiency, we have a breach of contract, and recourse is available to us. We purchased the car wanting and expecting it to work just as the salesperson and owner's manual guaranteed it would. If it doesn't, we have warranty rights as consumers to ensure that the problems are corrected, or that we recover the hard-earned cash we forked over for it. That's the deal.

When it comes to Congress and the product it delivers to the American people, our "wants" are discerned in a different fashion. As a nation of more than 300 million people, we have countless desires and expectations as individuals. Therefore, we have many different definitions of what amounts to our "general welfare." To really define that crucial term from our perspective as the customer, we must ask: What do Americans as a collective society really want from a work product of Congress? How do we prioritize which issues and problems we want our representatives to confront?

Fortunately, opinion surveys are constantly asking this question of the American people. And when we construct a composite of these poll results, we gain insight into what our country wants. Our responses form a sort of answer key that we can use to grade Congress. Individual polls only offer snapshots, and public opinion can frequently be volatile or uninformed. But when we compare responses over a longer period of time, we're better able to understand the nation's priorities.

A compendium of public polls taken over the last decade is displayed in the Appendix. These surveys were published by a wide range of news organizations, including CNN, Fox News, Bloomberg News, CBS, NBC, ABC, the Associated Press, Gallup, *The Washington Post,* and *The Wall Street Journal.*

Some of these surveys ask open-ended questions, and others provide answer choices. And when we look at the responses, three major categories emerge as areas where we want to see the government, and specifically Congress, produce results.

Not surprisingly, jobs and the economy represent our most consistent priority across these polls. And when Gallup specifically tracks the "importance" of the economic issue annually between 2001 and 2014, even through its fluctuations we can see how highly Americans prioritize it (see Figure 4.1).

Figure 4.1 Percentage of Americans Mentioning Economic Issues as the Nation's Most Important Problem[4]

Selected trend—January 2001–present

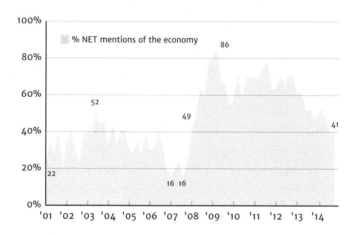

The economic issue cuts across party lines as well. In the run-up to the 2012 presidential election, an identical 48 percent of supporters of both Mitt Romney and Barack Obama pegged "creating jobs" as "very important."[5]

Of course this makes perfect sense, since survival and self-sufficiency are basic human desires. Americans are a generally hard-working people, and we want our country to have the sort of economy where it is possible to find a job and support a family. We want to know that if we work hard, we can advance, enjoy job security, and have a reasonable measure of stability in our lives.

During the first two weeks of 2014, Gallup conducted a national poll and asked the following open-ended question: "What do you think is the most important problem facing the country today?"[6] The three leading answers to that question were as follows:

1. Dissatisfaction with government/Congress/politicians; poor leadership/corruption/abuse of power   **21%**
2. Economy in general   **18%**
3. Unemployment/jobs   **16%**

Americans not only expressed serious concern about the economy but also registered a huge number regarding their disappointment in government. If it is not yet obvious that the two issues are closely intertwined, it soon will be.

While jobs and the economy together comprise the leading issue, we must note other popular responses connected with economic challenges: "budget," "debt/deficit," "taxes," and "energy and gas prices." No matter what one's opinion may be regarding policy prescriptions, all of these issues relate to the economy. So for the purposes of this discussion, they will fall under the umbrella of what we will call *economic well-being*.

Health care and its costs also comprise a major issue affecting our economic well-being. Of course, beyond how it touches our pocketbooks, the issue of health care is primarily about the state of our mental and physical health. Health is a huge concern in Americans' daily lives, and the polling numbers in the Appendix have consistently pegged health care as another one of the top three issues Americans want government to work to improve. And in 2014, one year after the official launch of the Affordable Care Act, Gallup still found Americans pegging it in the same top range.[7] As such, *health care* will be the second major category Congress is judged upon in this analysis.

National security is the third priority that Americans consistently want legislators to address. The term "national security" connotes a broad range of issues, and once again in the Appendix we see a number of challenges within this category that have been frequently mentioned in polling, including "the war in Iraq," "the war in Afghanistan," "terrorism," and the "situation in Syria." National security naturally includes public policy as it applies to other dangerous flashpoints where American intervention is required or considered. In addition, Americans have indicated their concerns over security-related issues such as veterans' affairs, intelligence gathering, and nuclear proliferation.

Toward the end of this chapter, a section titled "The Multiplier Effect" explores three more issues that exemplify the exponential effect that public policy challenges have on one another. We will see how the issue of education affects our economy, our national security, and the poverty rate in our country. Immigration policy will be examined in the context of its effects on the preparedness of our workforce as well as border security. Finally, we will examine the highly charged issue of gun use in America. Polls usually categorize these challenges separately, but they are all related links in the American chain—and weakness in one area often puts strain on the others.

Naturally we bear our own shares of individual responsibility in the collective effort to make our country great. But all of that happens within the rules of the road set up by our government. Members of the U.S. Congress are obligated to create and pass legislation that allows, rather than impedes, our individual capacities to reach these basic goals and quality of life.

So just how poor is the product? How secure are we—economically, physically, and nationally? We have reviewed the record low amount of legislative production in Congress. We have reviewed Americans' record low level of public confidence in Congress, and we know that Article 1 directs our legislators to provide for our "common defense and general welfare." But how justified are we in feeling such disgust for the actual end product?

We now take a look at Congress's performance, issue by major issue, as well as at some of the subordinate issues. Of course, the following examination is taken at a specific moment in time; although these challenges have been central concerns for many years, our world is also constantly changing. Americans' priorities will continue to evolve, as they always have. Nevertheless, observing the recent state of our nation on these issues, and particularly the trends, may help us generate some of that passion we will need to confront the problem.

As tempting as it may be to jump ahead to the question of *why*—we're going to stay focused here on the *what*. As we think about our past, as we experience our present, and as we contemplate our future, just how are we faring in America?

ECONOMIC WELL-BEING

The phrase "the American Dream" was popularized more than eighty years ago by a successful businessman and historian named James Truslow Adams. While most of Adams's books were about his beloved New England, in 1933 he broadened his canvas and published *The Epic of America*. In that book the author defined the "American Dream" as a land where "life should be better and richer and fuller for everyone, with opportunity for each according to ability or achievement."[8]

Truslow's words will sound familiar—they harken all the way back to the historic prose in our Declaration of Independence. As Americans, we grow up learning about our country as the vaunted "land of opportunity." The "American Dream" often conjures up romantic images of the classic rags-to-riches story that is still possible in a country blessed with so many natural advantages. For so long, the possibility of rising has been a big part of what made the United States such a dream destination for millions of aspiring immigrants.

In broader economic terms, this theme has come to be known in our country as "upward mobility." To millions of Americans, the dream is about having at least a baseline opportunity to improve one's own life. It is about living in a country where anyone can work hard and rise up. Where everyone has a fair crack at achieving economic advancement. Where if enough effort is exerted, a job can be secured. Where you can earn a paycheck that will sustain a reasonable standard of living for you and your family.

John Cox heard that story of America growing up on a cattle ranch in the 1960s. John began working when he was 12 years old, and it wasn't a choice. In cold winters he would wake up at four a.m. to feed the cows before heading off to school. Then more work on the ranch awaited him and his brother in the evenings.

John's parents told him over and over to work hard, achieve a college degree, and try to put away money for the future. John remembers, "I was raised from childhood to pursue the 'American Dream,' and to believe that the United States of America was the greatest nation on earth. My father, grandparents, school, church, and community instilled this American Dream mantra in me."[9]

His father always told him, "Take care of the job, and the job will take care of you." And that's what John did. He worked to pay his way through college, as a commercial fisherman in Alaska, sweeping volcanic ash in Washington State, whatever jobs he could find. Sometimes John worked two jobs at once, and he was proud to get his degree without owing a dollar to his family or to the government.

John became a cost accountant and invested in a home in Newberg, Oregon. He hoped to one day pass it down to his son Geral, who was born with Down's syndrome. John played by the rules, paid into his 401(k), lived within his means, and always tried to maintain what he called an "emergency fund."

Between 1972, when John first started working on that cattle ranch, and 2008, he was never without a job. But when the Great Recession rocked the economy, John was laid off from his accounting position that was paying $60,000. He'd never had trouble finding work before, so he wasn't too spooked. But when two months stretched into two years of unemployment, despite his best efforts, John was forced to use his emergency fund and cash in his 401(k) to keep up with bills. Finally, in 2010, the same proud man who was raised on the values of hard work and self-sufficiency broke down and surrendered. He applied for unemployment benefits. He hated it.

Year after year, John kept looking for work, ready to accept any job and all too prepared to take a substantial pay cut that would likely be part of the deal. But work was incredibly tough to come by, and the home he had planned to keep living in with his son was threatened with foreclosure on more than one occasion.

In early 2013, John Cox and several other families were profiled in a documentary called *American Winter,* about the nation's "alarming trend toward a disappearing middle class."[10] A few months after its premiere,

U.S. Senator Jeff Merkley (D-OR) invited John to testify at a hearing in Washington titled "State of the American Dream—Economic Policy and the Future of the Middle Class." He agreed to make the trip and share his experience with the committee.

Facing the panel of senators in the Capitol, John said he was grateful for the chance to speak, and pointed out that he was merely a "humble representative of the millions of families that have been placed in dire straits since the recession." And in his own humble way, he then told a story that in his darkest dreams he never could have imagined would be his.

Toward the end of his remarks, John stepped out of his narrator role and expressed a personal frustration that had been building for five years:

> I know first hand that help for homeowners facing foreclosure is seriously lacking. The federal government bailed out all the banks and then the banks simply pocketed the money without any penalty, and without helping folks like me all across this country. Due to no fault of our own, people like myself are drowning without a life preserver being thrown our way. What happened to that ship that we call the "American Dream?"[11]

John Cox's story is not unique. Over the last four decades, and especially the last fifteen years, millions of working Americans have found themselves face to face with this same brand of economic plight. But it's not just unemployment. It is a slow burn that starts taking its toll on working folks long before the specter of joblessness creeps up.

Our national economy has undergone steady changes that have conspired to push working Americans to the edge of the fiscal precipice—and often over it. Between 1973 and 2011, labor productivity in the U.S. actually increased by 80 percent, yet the real median hourly compensation for workers rose by just 4 percent (10 percent when all employment benefits are included).[12]

If that sounds out of whack, the conversion into dollars and cents is more dire. In their comprehensive research on how government policies have pulled down the middle class, political scientists Jacob Hacker and Paul Pierson further quantify what Americans have really been earning.

They report that between 1979 and 2006, "the average income of the poorest 20 percent, or quintile, of American households rose from $14,900 to $16,500, a meager 10 percent gain over 27 years, even after taking into account government taxes and benefits and private employment based benefits ... The middle quintile of households saw their inflation-adjusted income rise from $42,900 to $52,100—a gain of 21 percent."[13] When inflation is factored in, this amounts to an anemic 0.7 percent gain in income.

Even more sobering, they report this sliver of an increase is a result of additional hours worked, as opposed to actual gains in wages: "Hard as it may be to believe, a typical entry-level worker (ages 25–34) with a bachelor's degree or higher earned only $1,000 more for full time, full year work in 2006 than did such a worker in 1980 ($45,000 versus $44,000, adjusted for inflation)."[14]

And while wages have remained relatively flat over the last three decades, the average tuition to attend a four-year college has shot up more than 250 percent.[15] The combination of these two trends forces students to borrow to the hilt to go to college. The result is a student debt total in the United States that topped $1.2 trillion in 2014 (second only to home mortgage debt). Yet even with this surreal gulf between nearly frozen wages and a skyrocketing college debt burden, Pew Research indicates that 94 percent of American parents still expect their children to go to college and achieve a degree.[16]

The first decade of the twenty-first century was particularly cruel to working families. The Center on Budget and Policy Priorities reports that between 2000 and 2011, median income for working age households fell by more than 12 percent to $55,640. Yet over that same period, the American economy experienced growth exceeding 18 percent.[17] Even in the four years that followed the official "end" of the Great Recession in June 2009, median household income dropped by 4.4 percent.[18]

Statistics can be sliced and diced in myriad ways, but you don't have to investigate too deeply to find a mountain of these dismal numbers—and they do not exist in some academic vacuum. These facts represent stark realities felt daily by millions of Americans. The Pew Research Center reported in September 2013 that 63 percent of us believed that "the nation's economic system is no more secure today than it was before the 2008 market crash."[19] That group included a majority of both Republicans and Democrats. Fifty-four percent of Americans believed "household incomes have hardly recovered at all from the recession."[20] In addition, Americans surveyed in the poll had firm opinions about legislation implemented after the recession: "Roughly seven-in-ten said government policies have done little or nothing to help the poor (72 percent), the middle class (71 percent), and small business (67 percent)."[21] Instead, people believed that policies were advantageous to large banks (69 percent), large corporations (67 percent), and wealthy folks (59 percent).[22]

Are they right? The question of wealth imbalance goes directly to a politically charged issue that has been polarizing our country for several years: income inequality. More and more, when Americans are asked, most see the gap as a real problem. Concern about income inequality is becoming a commonly accepted viewpoint that stretches across what used to be a conspicuous partisan breach on the subject.

In January 2014, Gallup asked Americans their satisfaction level regarding "the way income and wealth are distributed in the U.S." A total of 67 percent answered that they were either somewhat or very *dissatisfied*—once again including a majority of both Republicans and Democrats.[23] Americans' discontent stretched across all age ranges, as well as income and educational levels. In that same survey, 45 percent of Americans expressed dissatisfaction with "the opportunity for Americans to get ahead by working hard."[24] In August 2014, an NBC/*Wall Street Journal* poll revealed that 76 percent of Americans *did not* feel confident that "life for our children's generation will be better than it has been for us"—up from 60 percent in 2007.[25] More than a supermajority of the country is doubtful that the very definition of the American Dream still exists.

It is not just public perception. Americans' opinions that the economy is delivering rewards for only a small slice of the population is borne out by real numbers. Emmanuel Saez, an economist at the University of California, Berkeley who has done extensive work on the issue, released a report in late 2013 finding the disparity between the wealthiest 1 percent and the rest of the country the largest since the 1920s. Saez quantifies the yawning gap over the years 2009–2012: "Top 1 percent incomes grew by 31.4 percent while bottom 99 percent incomes grew only by 0.4 percent."[26]

And when we look at Saez's data charted across all the periods of economic expansion since 1949, we can see the stark reverse trend in the swing of income gains for the bottom 90 percent of earners as compared to the top 10 percent (see Figure 4.2).

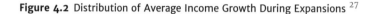

Figure 4.2 Distribution of Average Income Growth During Expansions [27]

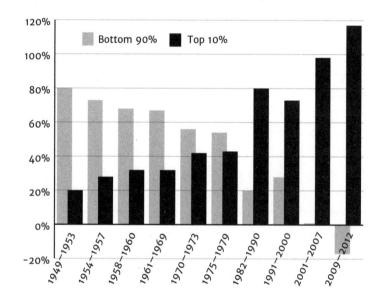

Such a glaring income divide raises an immediate question: Why? It would be one thing if the market just did what markets do and we had no choice but to live with the consequences. But economies do not live in a vacuum; they are shaped by an array of factors, including public policies. And on that score, the evidence suggests that our government—and in large part, Congress—is increasing inequity through its policymaking.

According to 2013 figures compiled by the Luxembourg Income Study, which examined fourteen developed countries using an income inequality measurement known as the Gini coefficient, the United States ranks tenth worst—before taxes and government programs are taken into account.

Once the actions of government are factored in, however, the U.S. shoots to the top spot as the most economically inequitable country.[28]

In other words, our widening income inequality is not merely the inevitable function of immutable economic principles that we are as unable to shape as the laws of physics. To a substantial degree, the divide is the result of policies enacted by our government—led by the legislative branch. And beyond the powerful effects of legislative decisions on taxes and entitlements, Congress has a variety of other policy tools at its disposal. Hacker and Pierson clarify this point early on in their economic analysis:

> Government actually has enormous power to affect the distribution of "market income," that is, earnings before government taxes and benefits take effect. Think about laws governing unions; the minimum wage; regulations of corporate governance; rules for financial markets, including the management of risks for high-stakes economic ventures; and so on. Government rules make the market, and they powerfully shape how, and in whose interests, it operates. This is a fact, not a statement of ideology. And it is a fact that carries very big implications.[29]

Those big implications are being felt in all fifty states. America has consistently boasted about how our combination of free enterprise and rule of law sets the stage for anyone to reach high and advance far, regardless of one's starting point. But our economy and our country no longer corner this market of upward mobility, if we ever did. In fact, by some measures of intergenerational mobility each of the following nations have moved ahead of the United States: Sweden, Germany, Spain, France, Norway, Australia, Canada, and Finland.[30]

It is a rough road that millions of Americans have been navigating in our erratic national economy. So many people are caught in this trap of stagnant wages in the face of increasing real costs for housing, food, health care, energy—so many of the basics.

One direction this road leads down is a dreaded situation that so many people never imagine they might experience—real poverty. It definitely came as a shock to John Cox. *How could this happen? I went to school and achieved my degree. I worked hard at my job. How did I end up needing to ask for assistance?* The truth is that poverty can get its clutches around just about any person or family in our current economy.

In 2012 the federal government defined poverty for an individual as an income of less than $11,490, with commensurate increases for additional individuals (a family of four amounting to $23,550).[31] In that same year, according to the U.S. Census, 15 percent of Americans (46.5 million people), including one out of every five children, lived in poverty. Ten million of those 46.5 million were working folks, and nearly three million Americans were working full time, yet still falling below the poverty line.[32] In 2013, the poverty rate ticked down half a percentage point. But in that same year, for the first time ever, American public schools reported that more than one million enrolled schoolchildren were homeless.[33]

It is an understatement to label this situation a failure. When 21 million American children are impoverished in a country as rich as the United States, something is inexcusably wrong. But our economic challenges go beyond the annual total number of people the government classifies as having fallen into the poverty category. Far too often, scores of Americans whose full-time work has allowed them to earn a satisfying quality of life still face a very precarious set of circumstances. So many working folks are driving down that same harrowing road, and although they may be surviving today, one unanticipated lane change can lead to a debilitating life change.

In July 2013, the Associated Press released a special report, "Signs of Declining Economic Security," that crystallized the new American predicament. The report led with the fact that "four out of five U.S. adults struggle with joblessness, near poverty, or reliance on welfare for at least parts of their lives, a sign of deteriorating economic security and an elusive American dream."[34] The report also forecast that by 2030, the overall rate will increase to 85 percent among working-age adults.

Another factor adding to this insecurity is the high cost of health care in our country—both for the insured and uninsured. We will investigate this further shortly, but it is essential to note the direct way in which health care bills can exacerbate already delicate financial situations for Americans.

A 2013 analysis on health care in *Time* magazine reported that 62 percent of personal bankruptcies are related to sickness or medical costs. Perhaps even more troubling, "69 percent of those who've experienced medically related bankruptcy were insured at the time of their filing."[35]

All of these numbers add up to a sobering conclusion: An enormous number of Americans are terribly vulnerable in our modern-day economy. So many of our friends and neighbors are one job loss away or one unexpected life event away from being either economically insecure or actually living in poverty. Potential solutions in response to the crisis will be debated, but the numbers and the realities are undeniable.

———

The troubling trends that have taken a toll on so many Americans' economic well-being touch off a larger discussion about our country's long-term, unfunded liabilities and the amount of national debt being driven by these massive commitments. Economists and legislators from each end of the political spectrum will deliberate over the urgency of the situation, but sheer arithmetic confirms it is a very real problem.

For millions of American retirees, Social Security and Medicare are increasingly important public supports that were passed long ago by Congress and guaranteed by the federal government. The programs are incredibly popular, for obvious reasons. They are also forecast to face severe shortages.

During the summer of 1935, both the House and the Senate voted overwhelmingly to pass The Social Security Act (officially now known as the OASDI—"Old Age, Survivors and Disability Insurance"). As President Franklin D. Roosevelt signed the new program for American retirees into law, he announced: "We can never insure 100 percent of the population against 100 percent of the hazards and vicissitudes of life, but we have tried to frame a law which will give some measure of protection to the average citizen and to his family against the loss of a job and against poverty-ridden old age."[36]

And that's just what it did. For decades, American workers have contributed payroll taxes to the IRS. Large proportions of this revenue then get deposited into a number of federal insurance trust funds, which in turn pay out benefits to current retirees. In the year 2014, 59 million Americans received Social Security, an expenditure of $863 billion that kept more than 20 million seniors over the age of 65 from falling beneath the federal poverty line.[37]

Thirty years after passing Social Security, in 1965, President Lyndon Johnson signed Medicare into law. Its simple goal was to provide health insurance coverage to seniors age 65 and above, without regard to their medical past. Over the years the program has been modified and now includes components that provide benefits for hospital insurance, supplementary medical insurance, and prescription drugs. Hospital insurance is financed by dedicated payroll taxes, like Social Security, while Medicare's supplementary medical insurance and prescription drug components are funded by a combination of premiums paid by beneficiaries and general revenues, such as income taxes. Notwithstanding the overall problems with health care in the United States, which we will get to shortly, Medicare has unquestionably been a substantial and often critical support for the millions of Americans it covers.

These two social insurance programs worked very well for years, both practically and actuarially. However, more recently the fiscal pendulum has been swinging in the opposite direction due to an aging population and rising health care costs. The federal government acknowledges this fact annually. In its "Summary of the 2014 Annual Reports," the Social Security and Medicare Board of Trustees explain:

> Neither Medicare nor Social Security can sustain projected long-run program costs in full under currently scheduled financing, and legislative changes are necessary to avoid disruptive consequences for beneficiaries and taxpayers. If lawmakers take action sooner rather than later, more options and more time will be available to phase in changes so that the public has adequate time to prepare. Earlier action will also help elected officials minimize adverse impacts on vulnerable populations, including lower-income workers and people already dependent on program benefits.[38]

Social Security and Medicare are enormous federal programs that comprise an extremely complex issue. Dense volumes have been written about these respective long-term challenges for the country, and there are no easy answers. Again, though, the objective here is to first evaluate the product—the present and likely future conditions of these legislative programs that have been so essential to so many Americans' economic well-being. Both may be in far more danger than indicated by the relatively benign language from the government cited above. And the potential financial damage each may cause stretches beyond direct impacts on beneficiaries.

Let's start with Social Security. Over the years, Social Security has accumulated nearly $2.8 trillion in its trust funds. For many years, the combined revenue from payroll taxes and interest paid on the trust fund savings has been more than enough to pay for benefits.[39] The trust funds are built up as a cushion for the disproportionately huge number of baby boomers expected to retire over the next 20 years. In 2010, Social Security benefits exceeded payroll tax revenue by $49 billion, although the program still ran a surplus when interest payments to the trust funds are included.[40] By 2020, however, annual Social Security benefits are projected to exceed the annual combined revenues from payroll taxes and interest payments. According to the administration's forecasting, if Congress does not take action to confront this problem, that trust fund will be bankrupt by the year 2033. If that happens, Social Security would only be able to pay 77 percent of scheduled benefits with the payroll taxes it collects in 2033.[41]

This troubling projection would have terrible implications on benefits for American retirees, not to mention the potential impact on the overall economy, depending on what measures are taken in an effort to brace the system. For years Congress has known that this issue requires serious attention. And according to Harvard University's Institute for Quantitative Social Science, when additional health and demographic factors are taken into account, the trust funds will need to pay out "$800 billion by 2031, more than the current annual defense budget—and that the trust funds will run out, if nothing is done, two years earlier than the government has predicted."[42]

The Medicare program is soaking in even hotter water, due to financial pressures from both rising health care costs and an aging population. In early 2014, the Centers for Medicare and Medicaid Services reported that total health spending in the United States—private and public—in 2012 amounted to $2.8 trillion ($8,900 per person). Although this dollar amount increases every year, the relatively good news was that for the fourth year in a row health spending grew at a slightly smaller rate as a share of the economy. Political disagreement about whether the Affordable Care Act caused this slim drop continues. The authors of the report say that the jury is still out on whether the decrease was due to an actual structural change that will sustain itself in future years.[43]

Either way, though, the math looks awful, because the growing number of Medicare beneficiaries increases the program's total costs. The number of new enrollees in Medicare jumped by 4 percent in 2012—the highest one-year increase in four decades. The Centers for Medicare and Medicaid Services reported in 2012 that the Affordable Care Act will extend Medicare's solvency by eight years.[44] But the SSA Board of Trustees still forecasts that the Medicare hospital insurance trust will be insolvent by 2030 (three years earlier than Social Security), triggering cuts in benefits for millions of seniors.[45]

Americans themselves have their eyes wide open about this danger. In 2011, Gallup asked, "How long do you think it will be until the costs of the Medicare and Social Security programs create a crisis for the federal government?" Thirty-four percent thought it already was a crisis, and a total of 86 percent said they believed the programs would be a crisis for the country within the next twenty years.[46]

It is hard to underestimate how crucial these benefits are to tens of millions of American seniors. Without them, poverty can strike quickly. We understand this threat to our quality of life in a visceral way. But the troubled trajectory of these social insurance programs also harms a larger measure of America's economic well-being, one that feels far more removed: our national debt and annual budget deficits.

Social Security and Medicare together accounted for a massive 38 percent of the nation's annual expenditures in fiscal year 2014. We simply do not collect enough federal revenue each year to cover that staggering

38 percent for Medicare and Social Security, plus the 62 percent we pay for everything else in what amounted to a $3.5 trillion federal budget in FY 2014.[47] We spend far more than we have. And it is the U.S. Congress that passes these programs, sets tax policy, and appropriates what our country spends.

The shortfall each year between what our government brings in and the larger amount we actually spend is our annual budget "deficit" ($483 billion in FY 2014).[48] The total running sum that we owe to lenders is our "national debt." At the beginning of 2015, total U.S. debt owed to public lenders climbed to just over $13 trillion. When intragovernmental debt is added, meaning the money the federal government has borrowed from itself in accounts such as the Social Security Trust Fund, our national debt exceeds $18 trillion.[49] The simplest conclusion we can draw from these facts is that our country isn't paying its own way. And to a substantial degree, we are using other countries' dollars (or yen, or rubles) to promote America's general welfare.

It is easy to get lost in all of the numbers and public arguments when it comes to debt and deficits. Terribly difficult challenges invite big disagreements in Congress about how urgently we ought to reduce our annual deficits right now—this minute. One side of the divide asserts that the deficit has been dropping in terms of real dollars in recent years, and that the emphasis right now should be on investment that boosts employment and therefore strengthens the overall economy, which in turn would increase government receipts to our treasury. Others say that the overall national debt and the interest sums we pay are ridiculously high amounts, and that they result in a crippling effect on the economy and a degrading of America's competitive edge.

Maya MacGuineas, President of the nonpartisan Committee for a Responsible Budget warns: "The federal debt is the nation's most pressing economic problem because our dangerously high debt levels are a threat on every issue—be it jobs, growth, competitiveness or public under-investment. The deficit is already harming the economy, and could eventually lead to a devastating fiscal crisis."[50]

But just how much debt constitutes a "dangerously high level"? For decades, eminent economists have debated this issue, and for decades no one philosophy has been proven to be entirely factually correct. Deficit spending is not an unequivocal evil in and of itself. Again, the economy is a massively complex entity, with thousands of constantly changing nuances and moving parts. Even former Chairman of the Federal Reserve Ben Bernanke, who is fully in favor of sound long-term planning to reduce the debt, underscored that the issue cannot be interpreted in black and white: "Neither experience nor economic theory clearly indicates the threshold at which government debt begins to endanger prosperity and economic stability."[51]

Instead of judging by the total dollar figure, many economists and policymakers therefore zoom in on a more relevant metric: *overall debt burden.* We measure America's debt burden by comparing our public debt to the total value of everything else that the country has produced over the course of the last year (commonly referred to as our "gross domestic product," or GDP). This debt-to-GDP percentage is relevant because it indicates America's ability to repay all of the loans we have received. Between 2001 and 2012, our national debt increased immensely, by more than $10 trillion. More important, though, our debt burden climbed to more than 70 percent—the first time this has happened since the end of World War II.[52]

Our annual budget deficit decreased in 2014, and the national debt will shrink slightly as a share of GDP over the next few years. However, the Congressional Budget Office makes clear that if policies on spending and taxation continued unchanged over the long term, the national debt "would be on an upward path relative to the size of the economy, a trend that could not be sustained indefinitely."[53] The concrete being poured on this perilous path comes mostly from the same two social insurance programs we noted are already running out of money.

Congress has been unable to pass legislation that would meet and improve these long-term challenges in a substantial fashion, so we constantly hear talk about an elusive "Grand Bargain." But Congress rarely even passes an annual budget by the September 30 scheduled deadline—it has happened only four times over the last three decades.[54]

Americans' economic well-being, both in terms of personal stability and national solvency, is a challenge that demands more effective public policy. The data over the last thirty years make it clear: Far too many

Americans are either unable to find a job or are working every day to earn incomes that do not meet current costs of living. True, the economy has become globally interconnected, and forces beyond our shores—and beyond the reach of government—substantially influence the slide we have seen at home. But what is also true is that our legislative branch has a great degree of control over how the economy works. Congress has missed opportunity after opportunity to improve and protect Americans' prospects. We will soon be examining how and why.

HEALTH CARE

Throughout the United States, we have a great many excellent hospitals, general and specialty medical practices, as well as outstanding medical universities. Training and research programs at these schools continue to graduate highly skilled and well-intentioned medical professionals. From general practitioners to surgeons, specialists, and researchers, America has produced thousands of accomplished doctors who are expert at what they do. At the same time, so many of these dedicated professionals fully realize that the work and service they provide as individuals cannot alone protect our country from the negative aspects of the collective health care "system."

Dr. John Noseworthy is one of these individuals. Noseworthy grew up in Melrose, Massachusetts, earned his M.D. in neurology in Nova Scotia, Canada, then obtained additional training through a research fellowship at Harvard University. In 1990 he joined the Mayo Clinic, a renowned not-for-profit health care system that operates in six states and serves more than one million patients every year from all 50 states and 150 countries. In 2009, Noseworthy became president and CEO of the $8.5 billion Mayo system.

Of late, Dr. Noseworthy and his team have been trying to put Mayo's 150 years of experience into the service of analyzing and diagnosing America's health care landscape. When asked in late 2013 about the impacts of the controversial Affordable Care Act (ACA), commonly referred to as "Obamacare," Noseworthy described the health care legislation as limited because it mostly affects Americans with insurance. Taking a broader view, he explained:

The Affordable Care Act, on which we're all putting so much attention at the moment, is in the context of an anemic recovery in our economy and a marked shift in the demographics of the American people, with the aging population, plus the prevalence of chronic disease, the rising costs of health care, the rising costs of research. All of that contributes to an unsustainable health care system. It's too costly—we're spending too much on health care.[55]

We've already touched on the surge in our country's senior citizen population as one reason health care spending is accelerating at a faster rate than our GDP. This rising rate has lessened somewhat since the passage of the ACA, although the degree of causation between the two continues to be debated. But beyond the demographics, Noseworthy zooms in on another huge aspect of America's health challenge: "We're spending too much on health care because it's fragmented and the quality is so uneven in our country. There are pockets of outstanding health care, and there are other places not at that level. There are highly efficient, high-quality health care groups, and others that are expensive and don't deliver that quality."[56]

One of his colleagues, Dr. Toby Cosgrove, president and CEO of the Cleveland Clinic, expanded on Noseworthy's observation: "We've got to learn how to be more efficient. The health care system in the United States is not really a system. It's a whole bunch of cottage industries."[57]

Cosgrove zeroes in on a critical point when he says we don't have a real "system," a word Merriam-Webster defines as "a group of related parts that move or work together." So the word "system" to describe health care in America is a misnomer (remember this definition, for it will be the very heart of our next chapter). Without a more integrated system, quality of care varies greatly. As a result, many millions of Americans receive overpriced care with subpar outcomes. This often leads to additional health crises. It is the worst kind of domino effect.

In the U.S. we spend far more than any other wealthy country on health care, both on a per person basis and as a percentage of our economy (and for years many of these countries have provided coverage for all of their citizens). A research study in 2013 by the Commonwealth Fund reported that "the U.S. spends $8,508 per person on health care. That is nearly $3,000 more per person than Norway, the second highest spender."[58] Sadly, the study also reported, "In 2013 more than one-third (37 percent) of U.S. adults went without recommended care, did not see a doctor when they were sick, or failed to fill prescriptions because of costs, compared with as few as 4 percent to 6 percent in the United Kingdom and Sweden."[59] In America, the average cost of a hospital stay is $18,000—nearly three times as high as the $6,200 average for the thirty-three other countries in the Organisation for Economic Co-operation and Development (OECD).[60]

So just what are all these high prices that add up to such exorbitant health care bills? Well, consider: One Plavix pill, which is used to treat heart and chest issues, costs four times more in the U.S. than it does in Spain. Lipitor, a drug used to treat cholesterol and prevent strokes, costs twenty times as much here as it does in New Zealand. A coronary bypass procedure costs approximately $67,000 in our country. The same procedure costs $16,000 in France. A far less complicated surgery, an appendectomy, costs about $13,000 in the U.S.—more than double the price for the same procedure in nine other developed countries. An M.R.I. scan that costs $1,100 here carries a price of just over $300 if you're in the Netherlands. Bottom line: America has been spending an *extra $750 billion* per year on health care versus other developed countries (even when income and cost of living are factored in).[61]

And if these products and procedures don't seem serious enough, consider the price for cancer drug treatments. One out of every three families in America is affected by cancer. And yet even with expanded insurance, cancer is one of the leading causes of bankruptcy. It all comes back to the non-system and the law. Dr. Hagop Kantarjian, who leads the nation's largest leukemia practice at the University of Texas Cancer Center, explains: "This is unique to the United States. If you look anywhere in the world, there are negotiations, either by the government or by different regulatory bodies to regulate the price of the drug. And this is why the prices are 50 percent to 80 percent lower anywhere in the world compared to the United States."[62]

In the 2013 film *Nebraska*, Bruce Dern plays a craggy old man who mistakenly thinks he's won the jackpot through a slick solicitation gimmick. After he bloodies his head in an accident and is taken to the emergency room, he randomly says to the ER doctor, "I won a million dollars." Without missing a beat, the doctor shoots back, "Congratulations—that'll just about pay for a day in the hospital." The punchline works because it's an inside joke that the whole country is in on. But in the real world, it's a punch in the face.

Again, the Affordable Care Act is an imperfect yet ambitious effort to solve one big part of our health care crisis by expanding insurance. Future effects of the ACA will take time to accurately decipher. Both supporters and opponents of the law agree that defects within the law need to be addressed, and we will return to this in Chapter 6. But even for Americans who are "covered," what are we actually receiving? Certainly not the full value of that $8,508 per person. Hacker and Pierson's research reveals that

> the United States has fewer doctors, hospital beds, and nurses per person than the norm among rich nations, and Americans (while less healthy overall), visit doctors and hospitals less often and have shorter hospital stays. Indeed, by some measures our health care looks surprisingly substandard. For example, recent analyses of 'amenable mortality'—deaths that could have been prevented with timely care—find that the United States has the highest rate of preventable death before age seventy-five among rich nations, and that it is falling farther and farther behind.[63]

In possibly the most authoritative evaluation of our poor health in America, we can look to the study commissioned by our very own government. In 2013, citing America's high average health cost per person and the fact that "Americans have been dying at younger ages than people in almost all other high-income countries,"[64] the U.S. National Institutes of Health directed the National Research Council and the nonprofit Institute of Medicine (IOM) to investigate the "U.S. Health Disadvantage."

The first glaring finding from the IOM:

This health disadvantage exists at all ages from birth to age 75 and that even advantaged Americans—those who have health insurance, college educations, higher incomes, and healthy behaviors—appear to be sicker than their peers in other rich nations.

The report is the first comprehensive look at multiple diseases, injuries, and behaviors across the entire life span, comparing the United States with 16 peer nations—affluent democracies that include Australia, Canada, Japan, and many western European countries. Among these countries, the U.S. is at or near the bottom in nine key areas of health: infant mortality and low birth weight; injuries and homicides; teenage pregnancies and sexually transmitted infections; prevalence of HIV and AIDS; drug-related deaths; obesity and diabetes; heart disease; chronic lung disease; and disability.[65]

This set of findings drives home the point that our nation's health and health care are problematic. However, the IOM study's conclusion covers a range of outcomes that have a number of causes and are not solely driven by the health care "system" (or lack thereof). Accordingly, and redolent of parts of the "economic well-being" evaluation above, the study's results introduce policy questions that stretch beyond just health policy. Deaths from drugs, murders, obesity, and various other causes cannot, and will not, always have a corresponding policy solution in the area of "health care." But as we can see, a great many of the laws Congress passes work in concert with one another to meet the nation's problems—to the extent they get passed. All of these issues are constantly bumping into one another, but that cannot be an excuse for ineffectiveness. In fact, the very complexity of these problems demands an optimal process and response from our lawmakers.

The bottom line on health care in our country, as the research confirms, is that we are not even close to receiving a commensurate bang for our buck—and far too many of those bucks are being squandered. As rich a country as we are, our overall health is poor. Certainly many of our own actions and decisions as individuals play a large role. But Congress's power to legislate for good and bad in this area is undeniable. Dr. Cosgrove from the Cleveland Clinic once again clarifies:

> One of the things Medicare has got to do is incentivize people to take care of themselves. We're not going to be able to control the costs in the United States unless we deal with the epidemic of obesity, which is now 10 percent of the health care cost in the United States and gradually going up, including diabetes, etc. So we need to have incentives for individuals to take care of themselves, and that's not really as big a part of new law as it should be.[66]

The lack of effective legislation on health care year after year has diminished the physical state of our nation, not to mention our fiscal state. ACA supporters claim credit for the slightly lower rate of health care spending since 2010. But even if this rate continues to slow marginally, analyses project that almost 25 percent of our GDP will be consumed by these costs two decades from now. Nightmare proportions.[67]

Dr. Noseworthy knows this and reiterates that despite a laudable benefit in covering Americans with insurance, Congress has many more rungs to scale:

> The Affordable Care Act will take its own path. What we really need to do is the next series of steps ... There are things government must do. First of all they need to modernize the payment system, modernize Medicare, they have to find a way to enable us to bring technology across state borders, to fund the NIH, and ultimately, the nation has to have the courage to step up to the looming insolvency of Medicare. That's what's pushing everything.[68]

Health care and the economy are highly interconnected. Stagnant wages make health care unaffordable for many. Expanded health insurance is starting to provide relief, but the stratospheric costs of many services and medications still squeeze health care consumers. Out-of-whack expenditures and inconsistent quality across the *non-system* conspire to put pressure on the federal budget. And then the billions we borrow in that budget to cover future health care and social insurance commitments jack up our debt and hurt our economy in the present.

In fact, Congress's poor legislative performance on the preceding two issues, the economy and health care, is particularly relevant as we transition to the next two sections in this chapter—America's national security and the multiplier effect. Just as health care and the economy ping pong off each other and cannot be separated, a variety of domestic and international issues ultimately intersect as we take the measure of our strength as a country.

NATIONAL SECURITY

The term "national security" is as old as the Constitution, but the issue is obviously a great deal more complicated today than when Alexander Hamilton first referenced it in *Federalist 29*.[69] Certainly one portion of one chapter of one book cannot come close to comprehensively evaluating how secure the United States is as a nation. It is far more wide-ranging than most public policy issues—we live in a big world—and with matters of life and death front and center, national security is a genuinely subjective topic. No one single method or measure can be used to judge our level of security, and a vast range of competing opinions exist on what are the best approaches to achieving safety and security for our nation.

Additionally, two conspicuous political features of the national security issue can make it seem more difficult to analyze and evaluate when looking at the performance of Congress. The first is the historic tension in our system between the powers and responsibilities of the president versus Congress in their respective duties to protect America. The U.S. Constitution designates the president as commander-in-chief, granting him the clear authority to command the armed forces, to appoint ambassadors, and to negotiate treaties. Congress has the power to declare war, "to raise and support armies," "to provide and maintain a navy," and "to regulate commerce with foreign nations." Importantly, Congress also has the authority through its powers of appropriations to continue or discontinue the federal funding that pays for these efforts.[70] Finally, Congress has the onerous yet essential obligation to exercise responsible oversight over the executive branch departments charged with achieving national defense goals.

More than two centuries later, the struggle for power over national security concerns has only become more fraught with questions and controversy. The reach of the executive branch has continually expanded beyond the Department of Defense (DOD) over the decades and now includes the Central Intelligence Agency (CIA), National Security Agency (NSA), Department of Homeland Security (DHS), Department of Veteran Affairs (VA), and a variety of other agencies that play roles in maintaining America's strength and security. Congress has the ever-increasing responsibility of *oversight* of these departments—to ensure that executive efforts are on the level and are being practiced responsibly, lawfully, and (hopefully) with a reasonable degree of efficiency.

The second political feature that makes national security a tricky issue in this context is the philosophical differences the political parties have historically had regarding America's military assertiveness—about both the size of our armed forces and their deployment. Americans would like to think that our leaders' differences end "at the water's edge." And sometimes they do. But other times, the imperative of protecting America and our standing in the world elicits passionate positions—often based on principle, other times on politics. In recent years, more so on politics.

We Americans like to think of our country as the "leader of nations." And in so many ways, our government remains a great power. But our government has also made decisions in recent decades that have called into question the wisdom of our international leadership. Such questions come from many corners of the world, but perhaps none are more important than those emanating from right here within our own borders.

As we begin this section on national security, which is to a great degree about protecting the U.S. from international threats, we must place the subject in perspective. Conventional views of America's national security system focus on three major components: defense, intelligence, and foreign policy. The product of our policies in these areas, however, is about far more than being able to say that our country has not been attacked in X number of years or had X number of casualties. Looking more deeply, what are the ways in which we are pursuing the goals of security, which include our state of preparedness, the actual costs associated with our decisions and actions, as well as the opportunity costs associated with inaction?

In America's current political atmosphere, it can be easy to generalize the left and the right's respective philosophical stances on national defense according to long-held stereotypes. But doing so clouds the discussion and ignores important facts. Both Democrats and Republicans, whether in the White House or through the power of congressional majorities, have each had historic successes and devastating failures in their efforts to protect the country. Pointing the finger at one party or the other is easy, but it is also increasingly off-putting to the growing political middle of the country. Consequently, in recent years an increasing number of rational voices have come forward to voice informed, nonpartisan criticisms of Congress's performance on national security—regardless of party affiliation.

Two respected institutional voices on this subject are the bipartisan Center for Strategic and International Studies (CSIS) and the nonpartisan Council on Foreign Relations (CFR). Each institution's leadership includes policy experts from both ends of the political spectrum as well as points in between.

Kay King is one of those experts. King has worked in senior advisor positions in foreign relations in the U.S. Senate and U.S. State Department and as a vice president at both the CSIS and CFR. In 2012, with the backing and counsel of a bipartisan CFR committee, King authored the special report *"Congress and National Security,"* in which she lays out a broad critique of Congress's performance since the end of the Cold War:

> It has relinquished its authority concerning military base closings
> to a series of independent commissions, and it is often reluctant
> to cut wasteful weapons programs, thus undermining its own
> credibility. On questions of military intervention, it has frequently

deferred to the executive branch, failing to provide the scrutiny essential to a successful foreign policy. On matters of diplomacy, development, and intelligence, Congress has been inconsistent and occasionally counterproductive. In its appropriations role, it has failed to provide timely funding for diplomacy and development agencies, delaying the start of programs and the hiring of personnel, thus diminishing U.S. capacity around the world. In its oversight role, despite globalization, it has not overhauled the Foreign Assistance Act since 1985, impeding a coherent approach to overseas programs, and it has resisted making vital structural changes to the intelligence committees, undermining accountability in the intelligence community. In its advice-and-consent role, the Senate has taken ambassadorial and national security nominees as political hostages for long periods of time, depriving the nation of sufficient representation overseas and political leadership in government agencies.[71]

King's review is harsh, to be sure. Americans also have strong opinions about how Congress should equip and employ the various tools in our national security arsenal. So let's take a closer look at these criticisms.

Military spending has been an increasingly contentious subject in Congress in recent years. Ironically, it is the Pentagon that has wanted to eliminate or reduce various weapons systems and programs, whereas Congress has been pushing back. Because building military assets often creates jobs, in recent decades members of Congress traditionally wanted to protect defense programs in their districts. The national security industry increased fifty-fold during the Cold War, and members of the House and Senate Armed Services Committees consistently steered military spending toward their local constituencies.[72] Congressman L. Mendel Rivers (D-SC), who retired as chair of the Armed Services Committee, directed so much defense spending to his district that people joked that the city of Charleston would drop into the ocean from the weight of its military base.[73]

But the urgency to budget in a smarter fashion on defense is a far bigger priority today due to the sizable national debt and deficits. Yet

Congress keeps spending even as the Department of Defense advises against it. In 2011, former Secretary of Defense Robert Gates, who was appointed by President George W. Bush and reappointed by President Obama, cautioned the country: "We must come to realize that not every defense program is necessary, not every defense dollar is well-spent, and that more of nearly everything is simply not sustainable."[74]

But the trend continued the following year, with multiple projects receiving funding from Congress—again against the advice of the Department of Defense. In the state of Ohio alone, the Pentagon said it either did not want or need additional funding for the Global Hawk Block 30 drone program, the M1 Abrams tank, the C-27J cargo aircraft, as well as an East Coast missile defense battery. Members of Congress from both parties in Ohio pushed back hard on all of the spending reductions anyway, which added up to several billion dollars.[75] The same thing happens every year in states throughout the U.S.; taken together, it adds up. In 2012, according to the Office of Management and Budget, the U.S. Congress appropriated $682 billion in military spending—an amount more than the *combined total* spent by the next ten nations of Russia, China, the United Kingdom, Japan, France, Saudi Arabia, India, Germany, Italy, and Brazil.[76]

That $682 billion was roughly 20 percent of the federal government's annual budget. While defense spending fell to $613 million in 2013 due to budget cuts, that total was still more than double what the U.S. spent on defense in the year 2000, just prior to our entry into the wars in Afghanistan and Iraq in 2001 and 2003. A long and complex debate could ensue about what concrete benefits these two controversial military actions may eventually bring the United States and its allies. In spite of their contrary positions on the wisdom of the Iraq war and components of our engagement in Afghanistan, both President Bush and President Obama have expressed on numerous occasions that "history will be the judge."[77]

Rather than enter that difficult debate, we can consider the very important costs that we know our country has incurred, as well as some of the factors that contributed to our government's decisions to engage in the first place.

The most appropriate point to start is with the extraordinarily brave men and women who have answered the call to duty time and time again to prosecute these wars. It can be easy to lose sight of the fact that in our system civilian leaders decide when, where, and for how long American soldiers will risk life and limb.

"Operation Iraqi Freedom" claimed the lives of more than 4,400 Americans, and more than 2,300 died in "Operation Enduring Freedom" in Afghanistan. And of those soldiers who did make it home, more than 50,000 of them sustained injuries in battle. A visit to www.icasualties.org allows you to review documents with the names of the thousands of courageous U.S. patriots who made the ultimate sacrifice on our behalf.[78] It is the most sobering kind of reading imaginable.

These epic human costs have no true price tag, but we can measure the hefty financial costs of the two military conflicts. By early 2014, the United States had already spent more than $2 trillion to support combat operations, reconstruction projects, and other military personnel costs. Yet the spending does not end when the wars end.

In 2013, Harvard public policy professor Linda Bilmes released a study titled *The Financial Legacy of Iraq and Afghanistan*. A national expert on defense budgeting, Bilmes reports that taken together the conflicts will cost us between $4 trillion and $6 trillion when we include "long-term medical care and disability compensation for service members, veterans and families, military replenishment and social and economic costs."[79] In the context of our country's long-term fiscal outlook, these projected future costs are debilitating.

Although the "history will judge" proposition may take years to yield definitive answers regarding the wisdom of these two wars, Defense Secretary Robert Gates did comment about it as he finished his five-year service in the Bush and Obama administrations. Speaking to cadets in a speech at West Point in 2011, Gates remarked that "any future defense secretary who advises the president to again send a big American land army into Asia or into the Middle East or Africa should have his head examined."[80] And we must keep in mind that the "heads" in Congress have considerable power and responsibility when it comes to publicly debating, authorizing, and funding the continuation of any U.S. military engagement.

INTELLIGENCE

Whether or not the supporters or the critics of these military missions end up being on the right side of history, documents have proven that faulty intelligence presented by the executive branch in 2002–2003 led to the war in Iraq. Factually incorrect information about the Iraqi dictatorship possessing "weapons of mass destruction" (WMD) convinced majorities both in Congress and the country to approve the invasion of Iraq. By 2005, with the new knowledge of having been misled, a majority of Americans viewed the war as a mistake. Nearly ten years later, Gallup reported that the same majority continued to believe it was a mistake.[81]

But the George W. Bush administration does not alone own the Iraq intelligence fiasco. Remember what Kay King wrote about Congress's deferring "to the executive branch, failing to provide the scrutiny essential to a successful foreign policy."[82] Just as the Constitution and the War Powers Act give Congress the powers to fund military actions and to authorize the continuation of any war initiated by the commander-in-chief, Congress also has the obligation to provide effective *oversight* of these types of national security decisions. This oversight has been sorely lacking.

The National Commission on Terrorist Attacks Upon the United States (known as the 9/11 Commission), an entity created in 2002, investigated America's state of preparedness before the September 11 assault and provided recommendations to prevent future attacks. The bipartisan commission was chaired by former New Jersey Governor Thomas H. Kean (R) and vice-chaired by former U.S. Representative Lee H. Hamilton (D-IN).

Although the 9/11 Commission criticized the CIA and FBI under both Presidents Clinton and Bush, it clearly asserted that Congress was also culpable:

> Congress had a distinct tendency to push questions of emerging national security threats off its own plate, leaving them for others to consider. Congress asked outside commissions to do the work that arguably was at the heart of its own oversight responsibilities. Beginning in 1999, the reports of these commissions made scores of recommendations to address terrorism and homeland

security but drew little attention from Congress. Most of their impact came after 9/11.[83]

In July 2014, the Commission published *Reflections on the Tenth Anniversary of the 9/11 Commission Report.* In the report, again chaired by Kean and Hamilton, the Commission wrote that "Congressional reform is the most important unfulfilled recommendation of the 9/11 Commission."[84]

The first report urged Congress to reduce its out-of-control number of homeland security committees: eighty-eight. But ten years later this total had actually *grown to ninety-two.* The Commission asserted: "This balkanized system of oversight detracts from the department's mission and has made Americans less safe," adding that Congress has still never "enacted a final, comprehensive DHS authorization bill setting policy and spending priorities," and that it wastes DHS resources as a result.[85]

Dr. Loch Johnson, who at one time worked on oversight committees in both the House and the Senate, is now a professor and author at the University of Georgia. He described the members of the Select Committees on Intelligence as falling "into an oversight stupor. They forgot the warnings of Madison and the wisdom of the Constitution. Oversight came to mean rallying behind the president and the intelligence community to support the fighting that ensued in Iraq, Afghanistan, and against global terrorism. This was an amplification of a trend visible even before 9/11."[86]

In 2004, Senator John McCain (R-AZ) reinforced the 9/11 Commission's conclusions: "Everyone recognizes that the failure of congressional oversight was one of the reasons why we have some of the problems in the intelligence community today. Bob Kerrey said that the Senate was more interested—the old bulls were more interested in turf than national security. That's a very harsh assessment, but we really still don't have meaningful congressional oversight."[87]

The task of "oversight," even the word, can sound pretty bland and boring—even to those in Washington who are charged with the responsibility. More than three decades ago, former Speaker of the House Tip O'Neill noted this aversion when he observed that members of Congress "like to create and legislate, but we have shied away from the word and deed of oversight."[88]

Nevertheless, oversight is a huge and critical responsibility of our legislative branch. Through committee hearings, where experts and citizens alike can be called to testify, and through staff research, Congress investigates and performs oversight to ensure that the laws it passes are being carried out according to their original intent. The importance of this role must never be sold short. Congress is passing legislation to promote our general welfare—to promote the fiscal solvency and physical security of the American people. Rules of the road are meaningless without proper enforcement.

The responsibility of oversight is wide-ranging as it covers nearly all of the activities and departments within the sprawling executive branch. Among these, the purview of Congress includes monitoring the agencies that administer policies over food and drug safety, the environment, transportation, law enforcement, intelligence gathering, tax revenue, homeland security, and many others. And, just as significantly, Congress is charged with ensuring that the funds it appropriates for these functions are being spent in a prudent fashion.

In Lee Hamilton's book *Strengthening Congress,* the former U.S. representative emphasizes the importance of proper oversight:

> There is a lesson to be learned from events like Abu Ghraib and the economic meltdown, and it is this: Even in a democracy, things that happen in the shadows can end up having deep implications for the nation and for every American. For the press, it is a professional shortcoming when it fails to bring them to our attention. For Congress, it is a dereliction of its constitutional duties. It is Congress's responsibility to shine light on the workings of government, and to ensure that its actions really do reflect the generous and honorable nature of our country.[89]

Imagine all of the time it would take to be truly proficient at this Herculean task. Members of Congress don't have that time—not even close. There are reasons for this, and we are just pages away from defining The Problem that has helped to produce many of these poor outcomes. We pause at this point only to emphasize the importance of oversight.

The role congressional oversight plays is not always visible, yet it is truly pivotal to the government's pursuit of national goals. And when it comes to national security, Congress's failures are hardly confined to the 9/11 disaster.

Continuing down the track of oversight over America's intelligence community, it seems as though not much has changed a decade after the CIA "WMD" debacle. In fact, we may be in worse shape. In 2004, after the 9/11 Commission labeled congressional oversight "dysfunctional," it also unanimously recommended reforming the structure and powers of the intelligence committees. Congress changed a few things around the edges but did not adopt the Commission's major recommendations. As a result of this inaction, nearly ten years later, during the 112th Congress, the Congressional Research Service (CRS) reported that "the Bipartisan Policy Center's National Security Preparedness Group, Commission on Weapons of Mass Destruction, and Council on Foreign Relations—still concluded that oversight of intelligence remained 'dysfunctional' and 'counterproductive.'"[90]

All of these oversight lapses and the policy decisions that result add up to our national security product. Wars that claim thousands of lives change families forever. The long-run costs of these military conflicts, in the trillions of dollars, in turn affect other large-scale economic challenges confronting the country. Dysfunction within the agencies mandated to protect us have negative effects on America's state of preparedness, many of which are unseen and unfelt—until they're not.

Likewise, oversight failures also shape the methods and practices our law enforcement and intelligence-gathering agencies use in the realm of spying. The CIA was created in 1947. The far larger NSA was formed in 1952, with the stated mission to "provide an effective, unified organization and control of the communications intelligence activities of the United States conducted against foreign governments, to provide for integrated operational policies and procedures pertaining thereto."[91] When President Harry S. Truman created the NSA, it was classified, so Americans did not even know it existed. Over the years it has been jokingly referred to as "No Such Agency." But in the twenty-first century, covert spying by our intelligence community is anything but comedy.

To be clear, the CIA, FBI, NSA and other intelligence and law enforcement agencies do highly important work on behalf of Americans and almost certainly have thwarted many lethal attacks on our country that most of us will never know about. Thousands of people in these agencies are patriotic citizens who work every day to protect the United States. It is a balancing act. In late 2014, FBI Director and former Deputy Attorney General James Comey expressed this well when he was asked if Americans should feel safe at night when they hit the pillow:

> I think they should ... We are better organized, better systems, better equipment, smarter deployment. We are better in every way that you'd want us to be since 9/11. We're not perfect. My philosophy as a leader is we are never good enough. But we are in a much better place than we were thirteen years ago.[92]

Americans need these executive branch agencies to perform important, often heroic jobs to keep us safe. At the same time, the post-9/11 environment and its correspondingly enlarged sphere of preemptive intelligence efforts make Congress's watchdog function even more crucial. The rule of law is paramount. James Comey emphasizes this point: "The oversight of the courts and the oversight of Congress will be at the heart of what the FBI does. The way you'd want it to be."[93]

A tension between the country's need to spy for national security purposes and the unethical or unlawful overreach of these agencies has always existed. The protections that stand between the proper and improper use of these investigative powers are congressional oversight and investigative journalism. And sadly, it has been the media and whistleblowers, not our elected representatives, who have uncovered these abuses in far too many instances.

In the modern era, the Watergate scandal rates among the most prominent episodes of U.S. executive branch abuse of law enforcement and intelligence agencies. *The Washington Post*'s Carl Bernstein and Bob Woodward famously brought to light President Richard M. Nixon's illegal intelligence operation, which spied on Americans and amassed personal files on them for domestic political purposes.[94] Additional abuses in the

Nixon administration were uncovered, and in response, Congress passed the Foreign Intelligence Surveillance Act in 1978 and the Intelligence Oversight Act in 1980. The two laws respectively outlawed the execution of warrantless wiretaps and required prior notice be given to the Senate and House intelligence committees on all important intelligence operations. Ten years later, the illegal covert actions of the National Security Council in Nicaragua during the Iran–Contra scandal tested the legislative branch once again. In 1989, Congress provided an answer in the form of a new inspector general position within the CIA.[95]

But oversight failures continued, and in 2005 once again it was the press, not Congress, that revealed more legally questionable intelligence operations. *The New York Times* reported that, according to sources in the government, "months after the September 11 attacks, President Bush secretly authorized the National Security Agency to eavesdrop on Americans and others inside the United States to search for evidence of terrorist activity without the court-approved warrants ordinarily required for domestic spying."[96] In 2008, Congress passed a law that gave immunity to the telecommunications companies that had aided surveillance operations.[97]

Congress has shown similar recalcitrance or impotence on the issue of detainment policy in the war against terror. One week after September 11, 2001, Congress passed the Authorized Use of Military Force that gave the president, and by extension the armed forces and intelligence agencies, the power to use "all necessary and appropriate force" in going after those responsible for attacking the twin towers and the Pentagon. That loose wording led to controversial actions taken by the Bush administration on legally questionable detainment of "enemy combatants" as well as "enhanced interrogation techniques," otherwise known as torture. In 2005 and 2006, Congress passed the Detainee Treatment Act and Military Commissions Act to address some of these questions. These laws were not very clarifying, however, and the courts have been largely left to rule on detainee cases with scant congressional guidance.[98] Nearly fifteen years after 9/11, the argument over the legality and effectiveness of these methods continued between congressional committees and corresponding executive branch agencies.

We can see how over the last two decades the already tough job of oversight has only become harder in Congress due to its increased dysfunction. Rules surrounding access to classified materials can make the task trickier. Also, since 2001 America's national defense and intelligence industrial complex has ballooned, compounding the degree of difficulty in congressional oversight. But Congress itself has played a substantial role in the enlargement of these government agencies, and it has a commensurate responsibility to supervise them properly.

In 2010, *The Washington Post*'s Dana Priest and William M. Arkin explored the depth of this problem in their series "Top Secret America." In one of the pieces, "National Security Inc.," they detail "what amounts to an alternative geography of the United States, a Top Secret America created since 9/11 that is hidden from public view, lacking in thorough oversight and so unwieldy that its effectiveness is impossible to determine."[99] The reporters provide evidence of an exponentially larger national security state than we have ever seen in America. In approximately ten thousand locations across the country, more than twelve hundred government organizations focus on homeland security, intelligence, and counterterrorism, producing fifty thousand intelligence reports annually. Priest and Arkin report, "Many security and intelligence agencies do the same work, creating redundancy and waste."[100] That mountain range of manpower also includes "854,000 people with top-secret clearances," 265,000 of whom are contractors.[101]

One of those contractors with access to classified information, Edward Snowden, became famous in June 2013 for leaking the fact that the NSA had collected the telephone records of tens of millions of Americans. A 29-year-old high school dropout, Snowden instantly became notorious or illustrious depending on one's view of his actions. Through additional documents he disclosed, *The Washington Post* reported, "The National Security Agency and the FBI are tapping directly into the central servers of nine leading U.S. Internet companies, extracting audio and video chats, photographs, e-mails, documents, and connection logs."[102]

Former Senator John E. Sununu (R-NH) spoke for many Americans a month later when he declared: "Members of Congress have been quick to express their shock and dismay at his outrageous behavior. Doing so makes it easier to avoid the hard fact that they all knew—or should have known—about the lax oversight of these programs. I certainly did when I was in office."[103]

Snowden claimed he leaked the information to safeguard Americans' privacy and personal liberties. The legality of his actions will be adjudicated if and when he returns to the U.S. to face the justice system. Regardless, however, the revelations he pulled out of the shadows only reinforce the fact that congressional oversight is not finding, or may be allowing, high-level executive branch activities that are either illegal or improper.

Many of these fights over the issues of power and abuse within the nation's intelligence and law enforcement agencies can seem very abstract. They don't hit nearly as close to home as losing a job or health care—events that touch our daily lives in more tangible ways. Surveillance may seem harmless when it's happening to the other guy—right up until one of us is "the other guy." Certain laws are intended to protect us from the federal government's overreach and abuse, and members of Congress are obligated to conduct proper oversight to ensure that such abuse is not happening. There are many, even inside Congress, who believe that they are losing the battle.

Yet another battle we are losing also cries out for coverage—one where Congress must play both a serious role in oversight and in providing adequate resources. Arguably, that responsibility is the most important moral function our government is tasked with performing: taking care of the American warriors who have taken care of us.

U.S. VETERANS

Along Vermont Avenue in Washington, D.C. sits the U.S. Department of Veterans Affairs (VA). In front of the entrance, all visitors walk past a gold-lettered plaque that reads: "To care for him who shall have borne the battle and for his widow, and his orphan." These words were spoken by President Abraham Lincoln in his second inaugural address on March 4, 1865—one month before the end of the Civil War.[104] The VA's stated mission is to fulfill Lincoln's promise "by serving and honoring the men and women who are America's veterans."

That duty is an enormous responsibility and extremely difficult task. Over the course of our country's history, 41.8 million Americans have served in the military during periods of war. More than 650,000 have lost their lives in battle. Even prior to the twenty-first century conflicts in Iraq and Afghanistan, the number of surviving U.S. war veterans totaled 16,962,000.[105] The VA serves veterans, their surviving spouses and children, as well as uniformed service members. The department describes its range of services as including "disability, education and training, vocational rehabilitation and employment, home loan guaranty, dependent and survivor benefits, medical treatment, life insurance, and burial benefits."[106]

Of course, the VA is a department within the executive branch. Its leaders and the president at the top hold primary responsibility for its management and operational effectiveness. However, in much the same way that Congress has oversight and appropriations responsibilities over national security agencies, so it does with the VA. And despite the agency's best efforts, the soldiers who put it all on the line for us in dangerous war zones abroad are struggling when they return home.

That is, if they have a home. Although the total number of homeless vets has been slowly coming down since 2010, the U.S. Department of Housing and Urban Development still estimates that more than 57,000 of our veterans are on the streets and on their own on any given night.[107]

Recent years have seen highly publicized grilling of the VA over its incompetent handling of veterans' disability claims. In 2013, it took an average of 378 days for the VA to complete a claim. Once a claim has been pending for more than 125 days, it is considered "backlogged." Under heat for the glacial pace of care for veterans, then-VA Secretary Eric Shinseki instituted reforms that began to at least reduce the backlogs. But in 2014, almost 700,000 U.S. veterans and their families were still waiting on responses from the government.[108]

The VA's failings are not confined to the huge number of vets waiting for the aid they've earned. On February 10, 2014, a *Wall Street Journal* article exposed both the shortcomings of the VA and Congress's tardiness with regard to oversight: "In a rare show of bipartisanship, top members of the congressional committees that oversee the VA are increasingly frustrated with the agency in the wake of incidents ranging from a patient's death after an altercation with a nursing assistant in Louisiana to a deadly outbreak of Legionnaires' disease in Pennsylvania. Lawmakers say these episodes reflect a lack of accountability at the 1,700 VA hospitals, clinics, and other facilities."[109]

A few weeks later, a bill came up in the U.S. Senate to expand medical facilities (which would help reduce the disability backlog) and provide education and hiring programs for vets (who have a higher unemployment rate than the overall national rate). The funding in the bill totaled $24 billion. The Senate minority killed the bill.[110]

U.S. Veteran Paul Rieckhoff is founder of the veterans advocacy nonprofit Iraq and Afghanistan Veterans of America. After the bill's demise he told CNN it was all of a piece: "The Senate shenanigans capped a winter of discontent for our community in which Washington continually attacked military members, veterans, and their families. It used to be that vets could count on bipartisan support in Congress. But clearly, no more."[111]

The VA's annual budget in 2013 was $140.3 billion.[112] In general, requests from U.S. presidents to Congress to increase annual funding for the VA have met with success. Politically, it is a dangerous area for members to say "no." This may be changing. But whether it is a matter of funding or negligent oversight, there is no question that our veterans deserve better service. Every day, an average of twenty-two veterans commit suicide.[113] Thousands are homeless. Hundreds of thousands are awaiting medical care. The ones who are healthy are underemployed. These are our vets. Basic patriotism alone requires us to insist that our elected leaders demand and see to improvements in this situation. Our veterans have sacrificed, and they have suffered. We owe them.

Obviously, the hope going forward is to promote public policy that will not produce additional combat veterans. Of course, this is not a realistic notion. Both smart and dumb wars have been fought, and often judgments over which were which are made far more easily in hindsight. But the foreign policy decisions our government makes have the power to impact international relations, and by extension, the frequency with which we are confronted by questions over when using force is necessary.

The final piece to briefly cover in reviewing the national security product concerns international relations when options other than military force come to the fore—exactly what Kay King pointed out when criticizing Congress's foreign aid policy. Although our foreign aid bill is only one-twentieth the size of our defense budget (roughly 1 percent of the overall federal budget), both sides of the aisle acknowledge that it plays an important role in U.S. national security. Former Secretary of State Condoleezza Rice articulated this at the White House in 2008: "For the United States, supporting international development is more than just an expression of our compassion. It is a vital investment in the free, prosperous, and peaceful international order that fundamentally serves our national interest."[114]

America provides funding for international development through the U.S. Agency for International Development (USAID), which was created by the Foreign Assistance Act of 1961. But Congress must approve every dime, and once again, dysfunction dilutes both strategy and execution. In 2009, the ranking member of the Senate Foreign Relations Committee, Richard Lugar (R-IN), complained, "during the last two decades, decision-makers have not made it easy for USAID to perform its vital function."[115]

Lugar was actually kid-gloving Congress. In fact, it has been nearly thirty years since Congress passed comprehensive foreign aid legislation. Susan Epstein, a foreign affairs specialist at the Congressional Research Service, explains that such failure weakens the ability of the foreign affairs committees to conduct oversight. Moreover, reinforcing King's point, Epstein says the greater concern is the bigger negative effect inept foreign aid legislation has on our nation's overall strategy:

> Largely due to this and other highly partisan and contentious aid issues, congressional action on re-authorizing aid, which could have included revamping the primary statutory basis for foreign aid, the Foreign Assistance Act of 1961, continues to elude Congress. As a result, the act continues to be patched and amended to the point where it is now considered to be fragmented, cumbersome, and missing the mark on addressing today's overseas aid

needs or U.S. national security interests. It continues to contain Cold War references and objectives at a time when foreign aid could be more useful in countering regional instability, poverty, and terrorism overseas to act as a stronger national security tool for the United States.[116]

Epstein's description of the committees' failures is not only instructive as applied to foreign relations and national security but also to congressional committees in general. Whether it is foreign relations, intelligence, or armed services, the congressional process is not optimally serving the American people. Foreign policy decisions are never easy, both with regard to legislation and oversight. But when members of Congress do not have the time or the capacity to work together on these issues, the country suffers.

With the world's eyes always upon us, the ways in which the U.S. carries out its national security policies have implications far beyond any urgency of the moment. Our military budget is bloated, and the American people (as well as many of our leaders) have openly questioned not only Congress's decisions to fund it but the wisdom of our decisions to use it.

Defense, intelligence, veterans, foreign aid—all are areas where congressional oversight has been feeble or entirely missing in recent years. We have covered a handful here, and in truth, this represents just a tiny nick in the paint. But hopefully this cursory review makes the point: Ensuring that our defense, intelligence, and foreign policy systems are working both effectively and ethically matters in today's world of accelerating transparency. All of these pieces are interconnected. Our government has a lot of mess to address, and the first branch of government will need to step up in big ways.

THE MULTIPLIER EFFECT

In the first two sections of this chapter we witnessed both the pain and waste Americans are experiencing with regard to health care and economic well-being—as well as the relationship between these issues. We also observed the negative long-range implications these predicaments threaten to inflict on our national debt as well as our inability to keep commitments to our seniors. All of these challenges are connected, and our domestic strength—or weakness—on each of these issues has a huge impact on our overall national security. Our stability at home has far-reaching implications in terms of the larger role that the U.S. plays in the international community.

But it's not just the big-ticket issues. In the final section of this chapter we zoom in on three problems that are cited to a lesser degree in public polling—"single-digit" issues—where the defective congressional process is likewise not measuring up. The Appendix lists measures of Americans' concern about education, immigration, and gun use in our country. These unmet challenges do not exist in separate silos. Again, in ways that are seen and unseen, individual failures in the public policy sphere have powerful multiplier effects. And it all begins with our young people.

EDUCATION

George Washington Carver once said, "Education is the key to unlock the golden door of freedom." But in today's America, despite the hard work and best intentions of so many education professionals, that door to opportunity is deadbolted shut for millions of kids. The statistics are staggering. Each one represents a real life. And each setback sets up the next hurdle.

According to the National Assessment of Educational Progress, approximately two-thirds of eighth-graders perform below proficiency both in reading and in math (two years behind their peers in other countries). In civics, that figure rises to 75 percent. By the twelfth grade, nearly three out of four students cannot write proficiently. And every year, American schools see roughly 1.1 million students drop out.[117]

Seventy years ago, the U.S. high school graduation rate stood first in the world. By 2012 the OECD ranked America twenty-second out of twenty-seven industrialized countries. Measured against those same countries, our students ranked twenty-fifth in math, seventeenth in science, and fourteenth in reading. Naturally, and unfortunately, so many of our kids drag this baggage along with them to college—if they get there at all.[118]

Standardized testing indicates that only 25 percent of high school graduates begin college with proficiency in English, reading, math, and science. So one-third of them enroll in remedial classes when they start college. Forty-six percent complete college, ranking the U.S. eighteenth—and last—among countries measured by OECD.[119]

Much as with our health care analysis, other factors affect these education statistics. The poverty challenge discussed earlier is a glaring example, and another reminder, of the ripple effect that so many public policy issues have on each other in our society.

The first and most obvious result of educational failure is the brutal consequences it has on individual lives. More than 40 percent of dropouts under the age of 24 are without a job according to the U.S. Department of Labor. On average, those dropouts will earn only 5 percent of what college graduates will earn over the course of their lifetimes. A huge number of dropouts will battle poverty throughout their adulthood—and require social welfare supports from the government.[120]

A second result of this depressing educational gap is the withering effect it has on our economy. Our labor pool is underprepared for the ever-changing demands of American employers. Educational failures result in a reduced labor force, reduced productivity, and reduced tax revenue.

A joint study that surveyed more than four hundred employers across the country described the U.S. workforce as "woefully ill-prepared for the demands of today's (and tomorrow's) workplace."[121] Seventy-five percent described their employees who had achieved four-year degrees as lacking "excellent" basic knowledge and applied skills.[122]

But our high school dropout rate has the largest measurable drain on our economy. A report from the Alliance for Excellent Education quantified the costs. In *Dropouts, Diplomas and Dollars: U.S. High Schools and the Nation's Economy,* author Jason Amos reports that an annual class of high school dropouts (nationally) will translate into a loss of $319 billion in lifetime earnings. Amos further reports: "America would save more than $17 billion in health care costs over the course of the lifetimes of each class of dropouts had they earned their diplomas. American households would have over $74 billion more in accumulated wealth if all heads of households had graduated from high school."[123]

The biggest alarm bell, however, comes from a more comprehensive study released in 2012, *The Economic Value of Opportunity Youth.*[124] The authors define "opportunity youth" as Americans between the ages of 16 to 24 who have either "never been in school or work after the age of 16" or who "have not progressed through college or secured a stable attachment to the labor market." The study found a total of 6.7 million young people who "are failing to build an economic foundation for adult independence." The collective costs to the U.S. over the long term? When the loss of tax income over the lifetime of this population ("taxpayer burden") is added to what they will need and receive from the government ("social burden"), the total *economic burden of opportunity youth to our country totals $6.3 trillion.*[125]

An equally powerful example of the national importance and concern over education was emphasized in the 2012 CFR Task Force Report *U.S. Education Reform and National Security.*[126] The report's co-chairs, former Secretary of State Condoleezza Rice and former New York Schools Chancellor Joel Klein, point out how educational achievement is critical to maintaining America's competitive position in a globalized world. But then they tie the issue of education directly to America's *national security,* explaining that our country needs qualified men and women to enter the ranks of the government's armed forces, intelligence agencies, and foreign service.[127]

Those needs are not being met. Our poor education record negatively affects U.S. military preparedness in ways unbeknownst to most Americans. The Task Force Report quantifies the problem: "The 25 percent of students who drop out of high school are unqualified to serve, as are the approximately 30 percent of high school graduates who *do* graduate but do not know enough math, science, and English to perform well on the mandatory Armed Services Vocational Aptitude Battery."[128]

Even within the current military ranks, our officers' educational proficiency is coming up short. According to the CFR report:

> U.S. schools are also failing to prepare enough scientists, mathematicians, and engineers to staff the military, intelligence agencies, and other government-run national security offices, as well as the aerospace and defense industries. Today, less than a third

of American students graduate with a first university degree in any science or engineering field. More than half of these students have studied social or behavioral sciences; only 4.5 percent of U.S. college students, overall, graduate with degrees in engineering. In China, by comparison, more than half of college students receive their first university degree in science or engineering.[129]

Additionally, the Task Force reports that in spite of the innovation we see coming out of Silicon Valley, the U.S. does not have enough members of the military with the proper technical expertise to effectively fight cyber-espionage.[130]

We care about our kids, and we want to see them excel educationally so they might reach their full potential. But it is easy to see how their educational successes, or lack thereof, have consequences for the entire country. Here we see just another example of where one issue collides with so many others. Building the strength of the United States is a holistic, never-ending process.

IMMIGRATION

Educational performance is not the only issue area sapping our labor force, and by extension, our economic dynamism. Near universal agreement exists that our approach to both legal and illegal immigration is causing the country pain. The last major immigration legislation Congress passed was the 1986 Immigration Reform and Control Act (Simpson-Mazzoli Act)—a law whose consequences remain controversial nearly thirty years later. Yet no major reform package has been delivered by Congress in the intervening decades. Our immigration mess and all of its associated problems persist.

The reality is that America actually needs more immigrants to come to our country. The challenges described earlier in our social insurance programs are to a great degree driven by demographics. Strengthening these safety net systems will require an increase in our workforce that cannot be achieved without substantial inflows of new immigrants. At the same time, the U.S. is struggling to recruit and maintain a workforce that is highly skilled and technically proficient. But year after year, Congress shoots blanks on reform.

In their book *Immigration Wars,* former Florida Governor Jeb Bush (R) and Stanford University's Clint Bolick present the dual problems posed by the status quo:

> Our immigration laws are so complex, cumbersome, and irrational that millions of people have circumvented them and entered our country illegally, inflicting grave damage to the rule of law that is our nation's moral centerpiece. Others have either given up or tragically abandoned their hopes of becoming Americans or have gone home, and we have lost their energy and talent forever.[131]

Losing this "talent and energy" directly affects our ability to fill both low- and high-skilled jobs essential to our economy. The challenge is critical enough to the semiconductor company Intel that it actually employs a "director of immigration policy." His name is Peter Muller, and in a 2013 editorial in the *National Journal,* Muller explained the effects of the interminable wait for congressional action on immigration: "In the high-skilled arena, our ability to compete in the global marketplace is compromised. The information-technology industry struggles to find enough qualified U.S. workers to fill the key jobs necessary for continued innovation. Employees who obtain temporary visas must wait years before they can get a green card to allow them to live and work here permanently."[132]

More broadly, the administrations of both President George W. Bush and Barack Obama have touted the positive effect that immigrants have on the American economy. In 2007, the Bush Council of Economic Advisers released an immigration report stating: "Our review of economic research finds immigrants not only help fuel the nation's economic growth but also have an overall positive effect on the income of native born workers ... They make up 15 percent of all workers and even larger shares of certain occupations such as construction, food services, and health care." The Council went on to assert that immigration would likely have a positive long-term effect on our country's public budgets.[133]

Of course, the real issue holding back effective immigration legislation is the population of illegal immigrants in the United States and the political challenges they pose. In fact, the issue is so controversial that advocates disagree over whether to use the term "illegal" or "undocumented" in describing them. By any label, as of 2014, this population totaled 11.7 million. U.S. Census data indicate no real decrease over the last few years, in spite of the Obama administration's increased border enforcement and record new levels of deportations between 2009 and 2012 (roughly 400,000 per year).[134]

Overwhelming majorities of the American people support common-sense immigration reforms.[135] But every year, without fail, Congress fails. And every year that real reforms elude us continues to cost us. Possibly the best measure of the economic harm caused by inaction on immigration can be seen in what we are forecast to actually *lose* over the long term without it. In July of 2013 the CBO analyzed a comprehensive immigration reform bill originating in the Senate. The CBO projected that if passed into law, the reforms would increase GDP by $700 billion over the next ten years and by $1.4 trillion over twenty years (in today's dollars). The CBO also stated that the federal budget deficit would decrease by $850 billion over the next two decades. Additionally, the chief actuary of the Social Security Administration projected a $300 billion influx to the Social Security Trust Fund by 2023.[136]

Beyond long-term economics, America's antiquated immigration laws have immediate effects on our society. The conservative Heritage Foundation observes, "Even though they pose no direct security threat, the presence of millions of undocumented migrants distorts the law, distracts resources, and effectively creates a cover for terrorists and criminals."[137]

In general, high rates of immigration, including undocumented immigrants, do not contribute to a higher crime rate.[138] But in those infrequent cases where illegal immigrants do intend to inflict terrorist acts on American citizens, the holes in our current immigration system make it easier for them to do harm.

The most high-profile example of this weakness being exploited was the Al Qaeda attack on our country in 2001, as Lee Hamilton and Slate Gordon, both members of the 9/11 Commission, articulated before the U.S.

Senate Judiciary Committee in 2004. They explained that the U.S. government had not treated border security as a matter of national security. Hamilton presented specifics:

> Al Qaeda was very skillful in exploiting the gaps in our visa entry systems ... The Commission found that many of the nineteen hijackers were potentially vulnerable to detection by border authorities, for all kinds of reasons. Some made false statements on their visa applications, some lied, some violated the rules of immigration. One failed to enroll in school; two over-stayed their time. But neither the intelligence community nor the border security agencies nor the FBI had programs in place to analyze and act upon that intelligence on their travel tactics.[139]

A good share of the responsibility for these and other failures of identifying dangerous illegal activity belongs to intelligence and law enforcement departments within the executive branch. Ten years later, information sharing continues to be a problem across these agencies. But it is also true that Congress writes the laws that govern immigration and enforcement. Congress also has the oversight authority and responsibility to ensure that the policies are being properly executed.

Our messy immigration situation has left more than 11 million people in the country without documentation. This creaky system subtracts from our economy by thwarting legal immigration, weakening our workforce, and wasting billions of dollars in federal resources.[140] You can hear members of Congress acknowledge these facts and wrangle over solutions daily. And yet it has been nearly thirty years since a major bill has reached the president's desk and been signed into law.

GUNS

One more single-digit polling issue deserves brief coverage within the context of the multiplier effect. Like immigration, it is an issue that ebbs and flows in citizen consciousness and concern: gun policy. Do guns fall under the category of public health or national security? The answer is that the issue could easily fall under either. Alternately referred to as "gun safety" or "gun control" or "gun rights," depending on one's point of view, guns in America evoke passionate debate and sharp political division.

The numbers of guns and annual firearm-related deaths in the U.S. are indisputably and extraordinarily high. According to the Centers for Disease Control and Prevention, every year since 2005 gun deaths have totaled more than thirty thousand: more than four times the number of deaths in the 9/11 attacks or the number of American soldiers' lives claimed by the combined wars in Iraq and Afghanistan.[141]

Taken alone, however, that annual thirty-thousand-plus figure has no significant meaning beyond its shock value, to the extent that it still shocks. But when we compare America statistically with other developed countries, we see the frame pull into sharper focus. In late 2013 the *American Journal of Medicine* published a study titled "Gun Ownership and Firearm-related Deaths," authored by Dr. Sripal Bangalore of New York University and Dr. Franz Messerli of Columbia University.[142] In the study, they investigate crime rates, mental illness, and the prevalence of guns in an effort to try to draw conclusions about the causes of gun deaths. The alleged causes, of course, would move into a deeper policy discussion. But agreeing on the facts is the first step in setting the stage. They are part and parcel of the product.

Using multiple databases and comparing twenty-seven countries on a per capita basis, the study placed the United States at the top of the list both in guns owned per 100 people (88.8), and firearm-related deaths per 100,000 people (10.2). Meanwhile, the number of guns owned per 100 people in Australia totaled 15, Turkey 12.5, Italy 11.9, United Kingdom 6.2, and Japan 0.6. In all of those countries, the average gun deaths per 100 people was under 1.3—and in 17 out of the 27 countries the average was under 2.0.[143]

The fight to define the right to lawfully bear arms in the U.S. goes all the way back to our country's fight for independence and the drafting of the Bill of Rights. But the issue and its impacts have become far more complex than they were in 1788. Guns are part of our culture, and few believe that fact will radically change. But the violence resulting from the wrongful use of guns is also part of what is ailing our country, and when it comes to the straight-up questions of both gun ownership and deaths caused by people using guns, America is the clear and undisputed leader of nations.

BREACH OF WARRANTY

As Americans we prefer to think of our country as the "leader of nations" in a more positive fashion than topping the charts on gun deaths or the inflated prices of life-saving drugs. In many ways, we still are. But when it comes to rendering judgments on the maturity and effectiveness of our legislative branch, people around the world, not to mention here in the United States, have deep doubts about our congressional leadership. And while we have looked at economics, health care, and national security as three distinct areas, we also know that many of the problems in these areas are the result of a single issue—a troubling congressional product. They collectively determine how strong we are as a country.

The earliest pages of this book established the concept that a public pact exists in America between the government and its citizenry. We further established that members of Congress, who serve in what our founders designated as the primary branch of our government, swear an oath of office to uphold the U.S. Constitution. We know, therefore, that our representatives are pledging to work to "establish justice, insure domestic tranquility, provide for the common defense, promote the general welfare, and secure the blessings of liberty to ourselves and our posterity."[144] And finally, through our common history, we know of the considerable powers and tools that are at our lawmakers' disposal to achieve these national goals.

We began this chapter by attempting to define that amorphous term: "general welfare." It is a phrase that has been fraught with ambiguity throughout our history, and there will not likely ever be one universally agreed upon definition. But a decade of public polling research tells the story of the American people's top priorities, the challenges we say we want Congress to tackle. These are the issues on which we are grading our legislators—a grade that has 80 percent to 93 percent of the country disapproving of the product. And no wonder.

We have seen our economy surrender into an accelerated slide over the last three decades. Wages for American workers lag behind the costs of living and costs of college. Hard work does not necessarily protect families from economic insecurity, or even worse, real poverty.

Health care in the United States costs a fortune. The Affordable Care Act has expanded insurance coverage, but we are still paying more for inferior outcomes compared with other countries that pay far less, in turn costing our entire *non-system* a whole lot more. If left unaddressed, this backwards process along with new demographic realities will render both Social Security and Medicare insolvent. These long-term debt threats conspire to boomerang right back on today's economic woes, yet the dirty laundry keeps on circling through the D.C. spin cycle.

The state of our nation's economic well-being, health care non-system, and other domestic failings directly affects the strength of America's position in the world. Educationally, our kids are falling behind in multiple subject areas versus our foreign competitors. Our immigration mess is costing us the people, talent, and skills that leaders in both the private sector and our military say we desperately need. And the decisions our government has made in national defense and foreign policy have cost us thousands of lives and trillions of dollars—with results that a majority of the American people have found highly questionable.

It wasn't always like this. In the twentieth century, the U.S. Congress produced a great many legislative achievements that made a positive difference in Americans' lives. In 2000, NYU professor Paul Light conducted a study on Congress in which he questioned 450 history and political science professors. From their responses, which analyzed more than 500 of the most significant laws passed by Congress from 1944–1999, Light concluded that "the federal government often succeeded in changing the nation and the world." Moreover, when the total legislation was culled down to a list of the top fifty laws, ranked by impact, Light found that of those laws, "even though Democrats controlled Congress for the vast majority of the past fifty years, only six can be tied to unified party control of government. Almost by definition, government's greatest endeavors reflect a stunning level of bipartisan commitment."[145]

What a difference a couple of decades makes. We've looked at poll after poll in which Americans indicate they believe that reasonable legislative productivity is a thing of the past. And now we know that our opinions are based in fact. We can look back at those historic accomplishments and then consider our current quagmire.

In 1948 Congress passed the Marshall Plan on a bipartisan basis, helping to rebuild European economies and improve stability after the end of World War II. Compare this to the critiques mentioned above about our broken foreign aid policy today.

In the late 1800s Congress passed two Morrill Acts to create and expand public universities through the land-grant college system. In 1944 Congress passed the GI Bill to help our veterans go to college, and in 1965 Congress passed the Higher Education Act to expand this type of support to many more Americans. Compare this to today where Congress bickers over small slices of education funding, and where America's student debt burden of $1.2 trillion has eclipsed even the country's total credit card debt.

In 1956 the Democratically controlled 84th Congress overwhelmingly passed the Federal-Aid Highway Act championed by Republican President Dwight D. Eisenhower, which created our essential federal interstate highway system. Today, the American Society of Civil Engineers gives America's infrastructure a comprehensive grade of D+, and concludes, "our infrastructure systems are failing to keep pace with the current and expanding needs, and investment in infrastructure is faltering."[146] The ASCE estimates we will need to invest $3.6 trillion by 2020 to repair these systems and structures; $200 billion alone to fix America's public schools.[147]

In 1965 Congress passed the landmark legislation that created Medicare along bipartisan lines: 307–116 in the House, and 70–24 in the Senate.[148] In 2010, through a poisonous political battle, the Patient Protection and Affordable Care Act was passed by a hair and without a single minority vote in the House or the Senate. Essential fixes to the flawed law are needed, yet any type of constructive conversation between the parties in Congress to make changes has been absent.

Very little good faith negotiation is happening in Congress. There is a glaring lack of dialogue and teamwork in an effort to craft and pass bipartisan legislative solutions. The practice of compromise between the parties to promote our general welfare seems to be a thing of the past. The process and the product are faulty. What we have on our hands is a breach of warranty.

Fortunately, our system provides us recourse when our government is not working as it was intended. In fact, there are two paths. The first is to elect new people to represent us in Washington, D.C. We have tried this approach over and over in recent decades, and it has not worked. Party control has swung back and forth like a tetherball, and with few exceptions, Americans do not believe that these "change" elections have substantially *improved the results or the product.*

No, the real problem is structural. It sits right inside the actual system. And so for Americans to be able to exercise the warranty remedies necessary to repair the product, we first need to understand the problems that are driving the dysfunction. We're going to need to wade into the weeds a bit, in order to yank out a few—straight from the root.

Part Two

5 The Problem

We have a republic that is no longer representative of,
nor responsive to the public. We need political reforms
and we need them quick.

David Walker, former U.S. comptroller general[1]

It is difficult to get a man to understand something,
when his salary depends on his not understanding it.

Upton Sinclair[2]

And so we arrive at that critical point in our search for answers that Spanish matadors might refer to as *el momento de la verdad*. But in this moment of truth, we are not facing one angry bull, nor for that matter, two treacherously sharp horns. The systemic problem that is weighing down our drowning Congress actually consists of *four* major defects, and one stubborn political fact. Here we will break it all down.

In Part I, we examined the depth of America's contempt for Congress, the promises that have been made to us, and the powers that have been granted to Congress to fulfill these written and spoken commitments. We also reviewed the relative state of our nation—our "general welfare" that Congress is tasked with promoting. And although it is true that the U.S. still proudly possesses outstanding people, talent, values, and wealth, we also know that we are falling behind—more like sprinting backwards—in meaningful ways that cause us pain everyday.

In the previous chapter, we noted that the laws Congress passes and the oversight it conducts are the inputs that move along an assembly line toward building a product. But if the parts on that production line are marred by flaws that degrade the original spirit and principles of our legislative system, how in the name of the framers would we end up with a quality product? We wouldn't. And as we've seen, we haven't. And the reason is because we have a skewed system.

We defined the word "system" in Chapter 4 as "a group of related parts that move or work together." In our legislative system, the major parts include: the representatives that Americans have a constitutional right to democratically elect, a congressional structure of two chambers that must work together to achieve mutually agreed-upon outcomes, and the power of majority rule as set out in the Constitution to activate decisions and pass legislation.

Now let's turn back to Merriam-Webster to explore the word "skew." Among the definitions the dictionary lists are: "1) to change (something) so that it is not true or accurate, 2) to make (something) favor a particular group of people in a way that is unfair, 3) to distort especially from a true value or symmetrical form."

Earlier, we heard the president of the Cleveland Clinic, Dr. Toby Cosgrove, emphasize that the United States does not have a health care "system" per se, but rather a series of unrelated cottage industries whose failure to interlock amounts to a health care "non-system." However tempting it might be to label our congressional wreck a "non-system" as well, that would be inaccurate. Instead, in Congress the system is riddled with defects that actually *do work together*—only toward overwhelmingly negative outcomes! The U.S. Congress is a *skewed* system generated by four defects that conspire to distort and counteract the congressional process.

In far too many cases, this leads to bad decisions or no decisions, inadequate laws or no laws, and the results cause our country to regress. We have a skewed system, subverting the process, generating a substandard product. Our twisted congressional system is not the fault of one person, or one party, or one entity. It has been tangled up over time, and it will take time to unravel.

THE "D.C. 4-3"

In the world of sports, the term "4-3" will make any knowledgeable fan think about professional football. For many decades, the 4-3 was the dominant defensive system that teams used in the NFL, and many still do. Dallas Cowboys Hall of Fame coach Tom Landry created the 4-3 in the 1950s, and then a variation of it called "The Flex," when he was still an assistant coach with the New York Giants. For those who aren't football aficionados, the workings of the system get a bit technical, but the upshot is that by using four linemen and three linebackers, the defense has more options and more flexibility on the field. These advantages empower the defense to be more effective against both the running and passing games of their opponents.[3]

Landry and his coaches set up the 4-3 as a rules system for his players to follow to maximize their prospects for success. Dallas won two Super Bowls and five conference titles under Landry. He still holds the league record for number of years coaching one team (twenty-nine). You could certainly say that his system succeeded in putting a pretty good product on the field.

On Capitol Hill, we have a 4-3 system, but not the kind you would brag about. In Congress, a handful of wrongheaded rules have led to the development of *four structural defects* that lead to *three negative effects* on

Congress's efforts to legislate and conduct proper oversight. The "D.C. 4-3" works to skew the system into dysfunction, and the four major defects are interrelated in ways that not only allow each other to exist, but in many cases *make one another worse.*

America is a politically divided country, and as we will soon examine, this rift poses big challenges for our federal government. But the D.C. 4-3 exacerbates this fact. It grabs hold of our polarized politics and then runs it through a meat grinder:

FOUR DEFECTS:

1. The Money Flood
2. Rigged Congressional Races
3. Two-year House Terms
4. The Senate Filibuster

THREE EFFECTS:

1. *Drives:* counterproductive outcomes
2. *Deters:* negotiation and compromise
3. *Distorts:* fair representation

The four defects in the D.C. 4-3 add up to a skewed system that makes it immensely difficult for Congress to arrive at constructive solutions. Unlike the Landry 4-3 Flex, the D.C. 4-3 wrecks the potential for flexibility and options. In many instances, the D.C. 4-3 pushes two political clubs that already have sharp philosophical differences even further apart. Other times, the two sides come together but for the wrong reasons. And the rigging inside the system has the power to distort the true will of the American electorate.

In the previous chapter we observed the exponential effect that policy issues have on one another. The defects in the skewed system operate similarly. The four structural impediments frequently build off of one another, and, by extension, damage the quality of the congressional process and product. In this chapter we will break down the four defects; in the next we will review specific examples of how the three negative effects influence policymaking and oversight.

Before reading the following analysis of the D.C. 4-3, one might object that removing any one of these obstacles will not thoroughly repair Congress. And that objection would be absolutely correct. In fact, it is the main point. Rather, *it is the collective, exponential strength of these defects that causes the damage.* And although we will not move into a platform of solutions until Chapter 7, logic already dictates that this difficult set of problems will require a correspondingly resolute set of responses.

BIG PICTURE

Former U.S. Representatives Mickey Edwards (R-OK) and Lee Hamilton (D-IN) served together in Congress from 1977 to 1993. Both congressmen experienced firsthand the problems caused by the D.C. 4-3.

Mickey Edwards describes the situation as soon as members of Congress are elected:

They begin by dividing into rival camps on the very day they are sworn into office. It is their differences—their partisan affiliations—and not their commonality as Americans that shapes the process. Compromise, an absolutely indispensable ingredient in a highly diverse nation of more than 320 million people, is seen as "sell-out"; rigid uniformity is praised.[4]

Lee Hamilton describes the atmosphere the skewed system creates:

There really *is* too much destructive partisanship on Capitol Hill. There *are* too many people in Congress who confuse their party's talking points with productive debate. Capitol Hill *can* find itself so hemmed in by lobbyists and the expectations of campaign donors that progress becomes impossible.[5]

The D.C. 4-3 takes decent, hard-working Americans who have a sincere desire to serve their country and forces them to behave like hamsters scampering on a greased wheel pegged to the maximum speed setting—with no "off" switch.

It all begins with begging for money, also known as "soliciting campaign contributions." Candidates must gulp down their pride and scramble to collect millions of dollars to even be competitive in a race for Congress. If they navigate the landmines of the superficial campaign game well enough to advertise their way into the House of Representatives, they must immediately start dialing for more dollars, because their next challenger will be attacking them in campaign ads in less than two years. Meanwhile, their party leadership is bearing down on them to vote in lockstep with the party, and, incredibly, to raise even more money to be doled back out to their political teammates.

In U.S. House races, outdated rules and new political realities conspire to rig elections. State parties maximize their political advantage through the shady practice of "gerrymandering": elected leaders using the power of their office to contort congressional districts by drawing boundaries that favor their respective candidates. Even worse, we still elect members of Congress through "winner-take-all" races in "single-member districts." This means general election voters get a choice of just two opposing candidates (and just two corresponding ideologies) for one congressional seat—in a country where a polarized national map makes most of the elections foregone conclusions before the campaigns even begin. These winner-take-all races not only distort American vote totals in terms of representation, they also have been helping to shrink the political center in Congress for two decades. As we will see, this rigged structure helps to drive hyper-partisanship—and deter congressional productivity.

Equally as corrosive are the expectations of the professional bagmen who rain down dollars on our representatives once they take office. Special interests are called "interests" for a reason. Lobbyist money talks while the voice of "one person, one vote," gets reduced to a squeak. In the Senate, an even higher cash price must be paid—to get the chance to do very little. Many U.S. senators have advanced from the scorched-earth culture in the House and, due to rules that are not even in our Constitution, may use the political machete known as the "filibuster" to deter the nation's business—with just a single threat of displeasure.

These four defects combine to generate a muddled atmosphere in Washington that is devoid of trust and loaded with obstacles. How can public leaders risk making courageous compromises to benefit the country when they face punishment from their own party and from the cash kings that pay for their campaigns? How can representatives have an honest conversation or constructive negotiation with their counterparts when scalding attacks and mockery lie in wait—usually broadcast through expensive TV ads that channel the power of a trained hypnotist? Pragmatic leadership becomes incredibly difficult. The haywire rules that drive the D.C. 4-3 allow for a tilting of the playing field that skews fair representation and deters rational dialogue and the passage of practical legislation.

Other meaningful factors affect the political process in Congress, but they are fairly immune to the wrong-headed rules in the system. Some of these impediments have developed over the course of many years. Unlike the D.C. 4-3, they exist for the most part outside of the system's formal structure.

First, the radically altered media landscape in recent years has contributed to the mess. A digital revolution has allowed information (or disinformation) to travel cheaply and at the speed of light. Anyone can be a publisher. Meanwhile, the traditional news organizations operate business models that are designed to attract the highest number of eyeballs to drive profitable ad rates. Cable networks are corporations, not classrooms. And despite some journalists' best intentions, the highly charged shout-fests on the twenty-four-hour "news" channels encourage many lawmakers to serve up sound bites for their bases, often reinforcing viewers' already fervently held beliefs.

Congress's ability to govern effectively is also challenged by a globalized economy, as well as large changes in the size of our country and its demographics. In addition, we have the perennial challenge of a large portion of the electorate that is unengaged. As outlined earlier, it will take a newfound passion—combined with time—to turn back that tide.

Finally, we have that stubborn political fact alluded to earlier. It is the 800-pound gorilla in the U.S. Congress: two deeply divided parties reflecting an increasingly polarized country. The political makeup of the United States has shifted considerably in recent decades. Since the 1960s, geographical diversity in the two political parties has been steadily evaporating. The South has turned more reliably conservative and the Northeast far more liberal. The deeper the hues of both red and blue in our states and congressional districts, the fewer the number of moderates we see being elected. And the weaker the political center, the more power we see moving to the party bases on each side of the aisle.[6]

As well, the ideologies of the two political parties have moved farther apart over the years. Political scientists Keith Poole, Nolan McCarty, and Howard Rosenthal have been studying political polarization for decades. Using a complex methodology called "DW-NOMINATE," the team has conducted research analyzing votes in legislative sessions going all the way back to 1877. In 2013, their data indicated that the polarization in 2011–12 reached a new high in both chambers, having doubled in the House since 1980. They also noted an important disparity in the shift: "Since the mid-1970s, Republicans have moved further to the right than Democrats have moved to the left. This rightward shift is especially dramatic among House Republicans, from a mean of 0.22 in 1975 to 0.67 in 2012." They dub this "asymmetric partisanship."[7]

This intense level of polarization in our country is tough stuff, but it is not insurmountable. The politics in our democratic system have never been easy, but in today's Congress, the problems in the D.C. 4-3 allow extreme partisanship to carry a disproportionately higher value in the legislative equation. We can't snap our fingers and wring out all of the disagreement between the left and the right. But we can attack the problems that exacerbate it.

The same perspective applies to the preceding challenges. We should be aware of them, for they matter in any discussion about improving Congress. But we must also keep in mind that, for the most part, they are independent factors. Privately owned media companies will cover the news any way they choose. Globalization is literally a global concept. U.S. Census numbers are not going to magically transform before our eyes. These factors exist *outside* of our formal system of elections and government. Consequently, we do not have a great deal of power to change them through reforming the rules.

However, what we are quite capable of doing is examining the *defects inside the system that are subject to change.* If we believe we have a breach of contract in terms of the poor product we are paying for in Congress, it only makes sense to investigate the reasons and then target the major causes that we do have control over correcting.

Many Americans believe that the political party they disagree with most is the culprit responsible for the shabby quality of the congressional product. But no matter where one stands on the issues, humility teaches us that there is no monopoly on wisdom. Common sense and facts do exist and can lead to practical solutions when we make a conscious choice to listen, think, and communicate honestly. Most Americans can engage in this kind of process. Now we're going to find out why so many members of Congress—even the ones who want to—cannot.

THE MONEY FLOOD

The lead-off defect in the D.C. 4-3 is the power of the almighty political dollar. In the New Testament, the Apostle Paul described money as "a root to all kinds of evil." In the campaign world, it is often referred to as "the mother's milk of politics." While the other three defects are harmful to either the House or the Senate alone, the money flood monster lays its greedy hands on every single one of our 535 members in Congress.

A trip back to the big screen starts us off here. In the 1998 political comedy *Bulworth*, U.S. Senator Jay Bulworth mistakenly believes he has a serious disease that will soon cut his life short. Much like that criminal suspect who has been granted immunity, the senator now feels free to speak the truth in his re-election bid without worrying about the consequences. So when he's asked at a large church meeting why he hasn't supported a bill that would help working folks to obtain fire and life insurance, he shocks the crowd with a deadpan display of raw honesty:

> Well, 'cause you really haven't contributed any money to my campaign, have you? You got any idea how much these insurance companies come up with? They pretty much depend on me to get a bill like that and bottle it up in my committee during an election. And in that way we can kill it while you're not looking.[8]

Now here's the not-so-secret, dirty little secret: that's how it really works. Campaign donors and special interests give gobs of money to members of Congress—and they expect results. Jack Abramoff was one of the most powerful lobbyists in our nation's capital for decades, before he was convicted and sentenced to six years in federal prison for bribing public officials. In 2011, after his release, "Casino Jack" was asked if it was easy to get what he wanted from lawmakers. He responded,

> I think people are under the impression that the corruption only
> involves somebody handing over a check and getting a favor. And
> that's not the case. The corruption, the bribery, call it, because
> ultimately that's what it is—that's what the whole system is ...
> I'm talking about giving a gift to somebody who makes a decision
> on behalf of the public. At the end of the day, that's really what
> bribery is. But it is done every day and it is still being done. The
> truth is there were very few members who I could even name or
> could think of who didn't at some level participate in that.[9]

But incredibly, most of this money dance is legal. Through laws passed by Congress (and occasionally ruled on by the Supreme Court), the system is intentionally set up to allow a slew of funds to keep rolling in. Incumbents need the dough to keep their feet on that spinning re-election wheel. The rules are rife with loopholes, and as long as legislators, campaign donors, and lobbyists don't flagrantly break the law and get caught for clearly expressed quid pro quos (as Abramoff did), just about anything goes. In every election cycle, the cash count climbs.

Let's start with campaign spending. In 2004, a *Washington Post* headline declared: "Cost of Congressional Campaign Skyrockets," estimating a new record average of more than $1 million to win a seat in the House—double the $500,000 it had cost a decade earlier.[10] In 2012, just eight years later, CNN offered this headline: "Cost to Win Congressional Election Skyrockets."[11] Sound familiar? Only now the price tag was $1.6 million—50 percent higher than 2004 and more than four times what a House seat cost in 1986. And the average toll required to get elected to the U.S. Senate in

2012 eclipsed $10 million for the first time ever. In 2014, a North Carolina Senate contest set a new high for a single race—more than $113 million was spent.[12] None of these records stand for very long.

When we extrapolate these numbers into national totals and compare them to years past, the incline is eye-popping. Back in 1974, the total money raised and spent by all House and Senate campaigns was $77 million.[13] In 2012, that figure was more than *$1.8 billion.*[14] On top of those dollars collected by the campaigns, political action committees (PACs) spent more than $400 million in 2012 to express their preferences—a far cry from the $34 million that PACs contributed back in 1978. And then we have the millions of dollars that the two national political parties reel in and then shell out to members. All legal.[15]

And there's more. Much more. Lobbying money. Special interests throw in huge sums of cash to their lobbyists to purchase access to lawmakers. The official total spent on lobbying in 2013 was $3.2 billion. This figure is "official" because it is tracked through the 12,281 lobbyists who are officially "registered." The catch? Not all lobbyists are registered. Some classify themselves as "strategic advisors" or "historians," and there is no penalty for evading registration. American University professor James Thurber has been studying lobbying since the 1980s. He estimates that the real number of lobbyists is more like 100,000—and that they generate closer to $9 billion.[16]

All of this lobbyist cash is doled out strategically. Return on investment is the goal. A 2009 report in the *American Journal of Political Science* revealed that for every $1 that a lobbying firm injects into the system on tax policy, the benefit to the clients ranges from $6 to $20.[17]

The lobbying tango continues for many members of Congress when it is time to launch their next career: lobbyist. Between 1998 and 2004, 43 percent of U.S. senators and representatives who left office slid into positions at lobbying firms—a 40 percent jump since 1973.[18] Connections and relationships are financially valuable in Washington, D.C.—for the lobbyists who give the money, and especially for former members of Congress whose pathways back into the corridors of power are even more direct. U.S. Representative Jim Cooper (D-TN) says it best: "Capitol Hill is a farm league for K Street."[19]

The accelerated pace of the money chase in Congress did not happen by accident. It started in the 1970s when the rise of television advertising enabled politicians to cut through the clutter and speak directly to voters in strategically created thirty-second spots. Armed with polling data, congressional candidates and their hired-gun consultants could now craft ad messages tailored to specific voting blocs. The race was on to raise more dollars than your opponent—in primaries and general elections—so that you could buy the highest number of gross ratings points on TV and drown out the voice of your competitors. The speed setting on the greasy wheel had been shifted up a notch.

Then the "Gingrich Revolution" pushed it to the next level. In his successful effort to win the Republican House majority in 1994 and during the years that ensued, Newt Gingrich changed the game by pressuring his members to raise money not just for their own campaigns, but also for their party. This was the beginning of a new era that saw a heightened urgency for both Democrats and Republicans to pull in even more money to help colleagues of the same political stripe win races. In the 2014 cycle, Speaker of the House John Boehner (R-OH) and Minority Leader Nancy Pelosi (D-CA) each helped to raise over $100 million on behalf of their respective party committees and candidates.[20] Former U.S. Rep. Mickey Edwards (R-OK) watched the escalation from the inside, and he says that beyond the increased time suck, there was another ugly consequence:

> To meet these demands, and to increase their chances of gaining a committee chairmanship or a leadership position within the party, members began to exert fund-raising pressure of their own, leaning hard on those members of the business and professional community whose profitability could be seriously affected by the passage or the non-passage of specific legislation.[21]

This pressure gets ratcheted up election after election, so much so that now the national parties primarily judge the viability of their own new candidates for Congress based on how much money they can raise. If the challengers are not deemed to be financially competitive, the parties will not open up the cash spigot.

And once new members do get elected, the parties crystallize the money priority more formally. On November 16, 2012, a week after election day, freshman Democrats arriving at their D.C. orientation received a very clear message. A PowerPoint presentation (shown below in Figure 5.1, obtained by *Huffington Post*) instructed members to make sure they were on the phones asking for money at least four hours a day. If twenty hours per week seems like a lot, keep in mind that such a figure is a recommended minimum, and many members are compelled to spend up to *forty to fifty weekly hours* on the money hunt. After floor votes on Capitol Hill, representatives can often be seen scurrying off to their party headquarters to start the dialing. Then members are expected to transfer tens of thousands of dollars back to the parties. This is how you move up the committee ranks to amass more power. The wheels keep spinning.

Figure 5.1 Model Daily Schedule While in Washington, D.C.[22]

In *Federalist 57*, published in 1788, James Madison wrote: "The House of Representatives is so constituted as to support in the members an habitual recollection of their dependence on the people."[23] A strong tie to citizens is one of the cornerstones of our system. But when the bulk of the money flooding into our nation's capital comes from the thin slice of folks who can afford to give it, that sacred democratic principle of "dependence on the people" gets violated in breathtaking fashion.

Harvard Law Professor Lawrence Lessig, a campaign finance reform activist and author of the comprehensive book *Republic Lost,* calls the moneyed climate in Washington a "gift economy." He explains that the rules in our system allow for all kinds of shadowy, indirect exchanges that put members of Congress in the position of being dependent on the money, as opposed to the American people:

> To see this, think again about the dynamic of this platform: the crucial agent in the middle, the lobbyists, feed a gift economy with members of Congress. No one need intend anything illegal for this economy to flourish. Each side subsidizes the work of the other (lobbyists by securing funds to members; members by securing significant benefits to the clients of the lobbyists). But that subsidy can happen without anyone intending anything in exchange— directly. "The system" permits these gifts, so long as they are not directly exchanged. People working within this system can thus believe—and do believe—that they're doing nothing wrong by going along with how things work.[24]

Thus does Congress operate. Whether it's campaign cash or lobbyist money or a mix of both, the "gift economy" distorts the system. The players who want political favors know they had better write checks big enough to be top of mind—or else. Here's how former Shell Oil President John Hofmeister describes the corruption:

> There's a huge price to not paying the price of the campaign request. There's a price in terms of access. There's a price in terms of interest by the member. So if you haven't paid your price of entry, who are you? I've actually been asked by a member, "Who are you? Because I've never met you before. And now that the election's over you're coming to ask me for something? Where were you before the election?"... It's pay to play, and I agree with the word

extortion, as harsh a word as that is, it's an atrocity, that no one seems to care about, because it goes on and goes on and goes on.[25]

So we can begin to see how this first problem in the D.C. 4-3 skews the system and violates the original spirit of representative democracy outlined in our Constitution. In the next chapter we will examine specific examples of how big money drives counterproductive policy and how it deters other kinds of solutions that Americans say they want. But first, Martin Gilens, professor of politics at Princeton University, gives us an excellent bird's-eye view of the landscape.

In 2004, Gilens published a study on democratic responsiveness that looked at the relationship between income levels and the public policy proposals Americans want to see passed into law. Gilens analyzed 754 questions based on possible policy solutions in the U.S. between 1992 and 1998. Overall, Gilens found "that when Americans with different income levels differ in their policy preferences, actual policy outcomes strongly reflect the preferences of the most affluent but bear virtually no relationship to the preferences of poor or middle income Americans."[26]

Specifically, Gilens found that when 90 percent of poor and middle-income folks were in favor of a policy change, it would be about twice as likely to become law than if 10 percent of them favored it. But for the most affluent Americans, there was a four-fold increase. When the study more closely examined policy questions where there was a stark difference of opinion between income groups, a policy change was six times as likely to occur when strongly supported by high-income Americans, but there was virtually no effect when it was strongly favored by middle-income folks.[27]

Ten years later, Gilens joined with Northwestern University Professor Benjamin Page to publish another study with even starker conclusions on the power of money. Using a single statistical model to analyze 1,779 policy issues between 1981 and 2002, they found that the average American truly gets the crumbs. The policy preferences of "economic elites"—defined as Americans in the 90th income percentile—were fifteen times as important in determining policy outcomes versus what ordinary folks wanted. Gilens and Page deliver this upshot:

In the United States, our findings indicate, the majority does *not* rule—at least not in the causal sense of actually determining policy outcomes. When a majority of citizens disagrees with economic elites and/or with organized interests, they generally lose. Moreover, because of the strong status quo bias built into the U.S. political system, even when fairly large majorities of Americans favor policy change, they generally do not get it.[28]

It's a staggering conclusion, especially considering the millions of Americans who have fought and sacrificed for the right to be heard through the power of the democratic vote. Of course, Congress will sometimes need to make unpopular decisions that do not track directly with the voice of the people. In fact, the possibility of their doing so is an important feature of our form of government. But Gilens's conclusion—the majority does not rule; economic elites do—tells us all we need to know about how money pollutes and distorts the system.

And it gets worse. In 2010, the "Super PAC" was born—injecting yet another money malignancy into the system. That year, two court rulings, including the Supreme Court case *Citizens United v. FEC,* permitted Super PACs to raise and spend unlimited sums of cash contributed by corporations, unions and individuals. Hundreds of millions of dollars get spent by these groups on campaign communications. These independent expenditures, also known as "IE's," are messages that advocate for or against a candidate but may not be coordinated with any candidate or related campaign committee.[29] In the *Citizens United* decision, a 5-4 majority on the Court basically deemed corporations as having the same free speech rights as people when it comes to political campaign activity.[30]

Gigantic amounts of Super PAC money further drown out the voices of the majority, if we apply Gilens's research. A weighty 80 percent of Americans disagreed with the Court's decision, including one of America's foremost congressional experts, Norman Ornstein.[31] A scholar at the conservative American Enterprise Institute, Ornstein calls the *Citizens United* case the most destructive decision he has seen from the Court in decades. Ornstein believes the activity is nothing short of corruption and describes what it means for federal candidates:

Some alien predator group, and you don't even know who they are, parachutes in behind your lines, roadblocks all the television time with twenty million dollars to destroy you. So you better go out and raise twenty million dollars in advance for insurance against that happening, or you find your own sugar daddy, which means more interests coming in. And when you're going out to raise that money, you do one of two things. You give something for it, or you shake somebody down.[32]

Aggravating this problem even further, we now have the danger of so-called "dark money." The system now permits groups to register as 501(c)(4) "social welfare" organizations that can raise huge sums of money to spend on independent campaign communications. Why is the money dark? Because under the U.S. tax code and recent interpretations by the courts, such groups have not been required to fully disclose their donors. So not only have outside groups gained outsized power in the process—we also don't know where a lot of this influence is coming from.

The danger to our democracy flowing from dark money became highly transparent in the 2014 cycle. Although the total amount of money spent on 2014 congressional elections was higher than the $3.6 billion in the previous midterms, the campaigns themselves actually raised less ($1.5 billion down from $1.8 billion). That decrease was overcome, however, by increases in money from undisclosed donors, partially disclosed donors, and PACs.[33] And of the total broadcast advertising dollars spent in the cycle, *55 percent of it came from undisclosed sources.*[34]

As we will see in the next chapter, this organizational money that floods into the system can drive irresponsible performance on some issues while freezing potential progress on others. U.S. Rep. Adam Kinzinger (R-IL) explains:

There's an entire industry in Washington that makes money on conflict. Some of these outside groups—you know, your Club for Growth types, and your Heritage Action, and your Freedom-Works—they go out and they fundraise by saying that Republicans aren't sufficiently conservative. Or they pick an issue to go to war on because they can stir the base and raise money on it and pay their big salaries. And what that does in the long run is it takes what would be a solid Republican agenda and causes chaos.[35]

It's an expensive obstacle course for members of Congress—a "gift economy" of unconcealed winks, back slaps, and favors galore. The money flood not only damages legislative policy, which we will examine in the next chapter, it also intensifies its sibling defects in the D.C. 4-3. It takes a lot of coin to be clearly heard blasting one's political opponent in an election campaign. And as soon as the winners arrive in Washington they must immediately begin navigating the pressures of re-election—which starts with the money. The greased wheel never rests. The situation is particularly bad in the House, which takes us to our next stop. The middle two defects in the D.C. 4-3—rigged races and two-year terms—dance with each other like they've been dating for a century. And their loony lack of logic will break your heart.

In an episode of the television drama *House of Cards,* the ferocious House majority whip Francis Underwood, played by Kevin Spacey, describes his job: "For those of us climbing to the top of the food chain, there can be no mercy. There is but one rule: hunt or be hunted."[36] A dramatic example of art reflecting life, his pronouncement might be a bit over the top if we applied it indiscriminately to every institution in our nation's capital. But in the U.S. House of Representatives, this mercenary sensibility is positively real. It is ubiquitous, continuous—and destructive.

Two major defects outlined in the D.C. 4-3 have helped turn the U.S. House of Representatives into an anemic object of scorn and derision in the eyes of the American people. The first, *the rigged nature of our congressional elections,* sustains the stale political divide on Capitol Hill, while distorting a bedrock principle of American democracy: fair representation. The other defect, *two-year House terms,* forces members of Congress to run even faster on that perpetual re-election wheel, increasing partisanship and deterring the art of creating and passing effective legislation. Each, in different ways, damages the integrity and quality of the congressional product. What the two defects share is a coincidental relationship with one of our nation's less celebrated founders, as well as a desperate need to be reformed. In this next section, we take on the first of these two problems in the U.S. House: an election format that has become rigged to create results that are unrepresentative—and dangerously predictable.

RIGGED RACES

A few rules in our system of congressional elections have developed into a structural defect that now diminishes fair representation in the U.S. House—and increases the ideological impasse. Some of the rigging is intentional, while some of it has evolved organically over time due to multiple factors. The rigged nature of our election process is troubling both because of the constitutional principle it violates as well as the legislative progress it prevents.

As we peer into the long-standing rules that have allowed this defect in the D.C. 4-3 to flourish, we must note that we are dealing with a plural. Four central ingredients make the recipe for rigging so powerfully destructive; one of these—a national map that has become sharply politically polarized—has nothing to do with the rules. To a great degree this polarization has resulted from our own geographical settling. Author Bill Bishop writes about this in his book *The Big Sort*: "As Americans have moved over the last three decades, they have clustered in communities of sameness, among people with similar ways of life, beliefs, and in the end, politics."[37]

Sorting is an external ingredient that gets exponentially inflamed when poured into the electoral pan with: 1) winner-take-all general elections in single-member congressional districts; 2) primary elections that limit voters' choices; and; 3) the manipulative practice of political gerrymandering, which further distorts an already distorted process.

The U.S. Constitution does not forbid any of these three rules or practices, but neither does it require any of them. Each has evolved over time, and in various forms. But over the last several decades, these problems have escalated to a point where we can see and feel the damage they are doing to Congress—and they all work in conjunction with one another. The age-old rigging strategy of gerrymandering gets a lot of scrutiny in political news coverage, and for good reason. But we start with the rules that draw far less attention yet play the largest role in the congressional vortex: winner-take-all elections in single-member congressional districts.

ONE PERSON. ONE VOTE. ONE REPRESENTATIVE?

The ideal of every American having a vote in our democracy was not something that existed in a real way for many years. The truth is that large segments of our population had to fight for the right to vote and be heard. In 1964 the Supreme Court cited "one person, one vote," as the guiding principle in its decision requiring legislative districts to be apportioned in equal population sizes.[38] But even if all of our districts were perfectly equal in terms of having precisely the same number of constituents, that would still not ensure true voter equality. And the rules are the reason.

In our system, single-member congressional districts combine with geographical political shifts to dilute and distort that powerful ideal of "one person, one vote." Just as harmful, the rigged nature of our congressional races is then converted into a hyper-polarized U.S. House where constructive negotiation and compromise are rarities.

Congressional elections in the United States are conducted on a winner-take-all basis. This means that whether a candidate wins with 95 percent of the vote or just over 50 percent (or even less when there is a plurality winner), that candidate's supporters receive 100 percent of the representation, while voters who made different choices on their ballots come away with nothing. When we combine winner-take-all rules with the geographic sorting and increased partisanship among Americans, we get a formula that exaggerates the polarization of our national politics and distorts electoral outcomes.

Even worse, these winner-take-all races leave millions of voters in uncompetitive districts where they have no hope of electing a candidate who shares their views. Because of the political balkanization of America, exacerbated by the impacts of gerrymandering, the overwhelming majority of these elections turn out to be no contest at all. The results are preordained. If we're talking about "wasted votes," this is the true showstopper. *Winner-take-all House elections in single-member congressional districts* actually make it unnecessary for massive numbers of American voters to even show up at the polls, outside of fulfilling their civic duty. This rigging effect puts the two parties into a deep freeze once our representatives show up in the capital. Our method of nominating two candidates in primaries and then electing one representative in each congressional district essentially limits voter choices, shrinks the debate, and boosts partisanship. It all adds up to a powerful deterrent effect on any kind of productivity in the House.

Winner-take-all is the only possible outcome when we elect one politician to represent all of the people in a district, as our current representatives do. However, these single-member districts are not the norm in other democracies, and have not always been the norm in the United States. There is nothing in the Constitution that requires states to operate single-member congressional districts. In fact, for the first fifty years, many U.S. House seats were elected "at-large" in "multi-seat" districts. Voters could cast one vote for each seat up for grabs in a race. If five seats were on the ballot, then five representatives would represent the entire district or city or county (and many local governments in our country continue to elect their officeholders this way).

But because these seats in multi-member congressional districts were elected on a winner-take-all basis, the system suffered from many of the same problems we have today. A majority party or bloc of voters would have the power to sweep all of the seats in an at-large election, completely shutting out other substantial coalitions. So in 1842 Congress passed the first apportionment law that required single-member congressional districts, which was seen as a way to increase fair representation in Congress.

Apportionment laws usually deal with issues surrounding how many members of Congress a state will elect based on population figures. Congress passed additional apportionment legislation over the next century and some at-large elections were permitted. But in 1967, Congress made it clear: Every district in every state would elect a single representative to the House. This law was passed partly in response to the Voting Rights Act of 1965 and concerns that civil rights might be violated in the South through reinstatement of at-large, winner-take-all elections. Ever since that time, single-member districts have been the rule.[39]

Our Constitution has also never required primary races to be conducted by the two political parties—or, for that matter, that we even have parties in the first place. In the early 1900s, Progressives were the ones who advocated for and created primary elections. Primaries were seen as a positive reform at the time because party members could choose candidates through the power of their votes—versus the cynical old custom where political machines in back rooms handpicked the party nominees.

But a century later, public primary elections are now part of the problem, and we are the only country that still uses them. These days, a relatively small number of engaged voters from the ideological left and right turn out for two primaries to select the party nominees who will go head to head in November (primary voting has fallen by about 30 percent over the last fifty years).[40] The control that base voters have in the process can prevent a moderate candidate who comes in second from advancing to the general election, even if that candidate is likely to appeal to a far larger percentage of the broader electorate. The candidates chosen by primary voters are then unlikely to moderate their positions or reach out to the opposing party's voters in the general election, as in most districts the outcome is a foregone conclusion. Even worse, our own tax money helps to pay for these primaries!

In many states, independent voters who are not registered with one of the two major parties cannot even participate (even though they've helped to fund the election). And in forty-four states, "sore loser" laws prevent independent candidates who lost a primary from entering the general election—a real problem for moderates who might have more success in a general than in a primary.

A 2014 study by political scientists Barry C. Burden, Michael S. Kang, and Bradley Jones investigated the effects of the primary election process. Analyzing the states with "sore loser laws," they concluded, "These laws give greater control over ballot access to the party bases, thus producing more extreme major party nominees. Using several different measures of candidate and legislator ideology, we find that sore loser laws account for as much as a tenth of the ideological distance between the major parties."[41]

Debate continues about how severely party primaries affect candidates and the partisanship they bring to Congress. But we do know that almost all pairs of primary elections nominate just two candidates from opposing teams. Consequently, in the winner-take-all general election voters are left with a narrow, binary "choice" between a Democrat and a Republican. When you consider the broad spectrum of intellectual and ethnic diversity in the melting pot that is still America, it's not much of a choice at all. And in a country that has become more polarized geographically, it translates into an increasingly predictable red-blue split. We get a Congress where most representatives are more reliably and sharply partisan, and where fewer and fewer moderates can find ways to reach across the political aisle to forge compromise. We get congressional deadlock.

Examining the numbers will give us a better feel for just how entrenched party division has become in our winner-take-all, single-member districts. The most relevant statistical factor in determining the likelihood of one party winning a congressional district is the measure of how people voted in the most recent presidential election. The Cook Political Report has been measuring district competitiveness in this fashion since 1997. Cook explains that its Partisan Voting Index (PVI) "illustrates how voters' geographical self-sorting, even more than redistricting, has driven the polarization of districts over the last decade" (redistricting is the process of drawing congressional districts). The PVI defines competitive "swing districts" as districts where each party had an advantage of five points or less, and it revealed that the 2012 redistricting reduced the number of swing seats from 103 to 99. But after the actual 2012 elections, the PVI reflected the number of swing districts taking an even bigger drop, from 99 to 90. Looking at this statistic over time gives us the best context: Between 1998 and 2014, the total number of competitive congressional districts has *nosedived 45 percent: from 164 to 90* (see Figure 5.2).

Cook cites additional evidence of voters self-sorting geographically. In 2012 "76 percent of Democratic-held seats grew even more Democratic and 60 percent of Republican-held seats grew even more Republican, not taking into account redistricting." Cook can make this claim from observing geographical areas where the vote returns confirm that the electorate has simply become more homogenous—they vote for the same party. "For example, the boundaries of West Virginia's 2nd CD have barely changed since 1998, but its PVI score has shifted from EVEN to

Figure 5.2 The Decline of the Swing Seat[42]

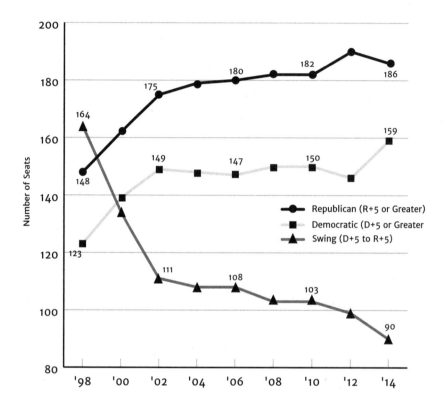

R+11 as its voters have moved away from the national Democratic brand. Likewise, Albuquerque's migration to the left has bumped the PVI score of New Mexico's 1st CD from R+1 to D+7."[43]

These regional shifts tilt congressional districts, often dramatically. Democratic districts with an average advantage of +7 points in 1998 jumped to +12 points by 2014. Republican leaning districts increased from +7 to +10. And as we will soon see, although gerrymandering has not caused it all, polarization does allow the state parties in power to worsen things by strategically drawing new lines on the map.[44]

What this all means is that in winner-take-all elections in single-member districts, most U.S. House races are no contest. Between 1996 and 2012, 95 percent of incumbent House members were re-elected.[45] Among all the winners in the 2012 congressional elections, the average margin of victory exceeded 36 percent. It is also easy to identify the geographical trends. Republicans carried all twenty-two House seats that were up for grabs in Arkansas, Oklahoma, Nebraska, Kansas, Wyoming, Montana, Idaho, and North and South Dakota. Meanwhile, Democrats swept the New England contests, winning all twenty-one seats.[46]

Constituents in the political minority in a district—voters who already know that the majority party has a race locked up—realize before stepping into the ballot box that their votes will be wasted. Different circumstances would occur in multi-seat districts, but in single-member districts where the winner needs just 50 percent plus one, all of the other votes basically go unrepresented. In all those districts rigged for one flavor of victory, a voter could wonder if there were even a practical purpose for showing up on election day.

At this moment in political history, the national map under our current system favors the Republicans. In 2012, Democrats won 1.4 million more votes than Republicans nationwide—yet the GOP secured 234 seats versus 201 for the D's. As we'll soon learn, gerrymandering accounted for roughly a dozen of the GOP seats in terms of distorted vote returns. But even when the effects of gerrymandering are statistically neutralized, the majority party in the House turned out to be the same party that won far fewer votes in the election. The skew in the system is totally transparent at this point. In 2014, the Republicans did win a majority of the overall vote with 52 percent, but it translated into 57 percent of the seats. That's what you get when you combine winner-take-all, single-member districts with geographical polarization: a distortion of American votes in U.S. House elections.

The year the Declaration of Independence was signed, John Adams said: "[A legislature] ... should be an exact portrait, in miniature, of the people at large, as it should feel, reason and act like them."[47] Winner-take-all in single-member districts has pulled us quite a distance from that founding principle.

Increasing the electoral safety of partisan candidates on both sides is one consequence, but another is the whittling down of the number of moderates we have in Congress. Here the distorted numbers translate into a troublesome political reality that drives so much of the inaction and failure described in Part I. A slightly more narrow "swing district" than the one PVI uses is where the share of the partisanship spans between 47 percent and 53 percent. By this measurement, in the 2014 election cycle, *in 388 House districts the partisanship favored one party by more than 53 percent.*[48] Members representing the majority in those districts do not have much incentive to work with the opposition party to negotiate and meet in the middle on legislation.

The safer that members of Congress are in their seats, the less they feel the need to compromise with their colleagues in D.C. And to compound this problem, we have a record level of ideological distance between the two political parties.[49]

The flip side of that huge slab of safe seats is the dwindling number of "crossover" members of Congress who have won a district where the partisanship landscape favors the *other party.* These are the moderates who can, well, moderate their positions on issues and legislative policy because they know they need to appeal to voters in both camps. We need these folks. According to FairVote, crossover Republican House members "were about 14.5 percent more likely to vote in a bipartisan manner than those residing in a competitive district." Similarly, Democrats representing Republican districts were 20.5 percent more likely to break from party ranks and move to the middle on proposed legislation.[50]

In 1993 there were 113 crossover representatives in the House. By 2014, *there were 26.*[51] That is a massive drop. We have nearly lost the political center in the U.S. Congress.

In his famous Farewell Address on September 19, 1796, George Washington cautioned future American generations: "The alternate domination of one faction over another, sharpened by the spirit of revenge natural to party dissention, which in different ages and countries has perpetrated the most horrid enormities, is itself a frightful despotism."[52] Our primary and general elections under a structure of winner-take-all, single-member congressional districts, take a polarized electorate and crystallize the division between the two parties. Imagine how our first president would reiterate his caution today—even before addressing the most blatantly obvious rigging tactic.

GERRYMANDERING

Elbridge Gerry, one of our nation's founders, had a long and, some would say, checkered career as a politician—a career that left a long-lasting and unfortunate legacy.

Gerry signed the Declaration of Independence but refused to sign the Constitution. He flip-flopped political parties and lost four races for governor of Massachusetts before finally being elected in 1810. After two men declined James Madison's offers to run as his vice-president, Gerry agreed to be his third choice. He died less than two years after they had won the White House.[53]

During his one term in office as governor, Gerry used his power to sign a law that redrew state senate districts in a way that favored his political party, the Democratic-Republicans. The tactic worked to staggering effect. In 1812, Gerry lost his re-election bid for governor. But in the same election, the newly convoluted map helped Gerry's party win the senate—even though the party's candidates *lost the overall vote.* The Federalist Party won the statewide vote total for the senate with 51,766 votes, defeating Gerry's Democratic-Republicans, who pulled in 50,164 votes. But due to the way Gerry's party had strategically scissored up the districts, it won *twenty-nine* senate seats to just *eleven* for the Federalists.[54]

This political event set the precedent for the electoral game-playing that has ever since created questions and doubts about whether voters' choices are truly being represented in our state legislatures and the U.S. Congress. A political cartoon that appeared in the *Boston Gazette* on March 26, 1812, depicted the ridiculous shape of the new congressional district of South Essex County, Massachusetts (Figure 5.3). Its resemblance to a salamander immortalized Elbridge Gerry in a way he never could have imagined.

Two hundred years later, state political parties are still gerrymandering and bending state and U.S. districts to their electoral advantage. We will bump into Mr. Gerry once again before we are finished talking about the House.

Figure 5.3 The Gerrymander, 1812[55]

At its core, gerrymandering is simply one party's strategic plan to waste as many of its opponents' votes as possible—in an effort to win as many legislative seats as possible. The practice has become so sophisticated that it now has its own lingo for describing how districts get fixed. Politicians can "pack" all the opposing party's voters into a single district so that a ton of those votes get wasted (since the winner only needs over 50 percent of the vote total). At the same time they can engineer a district to include a strong majority of voters from their own parties, while the rest sadly become known as "filler people." Legislators can also "crack" or break up problematic voting groups into different districts, diluting their power. They can even "hijack" a district by reconfiguring the lines to force two incumbent officeholders from the same party to face off against each other.[56]

To be clear, both the Democrats and the Republicans gerrymander congressional districts to enhance their holds on elections and political power. In Illinois, after the 2010 census, Democrats in charge of the state government masterfully gerrymandered new congressional districts. In the elections under the old map in 2010, Republicans had captured eleven seats while the Democrats had won eight. In the 2012 elections under the new map, the Democrats, although pulling in just over a majority (54 percent) of the overall vote, won twice as many seats as Republicans: *twelve to six*. In fact, if you take a look at the shapes of the Fourth and Seventh Congressional Districts in Illinois (Figures 5.4 and 5.5), it is easy to see why in 2012 the *National Journal* named them the fourth and fifth most gerrymandered districts in the country.[57]

Figure 5.4 Illinois' Fourth U.S. House District[58]

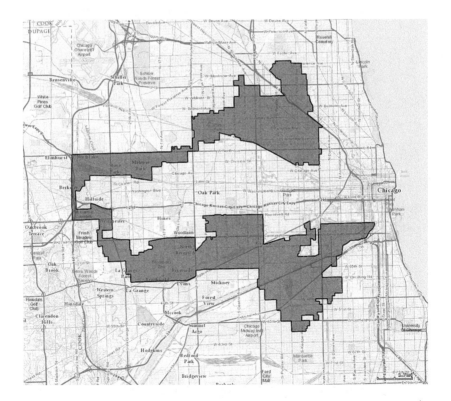

Figure 5.5 Illinois' Seventh U.S. House District

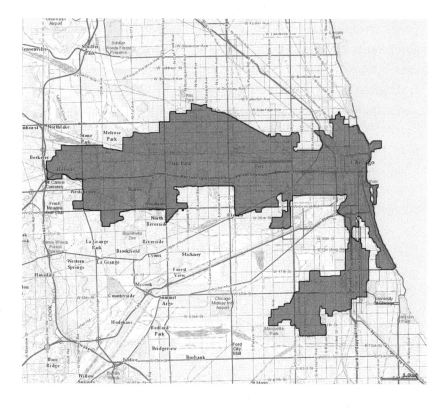

In late 2012, near the end of his last term in Congress, U.S. Rep. Steven LaTourette (R-OH) described the rigging in this fashion: "Some candidates don't even have to wake up on Election Day to win. I have not seen yet a redistricting proposal that is anything other than trying to favor one side over the other."[59] But LaTourette knows full well that his own party is guilty, too. In fact, nationwide in 2012, the newly gerrymandered districts helped Republicans to clean the Democrats' clock in congressional seat victories. We'll get to those numbers shortly.

We know that gerrymandering has been going on since Gerry himself, but only over the last few decades have we seen a substantial debate about its negative effects. Popular perception holds that gerrymandering forces congressional candidates to stretch ideologically further to their respective sides to win their party's nomination in primary elections. According to this theory, such candidates who go on to win general elections and head to Congress are then more stubbornly extreme once they arrive, due to the hardline primary races they've had to run to win the base vote in their gerrymandered districts.

Many political journalists, as well as officeholders—in each party—subscribe to this rationale. During the shutdown in 2013 forced by the House Republican Majority's refusal to fund the government, U.S. Representative Scott Rigell (R-VA) called gerrymandering "the principal cause of gridlock in Washington" and vowed reform.[60] A week later, former U.S. Senator Judd Gregg (R-NH) was more specific: "The House of Representatives is locked down ideologically because it's become stratified by gerrymandering of districts, so very little compromise is capable there."[61] Many of Gregg's colleagues from across the aisle, among then Senator Chuck Schumer (D-NY) and former Senate Majority Leader George Mitchell (D-ME), echo these sentiments.[62] And in 2014, former Supreme Court Justice John Paul Stevens not only expressed his belief that gerrymandering caused the shutdown, he proposed a Constitutional Amendment to render the practice illegal.[63]

The irony is that even though many incumbent officeholders blame gerrymandering—and their own party's use of it—as the cause of increased polarization in Washington, research has shown that its effects on the fierce partisanship in Congress may be overstated. The fact is that our country has been becoming more and more politically divided along regional lines for decades—that "big sort."[64] One researcher who has been studying polarization for years is Nolan McCarty, a political scientist at Princeton University. And although his work has consistently disproved that rigging of districts can be held largely responsible for congressional division, he nevertheless makes clear why he believes gerrymandering should be discontinued:

> The practice of elected politicians drawing districts for themselves
> and their political allies is an invitation to overt corruption. A key
> to any successful democracy is a widespread belief in the fairness

and impartiality of elections. Having incumbents participate in designing districts promoting their job security does little to enhance the legitimacy of American democracy.[65]

McCarty's emphasis on fairness and trust in the system is particularly important in light of recent analyses of gerrymandering's true effect: the distortion of American vote totals. To get a full grasp of this, we return to the Republican success in the 2012 election cycle—a process that actually started years in advance.

Prior to the 2010 redistricting (federal law requires states to redraw congressional districts every ten years to reflect new U.S. population figures), the Republicans crafted an official plan called "The Redistricting Majority Project" (REDMAP). REDMAP's own summary report proudly explained the opportunity they saw and took advantage of:

> As the 2010 Census approached, the RSLC began planning for the subsequent election cycle, formulating a strategy to keep or win Republican control of state legislatures with the largest impact on congressional redistricting as a result of reapportionment. That effort, the REDistricting MAjority Project (REDMAP), focused critical resources on legislative chambers in states projected to gain or lose congressional seats in 2011 based on Census data.[66]

The party executed the plan with great skill. In 2010 the Republicans beat the Democrats badly in state elections, resulting in their increased control of state legislatures from fourteen to twenty-five—and thus the privilege of scribbling new districts in most of them.

Of course, these efforts don't happen magically—and certainly not for free. Here we come to one way in which the problem of rigging races reaches back and overlaps with our first defect in the D.C. 4-3—the money flood. REDMAP spent more than $30 million to run this project to gerrymander the districts. A ProPublica investigation summarized the pay-to-play this way: "it's not cheap, and that's where corporations and other outside interests come in. They can provide the cash for voter data, mapping consultants, and lobbyists to influence state legislators, who are in charge of redistricting in most states."[67]

So what's the bottom-line result from all of this spending and strategic drawing? We already know that in 2012 the R's won the majority of seats, 234–201, even as the D's earned 1.4 million more votes. These are distorted results, to be sure, but just how much of the mismatch is due to gerrymandering? We do know that gerrymandering makes a difference. After all, in the states where Republicans drew the lines, their candidates won 72 percent of the seats with just 53 percent of the vote. Likewise, in the smaller number of states where Democrats had the power over redistricting, they won 71 percent of the races with 56 percent support.[68] Still, these stats do not take into account the "structural factors" that shape congressional districts, including our already polarized map, the power of incumbency, and also the high concentrations of Democratic voters in urban areas.

Fortunately, two mathematical analyses conducted following the election offer more convincing answers. Sam Wang is a professor of molecular biology and neuroscience and founder of the Princeton Election Consortium. Wang points out that in 2012, gerrymandered districts in five states in particular were huge drivers of the overall backwards results (see Figure 5.6).

Figure 5.6 Five States Where Partisan Interests Are Not Represented Fairly[69]

	D Vote	R Vote	D Seats	R Seats
Entire House	**50.4%**	**49.6%**	**201**	**234**
Arizona	45.6%	54.4%	5	4
Michigan	52.7%	47.3%	5	9
North Carolina	50.9%	49.1%	4	9
Pennsylvania	50.7%	49.3%	5	13
Wisconsin	50.8%	49.2%	3	5

Wang used computer models to split the 2012 state popular votes into thousands of unbiased "differently selected districts." This time the results came back right side up. In heavily gerrymandered Pennsylvania, for instance, Wang ran one thousand simulations that changed the 13–5 seat split to 10–8. Nationwide, the 234–201 Republican advantage moved to a more representative split, 222–213. In the state simulations, as well as nationally, the Republicans still held control, but the distributions were at least closer to the actual vote. Wang explains the Pennsylvania example:

> In this case, the structural imbalance is 9 − 8.3 = 0.7 seats. Partisan gerrymandering added a further imbalance of 8.3 − 5 = 3.3 seats. In other words, gerrymandering's contribution to Pennsylvania's partisan outcome was about five times as large as the effect of overall structural advantages.[70]

Wang's method measures "partisan bias"—the correlation of the overall vote to the share of seats won. Some critics have said that this is too general a standard, one of them being the frequent swing vote on the Supreme Court, Justice Anthony Kennedy.[71]

In response, in 2014 two researchers devised a new formula for measuring the effects of gerrymandering. Their solution may settle the matter—as well as assist in future efforts to draw districts more fairly where the will to do so exists. Legal scholars Nick Stephanopoulos and Eric McGhee argue in a study in the *Chicago Law Review* that the "efficiency gap" metric they have devised is far more effective in judging "the harm that is caused by gerrymandering"—for both the courts and the mapmakers.[72]

Unlike "partisan bias," which measures the difference "in the share of seats that each party would win given the same share of the statewide vote," the efficiency gap actually measures the *votes that are wasted.* Stephanopoulos and McGhee explain the efficiency gap this way: "It aggregates all of a plan's cracking and packing choices into a single number ... the difference between the parties' respective wasted votes is divided by the total number of votes cast, thus generating an easily interpretable percentage."[73]

By doing this, Stephanopoulos and McGhee can compare that percentage—that one number—with redistricting plans from past decades.

And that's just what they did. In 2012, they found that the average efficiency gap across all redistricting plans was 1.58—higher than any set of plans going back 40 years. In their words, "The severity of today's gerrymandering is therefore historically unprecedented."[74]

This picture of gerrymandering and its effects is meaningful in the context of examining the rigging of elections. Debates continue over how much it affects the hyper-partisan political environment on Capitol Hill. But let's be clear—it isn't helping. And the harm that we do know it causes by distorting our American votes and eroding our trust in the system is an unacceptable reality that cries out for reform.

Whether it's the record low number of moderates in Congress, or the record low number of bills being passed, or the record high distortion of American vote totals, the math alone tells us the system is in terrible condition. Primary elections that lead to two-nominee, winner-take-all general elections in single-member districts, joined with the practice of political gerrymandering, comprise a defective method of choosing our U.S. representatives.

The distorted election results travel to Washington where they are translated into deterrence. On Capitol Hill, the political environment is nothing short of hostile. The two parties clash daily over the same old philosophical differences. There is no third or fourth political party on hand to offer fresh ideas or build new coalitions, because single-member congressional districts prohibit smaller political minorities from enjoying their fair share of representation.

In Chapter 7, we will explore some ways to change that situation. Without reform, we will continue to receive a substandard congressional product. The wall between red and blue gets thicker and higher, and that's before we've even factored in the timing of elections in the House. Which brings us to the third defect in the D.C. 4-3—a rule as old as the Constitution, and one that accentuates the difficulties caused by each of the preceding obstacles.

TWO-YEAR TERMS

As promised, our story returns to Elbridge Gerry. Back in 1787, long before he was governor of Massachusetts, Gerry was a delegate to the Constitutional Convention. At that time, once-a-year elections were the norm for state offices. As the delegates debated the proposed length of U.S. House terms, they first agreed upon a three-year term. James Madison favored three years, seeing it as necessary "in a government so extensive, for members to form any knowledge of the various interests of the states to which they do not belong, and of which they can know but little from the situation and affairs of their own. One year will be almost consumed in preparing for and traveling to and from the seat of national business."[75]

But Elbridge Gerry pushed back and made the case for annual elections, emphasizing that the shorter the term, the more dependent representatives would be on the will of the electorate. Gerry described one-year terms as "the only defense of the people against tyranny." After all, these men had just fought a bloody war to vanquish an oppressively powerful and monarchic form of government. Ultimately, the delegates split the difference and agreed on two-year terms.[76]

Two centuries later, the U.S. House of Representatives is the only federal legislative chamber of any advanced country in the world that carries two-year terms.[77] This is a dubious distinction in a Congress carrying a national approval rate that hovers between 7 and 20 percent. And even if that polling number were doubled, or tripled, the two-year rule still wouldn't make sense today.

The time crunch of the two-year term puts restrictive leashes around the necks of our representatives in two major ways. First, members of Congress cannot let their focus wander very far astray from their next election, which actually takes place a scant twenty-two months after they are sworn in. These unremitting political considerations often force members to think less about how proposed laws or policies might benefit the country and more about how a decision may affect their chances of re-election. Secondly, with the heavy lift of job responsibilities that U.S. representatives are expected to perform both in Washington, D.C.

and back home in their districts, the constant campaign—including the time-sucking activity of scooping up campaign cash—steals countless hours from our leaders.

We begin with the lawmaking process. Two-year terms hold back both the legislative branch and the executive branch—the two branches that must work together. Tension between them really started drawing more fire in the second half of the twentieth century. In his book *Constitutional Reform and Effective Government,* James Sundquist recounts observations from leaders in both parties. In 1966, President Lyndon B. Johnson described things from the White House perspective: "You've got just one year when they treat you right, and before they start worrying about themselves … So you've got one year."[78]

By 1984, that perceived time horizon was compressed even further. With the GOP about to regain the presidency under Ronald Reagan and the majority in the U.S. Senate, Republican leaders explained how they needed to be ready to move with Indy 500 speed once sworn in. Addressing the issue of the deficit, Reagan's budget director, David Stockman, explained to the U.S. Chamber of Commerce, "In the cycle of the American political system, there is about a six- or seven-month window every four years when concentrated efforts need to be made to grapple with problems."[79] A few months later, House Republican Whip Trent Lott (MS) echoed Stockman: "We'll have six months, and that's all."[80]

So this tiny window not only holds back members of Congress by keeping their gaze on the next election, it also rushes the executive branch. In *The President's Agenda,* author Paul Light recounts how even President Nixon, a Washington veteran when he was sworn in, needed time when he entered the White House. A Nixon aide confessed that the administration "didn't have the organization to cash in" at the start of his first term. President Carter and his staff, mostly newcomers to Washington, suffered from the same problem.[81]

Five decades ago, both President Johnson and President Dwight D. Eisenhower decried two years as being too short to allow representatives to properly focus on and succeed in their role as legislators.[82] With every passing congressional session, the political challenges for lawmakers in the House only become more difficult.

Robert Kaiser is an author and Capitol Hill correspondent who spent more than fifty years as a reporter and editor for *The Washington Post*. In his 2013 book *Act of Congress*, Kaiser explains why few members of Congress ever end up having put their personal imprint on a substantial piece of legislation: "Legislating is no longer the principal preoccupation of our legislators—politics is. Most commonly, it is politics by sound bite."[83]

In the midst of our hyper-kinetic media atmosphere, we know our defective congressional election system not only distorts representation in the House but also sustains the polarized right-left grudge match in Congress. The ideological breach that plays out publicly everyday is challenging enough, but when we toss two-year terms into the mix, we have a potent formula for dysfunction. If the short window of time available to get anything done already seemed minuscule in the mid- to late twentieth century when moderate representatives still existed, consider how hard it is now in our far more divided House. Legislators are already under pressure to stick to the party orthodoxy, but the constant campaign is an additional demotivating force. To compromise in Congress usually means taking political risk, and short-term election considerations work against exercising the pragmatism necessary to make deals and pass legislative solutions. Two-year terms force most members to always keep their guard up.

Beyond the fights over legislative votes that get most of the play in the media, U.S. representatives also have a range of responsibilities that exist outside the sphere of pure politics. Many Americans often forget, or may not be fully aware, of just how demanding it is to serve in the U.S. Congress. Members spend hundreds of hours in committee meetings and hearings—most of these far away from the TV cameras. To do their jobs diligently, representatives are required to read and study—not only bills and resolutions, but also the materials necessary to educate themselves to the point where they can make informed decisions. In 2010 the media chided members of Congress for not reading the weighty Affordable Care Act that stretched over 2,000 pages. This was *one bill.*

We know that members of both the House and Senate get sucked into the money flood. But two-year terms make fundraising for House representatives even more of an everyday urgency, taking away valuable time that could be spent governing. U.S. Representative Raúl Grijalva (D-AZ) spells out the conflict: "I try real hard to raise what we're going to need. Which is a problem, because [then] I can't contribute to everything else ... There's other things going on, and the consequence of you being on the phone four to six hours a day means that you can't have the opportunity to interact, to learn and try to get your point across on a policy level."[84]

U.S. representatives are managers as well, running staffs in their D.C. offices, in the committees they may chair, and back home in their individual congressional districts. Representatives shuttle back and forth to Washington every week, and "back home" doesn't just mean seeing their families. It means being the point person for seven hundred thousand constituents who can call, write, or show up for any reason at any time. In 1789, that number was roughly thirty thousand. Constituent service is a genuinely important yet far less frequently appreciated task that our elected leaders are expected to perform daily. On top of this, an endless parade of schools, community organizations, businesses, and local government bodies are constantly requesting members of Congress to attend their events and make remarks as a prized "local dignitary." It's almost hard to believe that all of this work leaves any remaining hours for U.S. representatives to navigate the grimy waters of the money flood. But we know all too well that they find the time to hunt for more cash. They don't have a choice. Election day looms.

Lyndon B. Johnson's observations above do not arise only from the perspective of the executive branch. Long before LBJ acceded to the White House, he had served a dozen years each in the House of Representatives and in the U.S. Senate—where, as Majority Leader, he earned a reputation as a master legislator. He experienced the legislative process from every angle within the two branches that together are responsible for passing the laws that guide our nation. In his "special message" to Congress in 1966, President Johnson announced his firm opposition to two-year terms, explaining that they require

most members of Congress to divert enormous energies to an almost constant process of campaigning—depriving this nation of the fullest measure of both their skill and their wisdom. Today, too, the work of government is far more complex than in our early years, requiring more time to learn and more time to master the technical tasks of legislating.[85]

Fifty years later, the work is even more complex. Technology is more complex. The world is more complex. If history is any guide, that trend will continue. The job in Congress gets bigger, not smaller. And it's never static. Our representatives are only human. They need the proper tools to excel in their work, just like the rest of us. Time is a precious tool. U.S. representatives don't have enough of it between elections. Two-year terms are historical artifacts. This rule from our Constitution is obsolete, and ripe for reform.

SENATE STANDSTILL: THE FILIBUSTER

In an interview near the end of 2013, Senator Tom Harkin (D-IA) offered a cold, hard truth: "A senator has his or her power not because of what we can do—but because of what we can stop."[86] This sad statement and its consequences for the country are largely due to the byzantine rules in the U.S. Senate that allow for the use and abuse of the notorious filibuster. This defect is the final offender in the D.C. 4-3, and in the early part of this twenty-first century, there's been a whole lotta stoppin' goin' on.

The excessive deployment of the filibuster has increased to the point where the Senate now sits at a virtual standstill. The filibuster rule, which is not even in the text of our U.S. Constitution, permits a single senator to delay or derail any proposed bill or executive branch nomination. In other words, not only potential legislative solutions but also the appointing of personnel to staff our government agencies and the courts—the inputs we need to flow along that national production line—can all be stopped or stalled to a crawl by just one person, in a country of over 300 million. It is the antithesis of majority representation.

Our founders designed the U.S. Senate to be the more deliberative legislative body. During the Constitutional Convention of 1787, James Madison wrote, "The use of the Senate is to consist in its proceeding with more coolness, with more system, and with more wisdom, than the popular branch." Soon after, the story goes that George Washington explained to Thomas Jefferson the purpose for creating the Senate: "We pour legislation into the senatorial saucer to cool it."[87] For many years, the U.S. Senate did serve the country in this fashion to a respectable degree. But recently, and most especially since the dawn of this century, the heightened filibuster antics in the Senate have turned that common sense concept of a "cooling saucer" into the moribund reality of congressional quicksand.

Although the Constitution allows the House and the Senate to write their own rules, our founders most certainly did not create nor ever intend for the establishment of the filibuster. In fact, its birth was nothing more than a historical accident. In 1805, Vice President Aaron Burr, who was presiding over the Senate, made a recommendation to simplify the Senate rulebook. Burr argued that the motion on the "previous question" to end debate on a subject was unnecessary, and the following year the Senate took his advice. This meant that the Senate did not have a rule that empowered a majority of the chamber to vote to cut off debate—and take action on a pending issue.[88]

It didn't seem like a big deal at the time, and it wasn't until 1837 that an actual filibuster took place on the Senate floor. It took the original form of the filibuster, a very rare occurrence where senators were required to stand for hours and keep flapping their gums to prolong debate (to delay or deter a vote)—the traditional filibuster immortalized by Jimmy Stewart's impassioned plea in the 1939 film *Mr. Smith Goes To Washington.*

Filibusters remained rare for decades, occurring only sixteen times between 1840 and 1900. In 1917, the Senate adopted another rule known as "cloture"—a device designed to allow senators to end a filibuster. The catch was that a supermajority, two-thirds of the Senate, had to vote for cloture in order to cut off debate. What this meant was that the support of sixty-seven senators out of one hundred on the floor would be necessary to force a vote on a bill or nomination, in a legislative body that was supposed to be operating through the will of the majority—fifty-one senators. The filibuster rule and its companion, the cloture vote rule, effectively transferred a great deal of unintended power to whichever party was in the Senate minority.[89]

We know that the effects of this historical accident were unintended because of the parameters set out by our nation's founders. In our original U.S. Constitution, only five scenarios require a supermajority from

Congress: the impeachment of federal officers, overriding a presidential veto, expelling members from Congress, ratifying treaties, and proposing constitutional amendments. The need for a supermajority was reserved for these exceptional circumstances. The rest of the country's business in our legislative branch was to be governed by majority rule.[90]

On this subject, in *Federalist 22,* Alexander Hamilton clearly expressed the danger in violating this principle:

What at first sight may seem a remedy, is, in reality, a poison. To give a minority a negative upon the majority (which is always the case where more than a majority is requisite to a decision), is, in its tendency, to subject the sense of the greater number to that of the lesser ... its real operation is to embarrass the administration, to destroy the energy of the government, and to substitute the pleasure, caprice, or artifices of an insignificant, turbulent, or corrupt junto, to the regular deliberations and decisions of a respectable majority.[91]

In *Federalist 58,* James Madison stated in even simpler language the consequence of requiring more than a majority: "The fundamental principle of free government would be reversed."[92]

The irony is that the Senate's composition, with two senators representing each state regardless of population, has from the very beginning bent back the principle of majority rule. In his 2006 book *Our Undemocratic Constitution,* Sanford Levinson explained the asymmetry:

Almost a full quarter of the Senate is elected by twelve states whose total population, approximately 14 million, is less than 5 percent of the total U.S. population. To put it mildly, there is simply no defense for this other than the fact that equal representation of the states was thought necessary in 1787 to create a Constitution that would be ratified by the small states. By definition, this means that the Senate can exercise a veto power on majoritarian legislation passed by the House that is deemed too costly to the interests of small states, which are overrepresented in the Senate.[93]

The filibuster adds insult to this imbalance. The accidental rule allows an even smaller minority of Americans, through "representation" by their senators, to put a stop to the policy wishes of an overwhelming majority. And due to the additional pretzel twisting of Senate rules in recent years, the dysfunction has developed to a point where *a single U.S. Senator* can threaten a filibuster or similarly put a "hold" on any pending legislation or nomination. Without "unanimous consent"—every Senator on the floor being in favor of moving forward—"the world's most deliberative body" is delayed from moving forward.

These blocking tactics drive two major consequences. The first is that legislative solutions proposed by the majority get fully thwarted. This happens when the majority cannot assemble the current threshold of sixty senators to vote for cloture, which would lead to a vote on the issue at hand. But the second result is arguably just as harmful. Even if the majority *can* muster sixty "yeas" to beat the filibuster, under Senate rules the minority can gobble up dozens of hours of Senate floor time—days—before a vote is actually permitted to take place. In the Senate, where time is precious and where most Senators only spend half the week in D.C., wasting full days on needless delays is a death knell to legislative progress.

For most of the twentieth century, use of the filibuster and the cloture votes required to kill them was still infrequent. In 1964, Southern Democrats in the Senate led a filibuster on the Civil Rights Act, sparking the "longest continuous debate in Senate history" until 71 votes were finally mounted to override it.[94] The sixty-four years between the creation of the cloture rule in 1917 and 1980 saw a total of only 161 cloture votes (an average of about five during each two-year session of Congress).[95] But as Figure 5.7 shows, starting in 1991 the filing of cloture motions by both Democrats and Republicans started to steadily increase, and we've had no less than sixty in every congressional session since.

In 2007–2008, the filibuster crisis in the Senate broke a new barrier. With the Republicans in the minority, a historic high of 112 cloture votes were required to break filibusters. That number decreased a bit in the following two sessions. But in the 113th Congress, with the GOP still in the minority, a new record of *167 cloture votes* was reached by the end of July 2014—more obstruction tactics in eighteen months than all of those the

Figure 5.7 Senate Cloture Motions Filed (to End Minority Filibuster)[96]

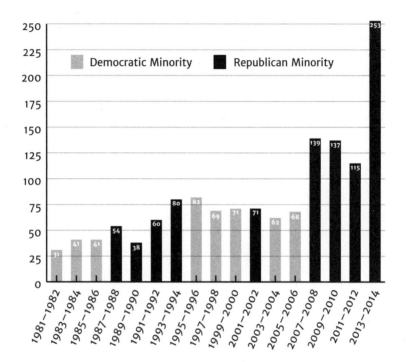

Senate had seen between *1917 and 1980!* By the end of that congressional session, yet another record high was reached with a total of 253 cloture motions filed.[97]

We have acknowledged that partisanship in both the House and the Senate is to a substantial degree reflective of our country's political divisions. But this breach gets magnified into legislative paralysis when Senate rules allowing for holds and filibusters are nakedly abused. We will look at examples of this in the next chapter, and how the severity of the problem in 2013 led to at least one reform in the way the Senate votes on nominations. But even after that rule change, the status quo still requires a supermajority to get to a vote on any piece of legislation. To pass laws. And in practical terms, even the specter of obstruction is the true deterrent. Author Ezra Klein broke this down in a column for the *Washington Post*:

The issue today isn't that we see fifty, or one hundred, or one hundred fifty filibusters. It's that the filibuster is a constant where it used to be a rarity. Indeed, it shouldn't even be called "the filibuster": It has nothing to do with talking, or holding the floor. It should be called the sixty-vote requirement. It applies to everything now even when the minority does not specifically choose to invoke it.[98]

And even when procedure requires the actual recruiting of sixty votes to break a filibuster, the minority would only need senators from twenty-one states. Due to the representational disproportion in the Senate, this means that a group of Senators, *speaking on behalf of just 11 percent of Americans,* can at any time block or delay an overwhelming majority.[99]

These backwards Senate rules allow for a massive distortion and skewing of the system. It is time to put a stop to all of the stopping.

———

In this chapter we have examined a set of rules that have led to four defects in our congressional system. The House and the Senate are deluged with a flood of money—and it's legal. Election rules and a polarized national map conspire to rig House races in a way that reduces competition, limits choice, and jacks up political division. Then two-year terms turn would-be legislators into perpetual candidates. The U.S. Senate is polarized as well, but in times past it has navigated its differences to pass mutually agreed-upon legislation. Today, both political parties—to varying degrees—abuse the rule known as the filibuster, establishing a disruptive veto point in our system that the founders never intended.

Using a wide-angle lens in this chapter, we have reviewed election results, scholarly research, and mathematical studies that collectively tell a story about the D.C. 4-3. We can see how four defects cause three negative effects—and each effect skews our system. We know that money *drives* poor outcomes, *distorts* elections, and *deters* voter trust. We know that rules in the House *distort* fair representation, and *drive* down the capacity for moderation. And we know that the filibuster *deters* the nation's business by *distorting* the will of the majority, a founding principle of our republican form of government.

We have been breaking all of this down from a distance, but of course the other essential part of this story is how all of this dysfunction plays out on the ground. And now we're ready to take a closer view—a look at some examples of how the D.C. 4-3 works (or more accurately, *doesn't* work) in the practice of policy and governance.

6 The Policymaking

The 112th Congress was almost universally derided as the worst ever. It was the most polarized body since the end of Reconstruction, according to one study, and I grew embarrassed by its partisan bickering, inactivity, and refusal to address the vital challenges facing America.

Former U.S. Senator Olympia Snowe (R-ME)[1]

T he crafting of policy and passing of legislation is supposed to be where the rubber hits the road in Congress. But far too often, the D.C. 4-3 empties the gas tank, impeding forward progress. Other times, well-heeled special interests glue the accelerator to the floor. The legislative vehicle flies by, but the masses of regular folks along the track barely get a glimpse, much less an influential word in the process.

We saw in the previous chapter, The Problem, how a set of rules has allowed for a skewing of the system that distorts campaigns, elections, and then incentives inside the nation's capital. In Chapter 4, The Product, we looked broadly at the state of our nation on the priorities that Americans say they want Congress to confront through public policy. Here we take a look at some actual examples where defects in the D.C. 4-3 have had the power to drive substandard results on some issues, while deterring Congress from forging compromise on other crucial issues.

Naturally, it is impossible to conduct an examination of political outcomes without evincing value judgments on various ideas. But on the following pages, we will see cases of both Democrats and Republicans excoriating members of their own team as well as their own product. The *process* takes center stage in this analysis. We don't always know for certain whether a potential solution that gets distorted or deterred by the D.C. 4-3 might have delivered benefits or detriments to the country. But we do know that without a logical process where legislators can practice the art of pragmatism on behalf of the people, our country will continue to fall far short of its potential.

WHEN THE FLOODGATES OPEN

In the previous chapter we learned just how much money flows through Congress. We heard both from outside interests who throw money into the system and from those on the inside who are waiting with catcher's mitts to collect the cash. These sources described the ways in which the dollar rush skews the overall legislative process. We also took a high level view of money's effect on our leaders. We know from Martin Gilens's and Ben Page's statistical research that "the majority does not rule" on hundreds and hundreds of legislative votes, when compared with the preferences of the economic elites who are influencing the system.

Now that we have an idea of how the "gift economy" works and the broad power that money exerts, we're going to descend down to ground level and look at specific cases where it causes product failure. Whether it is driving poor legislation or deterring potentially positive outcomes, the money flood deluges those important issue areas we observed in Chapter 4, where the U.S. has been flailing.

The biggest and most appropriate example to start with is the financial crisis of 2007–2008, which touched off the Great Recession. We learned earlier that between 2009 and 2013 median wages for workers actually dropped, the poverty rate increased, and that in 2014, 57 percent of Americans still believed they were living in a recession.[2] There were many reasons for the crisis, to be sure. But our very own federal government traced the causes back to the influence of the money in our system that *drove* poor legislation and weak regulation.

In 2011, the bipartisan Financial Crisis Inquiry Commission issued a comprehensive report and announced up front that the entire debacle could have been avoided. Among the causes included in the Commission's list: "more than thirty years of deregulation and reliance on self-regulation by financial institutions"; "an explosion in risky subprime lending and securitization"; "the growth of a shadow banking system—opaque and laden with short term debt"; "predatory lending practices"; "unregulated derivatives"; and a "lack of transparency."[3]

Specifically, the Commission asserted that legislation passed by Congress in 2000 prohibiting the regulation of complex financial derivatives "was a key turning point in the march toward the financial crisis." Without any oversight over these complex derivatives, the bundling of mortgage securities and Wall Street's heavy gambling on credit default swaps fueled the massive housing bubble that ultimately burst.[4] The Commission also noted that, although "government sponsored enterprises" like Fannie Mae and Freddie Mac along with our politicians' push to increase home ownership played a role in the crash, the larger problem was "the failure of the Federal Reserve and other regulators to rein in irresponsible lending."[5]

The credit rating agencies, particularly Moody's, were another big cause of the financial meltdown. Conflicts of interest as well as a lack of public oversight allowed the agencies to give their seal of approval to junk investments and faltering financial firms. Congress did not respond with accountability measures until way too late—2010. The financial industry had spent more than $3.5 *billion* to influence government decisions in the decade leading up to the crash.[6]

Henry Paulson, who served as treasury secretary under President Bush, agreed that the wrong regulatory system was in place in advance of the breakdown.[7] But even in cases where prudent government policies have been passed to maintain the strength of our economic institutions, if the regulators are not doing their jobs diligently, the system is every bit as much at risk. And who oversees the regulators? Congress. Who oversees the Federal Reserve, Securities and Exchange Commission, U.S. Treasury, FDIC, and HUD? They are all supervised by the U.S. House Committee on Financial Services, otherwise known as the "Cash Committee."

The Cash Committee has grown from forty-four members in 1980 to more than sixty and counting. Members of Congress from both parties are dying to get on the Cash Committee because it is the leader in bringing in cash—millions and millions from political action committees set up by lobbyists to represent all kinds of corporate interests. Democrats and Republicans alike need that cash to pay their way up the party leadership chain, as well as to pay for campaign ads in their next election.

And the PACs cover their own bets by throwing in chips on both sides of the aisle. In the 2006 cycle, when Republicans were in charge of Congress, corporate PACs contributed roughly 65 percent of their lobbying cash to the GOP. In the next two election cycles, when the Democrats had taken charge of both chambers, the PACs split their donations evenly between the parties.[8]

In 2013, five years after the crash, freshmen U.S. representatives from both parties lucky enough to be assigned to the committee started receiving hundreds of thousands of dollars from bank lobbyists and corporate interests. Four months into their tenure, Democrats joined with Republicans to vote to strike down some of the toughest financial protections that had been put in place for consumers by the 2010 Dodd-Frank banking reform law. Former U.S. Representative Brad Miller (D-NC), who had just retired after ten years on the Cash Committee, remembered how it was when he was a neophyte: "Freshmen are pushed and pushed and pushed to raise money—it's how they are judged by the leadership and the political establishment in Washington. It's only natural that it has got to be on your mind that a vote one way or other is going to affect the ability to raise money."[9]

It has been going on for decades. So it's no wonder that the Financial Crisis Inquiry Commission drew this stark conclusion about the cash and the crash:

> The financial industry itself played a key role in weakening regulatory constraints on institutions, markets, and products. It did not surprise the commission that an industry of such wealth and power would exert pressure on policy makers and regulators. From 1999 to 2008, the financial sector expended $2.7 billion in reported federal lobbying expenses; individuals and political action committees in the sector made more than $1 billion in campaign contributions. What troubled us was the extent to which the nation was deprived of the necessary strength and independence of the oversight necessary to safeguard financial stability.[10]

But how tough was the new Dodd-Frank legislation? Did all that lobbying cash coming in to lawmakers dilute its strength? And if provisions in the banking law are still under assault by moneyed interests writing checks to Cash Committee members, are we actually better protected? It's an ongoing debate, but serious doubts are easy to find. Adam Garfinkle was a speechwriter in the George W. Bush administration and is the founding editor of the conservative *American Interest*. Nearly three years after Dodd-Frank's passage, Garfinkle explained the ongoing danger, and also cited the money flood as the reason for it:

> It is still okay for well-heeled financial services businesses to bet against their own clients with their own money, and risk that of others at no real cost to themselves. Trillions of dollars' worth of derivatives are still unreported and unregulated. High-speed

trading, which now accounts for about 65 percent of all stock trades in the United States, is the new source for a range of insider abuses that are clearly wrong but not yet illegal; other countries have created limits, but the financial plutocracy has so far prevented legislative or regulatory action in the United States.[11]

Dodd-Frank also designated which large banks are to be categorized as "systemically important." Thomas Hoenig, vice chair of the FDIC and former president of the Federal Reserve Bank of Kansas City, believes this sustains the too-big-to-fail problem in our financial system, making us "less safe." Hoenig explained that the law would "further concentrate our financial system to these powerful few companies, and therefore make it even more fragile in the sense of financial vulnerability to the taxpayer. I don't think that's healthy."[12]

The same special interests that drove the legislation and lax oversight that led up to the economic collapse have been right back at the table in its aftermath. Four years after the Dodd-Frank reform, the SEC had still not enforced the new rules on the credit rating companies.[13] One year later, in December 2014, capital requirements at the big banks were still deemed to be too low. As changes were being proposed, U.S. Senator David Vitter (R-LA) announced: "Even the pro-megabank Federal Reserve has finally acknowledged that the status quo is only allowing the problem of 'too big to fail' to continue."[14] And that same month, Congress overturned a safety provision of Dodd-Frank that had required banks to use separate accounts—not federally insured—to trade risky derivatives. The measure was sneaked into a larger spending bill because the Cash Committee had originally passed it by a vote of 53–6. Citigroup lobbyists designed the legislation and, according to The Washington Post, JPMorgan Chase CEO Jamie Dimon personally called lawmakers to push for its passage. Both banks contribute millions of lobbying dollars. Simon Johnson, former chief economist at the International Monetary Fund, leaves no doubt as to why: "It is because there is a lot of money at stake. They want to be able to take big risks where they get the upside and the taxpayer gets the potential downside."[15]

As we read Lawrence Lessig's description of the manipulation of the Dodd-Frank banking legislation, we can see the David and Goliath nature of the problem:

In October 2009 there were 1,537 lobbyists representing financial institutions registered in D.C., and lobbying to affect this critical legislation—*twenty five times* the number registered to support consumer groups, unions, and other proponents of strong reform. A system that makes lobbyists the ticket to influence is a system that wildly skews the issues that will get attention. This, in time, will distort results.[16]

There are those words again: "skew" and "distort." The money flood drives counterproductive solutions, because the incentives are tilted toward narrow interests, as opposed to the majority—us. And beyond policy on financial regulation, the money flood also drives laws that skew and screw with principles in the free market that are supposed to benefit consumers. Legislation gets passed every year that arbitrarily drives up prices for Americans, while corporate political donors reap ridiculously profitable rates of return on their investment.

Agricultural subsidies and price supports are a depressingly powerful example of this corruption. Congress passes legislation that protects sugar and corn producers. The government subsidizes corporate dairy farmers (costing Americans more than 25 percent more to buy milk and cheese), and has stepped in to protect shrimp and banana producers—even cotton farmers. And most of these gifts in the form of market perversion go to the very richest of the world's corporate farmers. More than 70 percent of the subsidies go to just 10 percent of farm producers.[17]

The conglomerate Archer Daniels Midland (ADM) might be the best poster-child for this kind of market corruption. ADM's profits exceeded $69 billion in 2009. According to a policy analysis from the Cato Institute, more than 40 percent of the corporation's annual profits are derived "from products heavily subsidized or protected by the American government." The analysis also revealed that "every $1 of profits earned by ADM's corn sweetener operation costs consumers $10, and every $1 of profits earned by its ethanol operation costs taxpayers $30."[18]

This skewing of legislation toward the farming industry is also a perfect example of how one bad policy outcome impacts another—and the exponentially negative effect it can have on Americans. While some researchers will debate the relationship between obesity and subsidies for high fructose corn syrup, there is no question that there are more cheap junk foods on supermarket shelves than ever before. Obesity rates have reached record highs in recent years, which jacks up the health care costs we all know need to be moving in the opposite direction.[19] We may not want Congress to tell us what we can or cannot eat in a country where our freedom of choice is so highly prized. But for our leaders to actually take money and then incentivize wealthy corporations to shower the market with unhealthy products is just plain stupid by any measure.

Once in a while someone tries to speak up or stand up on this issue, but the money soon turns the effort on its head. In early 2014, Iowa Senator Chuck Grassley (R) took a political risk when he introduced legislation to place a hard cap of $250,000 on subsidy payments to wealthy farmers. But the final bill not only eliminated the cap, it also created additional price supports incentivizing farmers to overproduce and put taxpayers at further risk. Grassley summed it up: "A few people, with the single-minded intent to keep unlimited farm subsidies flowing out the door, proved Congress deserves its 12 percent approval rating."[20]

Once again the money had won. And Grassley's comment after the bill's passage was tame compared to the *Chicago Tribune*'s description:

> For special interests, it's party time. Trade protectionism for the domestic sugar business? Check. Government control of the milk supply? Check. Block grants for states to promote their growers of vegetables, tree nuts, and flowers? Check. One sweetheart deal after another in a bill that goes on for nearly 1,000 pages.[21]

What reward can Grassley expect to receive for his exhibit of statesmanship? He just might get turned out of office—perhaps even in a primary election—by the moneyed forces he stood up against. That's what happened to his midwest colleague, U.S. Senator Richard Lugar (R-IN), in 2012. One of the few remaining moderates in his party, Lugar was the target of those "predator groups" described in Chapter 5. Lugar's former Hoosier colleague from the other side of the aisle, Evan Bayh (D), said the defeat was a loss for Congress: "What's happened in the Senate is you have large sums of outside money that come in to endorse political orthodoxy. It happened to Dick Lugar in Indiana. Six million dollars came in against him."[22]

Health care is another area where we see corporate money skewing legislation, and costing us. The prescription drug lobby is a trenchant example, as it shows how Americans got the shaft two times in less than ten years—under both Democratic and Republican control of the government. According to the Center for Responsive Politics, the pharmaceuticals and health care products industry is the leading lobbyist sector in terms of money spent in Washington. Between 1998 and 2014, it invested more than $2.9 billion on political activity, an investment that earned a big-time profit margin, much of it in the form of our consumer dollars.[23]

In 2003, the Republican-controlled Congress passed "Medicare Part D," which enabled American senior citizens to purchase a full range of high-priced medications. The program was estimated to cost more than half a trillion dollars over a decade, with no increases in tax revenue to cover it. The kicker? The law actually forbade the U.S. government from negotiating with the pharmaceutical companies for better prices—even though the drug manufacturers used the patents they derive from the government to justify the prices they set. According to an analysis of corporate filings by Health Care for America Now, the drug companies pulled in a profit of $711 billion between 2003 and 2012, with their annual profit increasing 62 percent between the first and the last year.[24] We pay more money, and they make more money.

A key player in the cutting of that infamous deal was a congressman named Billy Tauzin from Louisiana, a former Democrat who had changed political parties, and who also chaired the House Energy and Commerce Committee. Right after he successfully pushed for the Part D law that drives the kinds of higher drug prices we reviewed in Chapter 4, he left Congress and walked straight into a $2 million per year gig as president and CEO of the lobbying group PhRMA, the Pharmaceutical Research and Manufacturers of America.[25]

That may possibly be the best single example of the warped revolving door world of corporate lobbying. We have seen some of the cosmic dollar figures spent by lobbyists, and now we can see the added incentives for lawmakers and their staff. They're not just worried about holding onto their jobs so they can keep sprinting on the wheel. Public service salaries just can't compete with the compensation offered by the influence peddlers, and it is an easy crossover move to get to the real money.

The Sunlight Foundation reports that between 1998 and 2012, the total number of contract lobbyists who had previously worked for the government nearly quadrupled from 482 to 1,846—including 128 who had actually served as members of Congress.[26] These are the people who influence the writing of our laws, or, in some cases, *actually write the laws.* In his book *Broken: American Political Dysfunction and What To Do About It,* Adam Garfinkle explains how a former head lobbyist for WellPoint, Liz Fowler, was instrumental in drafting the Affordable Care Act (ACA) and how former J.P. Morgan analyst Julie Chon wrote substantial parts of Dodd-Frank. Even more eye-opening, Garfinkle writes:

> A pristine revolving-door example of a contracting scam, rather than the writing of a law or a reg, concerns former Secretary of Homeland Security Michael Chertoff. When Chertoff left government, he became a lobbyist for Rapiscan, and was instrumental in getting that company's full-body x-ray scanners installed at airports. These machines may not be entirely safe, especially for pregnant women, and there's no evidence that they actually work to stop terrorists. But the government bought them anyway.[27]

In 2009, six years after Billy Tauzin pushed Medicare Part D, he was getting paid even more to run PhRMA. President Obama had promised as a candidate to reform D.C.'s money-laced lobbying culture and to negotiate for lower prescription drug costs. Tauzin was ready: By the time health care legislation came up for debate, PhRMA had 165 additional lobbyists (137 of them former government staffers) on its payroll who "flooded Congress with campaign contributions, and hired dozens of former Capitol Hill insiders to push their case." Democrats, in charge of both the House and the Senate, received the bulk of the $8 million pumped into the Capitol. Under pressure from lobbyists and the dependence they had purchased from Congress, the Obama administration held a series of back room talks with Tauzin and the pharmaceutical lobby. The final deal *prohibited* the government from "lowering prescription drug prices through Medicare negotiations, re-importation and quicker release of generics onto the market."[28]

"Obamacare" finally passed. The pharmaceutical industry agreed to $80 billion in cuts to drug costs and to support the legislation. But by handcuffing the negotiating power of the government, the drug companies saved $220 billion that could have been saved by the American health consumer and taxpayer. Preventing generic drug prices from going down is not exactly "promoting our general welfare." But the deal definitely improved Billy Tauzin's welfare. His salary in 2010? PhRMA paid Tauzin $11.6 million.[29] Or you could say that we paid him.

These two examples of insider legislative deals with the pharmaceutical industry also provide us the perfect opportunity to confront the question of congressional responsibility versus presidential responsibility. After all, wasn't the Prescription Medicare D legislation originally an initiative of President Bush? Didn't we just see how President Obama's administration buckled to the drug companies? Perhaps we did. But this does not absolve Congress. As we saw in Chapter 3, The Promises and the Powers, Congress was designed and designated in our Constitution as the first and leading branch of the federal government. Sanford Levinson reminds us that "divided government" originally meant the separation of powers, not the bitter partisanship between the parties it has morphed into over time.[30] Congress's powers to legislate and appropriate are forceful levers in the practice of governing—if Congress chooses to independently exercise them. But that is awfully difficult due to the rules in the system. We could fault the individual members for making a conscious choice to cave in and exchange gifts with those corporate interests both in the Part D and Obamacare episodes. But the foul dependency inside the system is the real problem. Members of Congress need that money to get re-elected and stay in power. They are pressured to keep getting paid—in order to keep playing. It happens inside the skewed game everyday. And in the end, Americans are the ones who get fleeced.

––––––––

The slush of money in the D.C. 4–3 doesn't just cause the reckless driving of poor policy. The billions of greenbacks coursing through the Capitol also skew the system by *deterring* rational dialogue and good faith negotiation. Senator Joe Manchin (D-WV) explained this deterrent effect in very clear fashion in a 2014 CNN interview:

> There's so much money involved … I go to work everyday, and I'm expected to raise money against the other side, if you will. So as a Democrat I go to work, I'm expected to raise money for the DSCC and my Republican counterparts and my colleagues are expected to raise money for the RSCC. That money is used against any Democrats or Republicans up for elections, and then we're even expected to go campaign against them. Now that doesn't add for a good atmosphere, for us to start next week, come back after all this stuff happens the week prior to that and say, "OK, will you work with me now, can you co-sponsor a bill." That's what's happening. The money has infiltrated and has driven us apart.[31]

Manchin's observation about the stagnant atmosphere on Capitol Hill is extremely important in our overall effort to analyze and unlock Congress. Our polarized political landscape is challenging enough, but Manchin is saying that the money flood inflates the conflict even further. The D.C. 4–3 fosters an environment in which U.S. senators and representatives are deterred from listening to each other, evaluating arguments on the merits, and creating effective solutions. Our founders intended to create a Congress where interests could be balanced to ultimately favor the national interest. Instead, far too often, even the possibility of negotiation and compromise is precluded. This deterrence constantly paralyzes Congress from passing laws that could promote our general welfare. It prevents Congress from making progress on all those challenges we saw Americans suffering from in our review of the product.

In their book *Winner-Take-All Politics,* political scientists Jacob Hacker and Paul Pierson make a powerful case about how wealthy interests have successfully pushed to restructure our economy, hurting average Americans. The term they use for the way members of Congress are deterred from passing policy is "drift"—"the passive-aggressive form of politics." Drift impacts all kinds of issues that affect our daily lives such as health care, financial regulation, taxes, federal investments in education and research, labor laws, and others. The authors explain that when current laws have been failing us or have become obsolete and require maintenance, "political leaders fail to update policies, even when there are viable options, because they face pressure from powerful interests exploiting opportunities for political obstruction."[32]

Hacker and Pierson cite the minimum wage as a prime example. We know from the data in Chapter 4 that wages for Americans, especially at the bottom, have not kept pace with the price of goods in our economy. Why haven't minimum wage laws been passed to account for this gap? According to their research, it is because

> intense opponents of the minimum wage have worked tirelessly and effectively to prevent it from being increased to prior levels or pegged to inflation (a proposal that came close to passing in the 1970s). This has been every bit as much a political fight as, say, the Bush tax cuts of 2001 and 2003. But it is a far less visible fight, resulting not in big signing ceremonies, but in nothing happening. Our point is that *nothing happening* to key policies while the economy shifts rapidly can add up to something very big happening to Americans who rely on these policies.[33]

Clearly Hacker and Pierson believe that raising the minimum wage is long overdue. The issue traditionally breaks along ideological lines. But like so many other policy decisions that directly impact Americans, the distorted climate generated by special interest cash deters even the possibility for representatives to have an honest discussion and negotiation on the issue.

We know that members of Congress get incentivized by lobbyists and outside interest groups to support their preferences and toe the party line (Gilens's research showed us how policy outcomes track with those preferences). But it gets even worse: now we see moneyed interests funding "objective research" that isn't even truly objective. The real goal is to frame information in a way that will sway legislators and opinion makers. Both sides of the aisle do it, with corporate interests and labor unions actually setting up these entities and throwing millions of dollars behind them.

It is not necessarily illegal, but it is certainly not always ethical. An egregious example of how this special interest activity can distort the debate occurred right in the middle of the minimum wage battle in 2014. An organization called "The Employment Policies Institute" (EPI), was set up by Richard B. Berman, an ad executive known for advocating on behalf of Corporate America. The EPI is a "nonprofit" that has no employees, yet it paid Berman's ad firm more than $1 million in 2012. EPI had just 11 major contributors that year, which included private conservative donors, as well as the restaurant industry.[34]

But beyond the questionable pay arrangement benefiting Berman, the EPI's research has come under fire for using narrowly chosen data that led to inaccurate conclusions about the effects of the minimum wage. Lisa Graves, executive director of the nonprofit watchdog Center for Media and Democracy, says EPI's questionable information only clouds the discussion: "They are trying to peddle an industry wish list, but mask it as if they are independent experts. They are little more than phony experts on retainer." John Weaver, a veteran consultant of Republican campaigns, agrees: "It is the way of Washington now—and that is unfortunate. Because if it's not dishonest, it's at least disingenuous."[35]

It would be logical to wonder at this point if members of Congress could just cut through all of this noise and get to a set of facts that both sides could agree upon. But that takes time—time that the money hunt steals. The issues confronting Congress are hard questions, and developing practical solutions requires study and intellectual creativity. The time squeeze deters this from happening. Former Senator Olympia Snowe (R-ME) described this reality after her retirement in 2012:

Congressional scheduling is now at the mercy of fundraising events ... There used to be a time when we would separate politics and policy at least for the first year after the election, to attempt to synchronize our legislative agenda on issues crucial to the nation before the campaign season of the second year. Now we are experiencing a perpetual focus on campaigns and fundraising.[36]

Whether or not Congress passes legislation to raise the minimum wage is not the overarching issue here. That is but one policy option in the area of economic well-being. As we observed in Chapter 4, Congress could employ a variety of policy alternatives to promote our general welfare. But generally they don't. We saw this in the Pew Center research in Chapter 4, where more than 66 percent of Americans said that the legislation passed since the recession has done little or nothing to help the middle class, the poor, and small business owners. At the same time, an average of 65 percent believed the policies have been beneficial to wealthy folks, large banks, and large corporations.[37]

These deterrents to communication, policy creation, and negotiation arise on issue after issue. When special interest paymasters restrain members of Congress from even considering the other side of an argument, how can they compromise on potential solutions to help the people? When countless hours spent begging for cash robs legislators of the time to actually legislate, how will they be able to craft laws that empower Americans to get a fair economic shot? The money skews and distorts Congress's capacity to trust, learn, think, and then act.

In the previous chapter we also reviewed Congress's failures in overseeing the executive branch. The time suck required by the cash hunt also puts a huge dent into Congress's ability to actually conduct proper oversight on legislative policy.

Think about the Financial Crisis Inquiry Commission's statement earlier in this section regarding the country being deprived of "the oversight necessary to safeguard financial stability." We know what that failure meant for our economy and its impact on American families. And we need not look far to find other examples of oversight failure, from CIA torture and secret domestic spying programs to Medicaid fraud and breakdowns in consumer protection. Far too often, Congress is not the entity that throws the penalty flag. The strongest example of this lax oversight may be the Veterans Administration scandal that fully emerged in 2014 where VA officials were "cooking the books" and lying about the wait times for severely injured veterans, some of whom died. The president and the American people did not learn about this shame from Congress—instead we were all alerted to the scandal from investigative reporting on CNN.[38]

Government oversight is hard. It is tedious and requires a substantial amount of attention span. The thousands of hours Congress spends soliciting money represent one way that the money defect challenges Congress's ability to conduct oversight. In addition, special interest cash can affect the *degree* of scrutiny oversight committees exert within their purviews. U.S. Rep. Miller admitted that "it has got to be on your mind that a vote one way or other is going to affect the ability to raise money." The same goes for oversight, as both activities are exercises of power.

One final deterrent effect resulting from the power of money is the negativity it inspires in all of us. Americans may not be able to articulate all the granular details we've been examining here that display money's effect on Congress—but we do instinctively know that the system just doesn't smell right.

Between 1964 and 2008, the American National Election Studies (ANES) asked Americans whether the government is run for the benefit of all or run for a few big interests. In 1964, 29 percent chose "a few big interests" while 64 percent chose "for the benefit of all." Forty-four years later, 69 percent chose big interests over 29 percent who selected our overall benefit.[39] We have seen a complete reversal in public perception on this question. And though ANES uses the word "government," it is not a leap to assume Americans are in large part making a judgment about their elected representatives in the House and Senate (who've registered a 7 percent approval rating). If voters are continually deterred from trusting a game they see rigged with cash, why participate? Why waste the time?

In a speech at Georgetown University in 2014, former President Bill Clinton said: "Somehow you have to find a way to establish trust among adversaries. Agreement is not nearly as important as trust. Trust predates everything."[40] This is not only true in terms of trust between our two parties in Congress, but also between the American people and the elected representatives in whom we place our trust. Money is the most visible problem in the D.C. 4-3 that deters this trust. It is already poisoning the capacity for our leaders to properly operate what was designed as a "representative democracy." It is also poisoning the people's capacity to believe in our own power to make a difference. The money flood is essentially drowning both the integrity and efficacy of our legislative branch. We need to throw it a line so that it may pull itself—and the rest of us—back up.

HALTED HOUSE

The defects in the D.C. 4-3 are all connected. They team up not only to help each other exist, but also to deter and distort progress on the policymaking end. And in some cases, they drive counterproductive legislation. We saw in the previous chapter how the flood of money swishing through the system makes big splashes daily in the U.S. House of Representatives. The REDMAP project reveals how money is required to rig congressional districts. The steep, record-breaking price of campaigns for House seats confirms that it takes mountains of money to get re-elected every two years.

Plenty of that cash is special interest grubstake, provided for a purpose. The interests who can afford to purchase access—on both sides of the aisle—push U.S. House Representatives to tilt in opposite directions on important public policy issues. As well, the increased partisanship and vanishing center fostered by our single-member congressional districts keep House members in their red and blue boxes. Accordingly, representatives must carry their respective party banners loudly and proudly. Once they are sworn in, it won't be long until challenger candidates will be publicly criticizing their performance.

These middle two defects in the D.C. 4-3, *rigged races* and *two-year terms,* combine to make everything more difficult in the lower chamber of our legislative branch. Each has its own power to deter and distort, but taken together, the power increases. So in this section we look at that collective capacity. The House gets ground to a halt, on issue after issue.

————

In 2012, freshman Representative Pete Gallego (D-TX) was one of only three Democrats who won a congressional district that had less than 47 percent Democratic partisanship.[41] Gallego's "crossover" election appeal defined him as one of those few remaining moderates in Congress—but he soon realized the swamp he had waded into. Six months into his first term, Gallego made the following observation about the shocking level of intransigence among his new colleagues: "If you walk in everyday and you tell your spouse, 'I don't care what your opinion is because we're going to do it my way because I'm always right,' then your marriage doesn't last very long—it's not much of a marriage."[42]

Less than a year later, House Republican Majority Leader Eric Cantor made the same analogy to marriage in his farewell speech as he emphasized "trying to strike common ground." Cantor had his comeuppance by being the first sitting majority leader to ever lose a primary—in this case to Tea Party candidate Dave Brat. (Financially, at least, Cantor did not suffer; after leaving office he glided straight into an investment bank that guaranteed him $3.4 million in compensation within 18 months).[43] Ironically, Cantor had been one of the Republican leaders whom Democrats had most blamed for extremism and legislative delays. Pundits debated why the staunchly conservative Cantor had lost, but one reason cited was his slightly softened stance on the issue of immigration reform just prior to the election—a hint that he was open to negotiation. In his ruby-red, gerrymandered Seventh Congressional District of Virginia, that adult attitude of keeping an open mind may have left his right flank wide open.

Cantor's loss caused many observers to conclude that the prospect of immigration reform was dead. The truth is that immigration legislation, like so many other common sense proposals, had little to no chance of getting through the House long before the more conservative Brat beat Cantor. Just one month into 2014, an NBC headline blared what so many in Washington already knew: "Shutdown: Both Parties Avoid Action Until After Elections."[44] NBC political editors explained how Republicans had taken immigration off the table, while the Democrats had removed the prospect of adjusting the increase in Social Security benefits in the budget, as well as "fast track" trade authority. Their conclusion: "both sides are deploying a do-no-harm strategy—all with less than nine months before Election Day 2014. It's just the latest reminder that Washington is not going to get *anything* major done this year. It's not even March 1, and both parties are waving the policy white flags."[45]

Two days later, *New York Times* columnist David Brooks broke it down further:

It's all bad for the country. So what are the things that are going to help the economy in the near term? Immigration would be a huge boost for the economy. Fast track, a trade deal across the Atlantic, across the Pacific, huge boost. Chained CPI would save a trillion dollars in the second decade off the federal budget debt. So these are all gigantic, very good policies where there is majority support, and where in the old days in Washington, you'd cobble together a bipartisan coalition, and get rid of the fringes. But right now the fringes have veto power, and nobody's found a solution to that.[46]

Soon after, we saw the immigration issue play out again when thousands of undocumented children from Central America were being illegally and dangerously brought into the United States. After two months of our leaders shouting about the urgency to provide a solution, Congress broke for its five-week summer recess on August 2 without even passing a short-term response to the problem. Instead, with the midterm elections only three months away, the hard-liners in the House majority drove a policy solution that didn't have a chance of full passage—and they knew it.[47] It was all for show for the party base, and it would have only been a stopgap measure.

Three weeks after the midterms, Senator Lindsey Graham (R–SC) described his frustration with continued House inaction on immigration policy: "Shame on us as Republicans for having a body that cannot generate a solution to an issue" that has national security, economic and cultural implications. "The Senate has done this three times. I'm close to the people in the House, but I'm disappointed in my party."[48] The United States has not seen "comprehensive immigration reform" passed since 1986. As we reviewed earlier, the economic potential that our country has lost over three decades is irrecoverable.

We have also seen congressional dysfunction deter the budgeting process repeatedly in both the 112th and 113th sessions of Congress. In the spring of 2012, two of the remaining moderates in Congress, U.S. Representatives Steven LaTourette (R-OH) and Jim Cooper (D-TN), co-sponsored a budget bill that included recommendations from the bipartisan Bowles-Simpson Commission to reduce the country's long-term national debt. The morning of the vote, the two congressmen said they had one hundred members from both parties supporting their budget. By the time of the actual vote that night, the number had fallen to just thirty-eight. LaTourette explained that liberal and conservative special interest groups pressured members on both sides into political submission.[49]

Former U.S. Comptroller General David Walker, who served from 1998 to 2008, describes how both sides of the aisle in Congress have been failing for years to face reality and strike a very necessary deal:

> The truth is, too many Democrats and liberals are in denial that we must reform social insurance programs to make them solvent, sustainable, and secure. Too many Republicans and conservatives don't acknowledge that given known demographic trends and rising health care costs, comprehensive federal tax reform will need to generate revenues above current and historical levels of the economy (GDP). The leaders of both major parties in Congress pay too much attention to the extreme factions of their political base rather than the desires of a significant majority of "We the People." In addition, both sides seem to not be very proficient at math.[50]

The increased visibility of the issue of debt and deficits in recent years may make it seem like the urgency of this problem is something relatively new. But more than twenty years ago in 1992, similar budget questions were being asked. At that time, with Democrats controlling both the House and the Senate, Senator John Danforth (R-MO) called out the two-year election cycle as the cause of inaction:

No sooner is that suggestion put forward than people are saying "Wait a second. Not now. No. Wait until next year. Let us not talk about controlling the entitlement programs, because this is an election year and we do not want to offend anybody by talking about the entitlements. That is too risky politically. We want to get through the election. Wait until next year."[51]

Although the breakdowns over the budget may have reached new lows, the trend is hardly unprecedented. For years we have seen childish haggles, delays, and shutdowns over the budget. In his book *The Parties Versus the People,* former Congressman Mickey Edwards (R-OK), speaking from his experience on the budget committee, laments that Congress engages in "a constant use of fallback 'omnibus' bills, short-term stopgaps, and 'continuing resolutions' that simply keep doing, for a while at least, what was done the year before, whether or not that addresses problems or allows sufficient oversight of federal agencies. Partisan warfare is exacerbated and Congress's ability to function is crippled."[52]

Congress's new levels of paralysis and governing by crisis have real negative effects. Stopgap budgeting omits the creative thought and planning necessary to actually benefit America in the long run. Genuine disagreements over the best courses of action on spending and taxes do drive much of the gridlock. But now the partisan tail of the extremes in the House is wagging the dog, snuffing out even the potential for rational compromise. In a fast moving, more interconnected world, inaction and uncertainty weaken the United States in major and unmistakable ways.

We saw this spelled out by the credit rating agencies in the summer of 2011. That moment was the first time that the recently elected members of the Tea Party pushed the Republican majority to use the debt ceiling as a tactic to force spending cuts in the budget. Without a debt ceiling increase, the U.S. government risked defaulting on its financial obligations already decided upon in appropriation legislation passed by Congress. After months of public squabbling, compromise still eluded the parties until July 31, two days before the date the U.S. Treasury said the government would run out of stalling mechanisms to pay the bills. According to the Bipartisan

Policy Center, delays had already been forecast to cost the country an estimated $18 billion in future costs.[53]

Beyond the public embarrassment and further loss of American confidence in Congress, the episode caused the U.S. credit rating to be downgraded for the first time in history. In its statement, Standard & Poor's made clear that the skewed political *process* was a driving motivator in the downgrade:

> The political brinksmanship of recent months highlights what we see as America's governance and policymaking becoming less stable, less effective, and less predictable than what we previously believed. The statutory debt ceiling and the threat of default have become political bargaining chips in the debate over fiscal policy ... [This] weakens the government's ability to manage public finances.[54]

Immediate effects of the downgrade included raising U.S. borrowing costs, pulling consumer confidence down by fourteen points, and decreasing growth in consumer spending from 0.8 percent to 0.1 percent.[55]

We also see the practical effects that inaction has on the federal agencies tasked with carrying out legislation passed by Congress. These are already large, unwieldy bureaucracies by their very nature. But when Congress provides unclear guidance and insufficient resources that the agencies require to do their jobs, Americans often suffer as a result.

Even before the 2013 government shutdown, the breakdown in the proper budgeting process and the indiscriminate sequestration cuts caused confusion for state governments, federal agencies, research labs focused on disease cures, and even the U.S. military. In June 2013 Defense Secretary Chuck Hagel told Congress that the uncertainty "from month to month, year to year, as to what our possibilities are for contracts for acquisitions, for technology, for research—the technological advantage that we have in the air and the superiority we have at sea, the training, the readiness—all of these are affected."[56]

State governors have likewise been exasperated with Congress's inability to negotiate and plan for the country. Two months before House

Republicans' insistence on defunding the health care law led to the budget stalemate that shut down the federal government, Republican Governors Scott Walker (WI), Phil Bryant (MS), and Jack Dalrymple (ND) warned their own party colleagues in Congress against the tactic of tying the two together. Even Mississippi Governor Bryant, who opposed the ACA and chose not to expand Medicaid in his state, urged members to be practical:

> Take the battle to the floor, debate it, do all that you can to get that bill passed because we believe in eliminating Obamacare completely, that's why we didn't expand it. But at some point perhaps we have to realize that the federal government—because of the support of our military, support of our public safety, our infrastructure—we have to have a budget.[57]

The shutdown itself gives us a good look at how all those polarized single-member congressional districts translate into a wide congressional divide in D.C. The day before the shutdown, the House editor for the *Cook Political Report,* David Wasserman, called out hyper-partisanship as the culprit for the impasse. Wasserman explained what he calls the "extreme index":

> Fewer than a third of House Republicans in 1995–96 came from districts that were at least ten points more Republican than the national average. Today more than half of House Republicans come from districts that are at least ten points more Republican than the national average on the *Cook Political Report*'s partisan voter index. So, we're talking about a situation where Obama has negative leverage. If he comes out and says he supports one thing, that drives the incentive on the right to actually oppose things more.[58]

The divide is powerful. We used to see Congress pass historic pieces of legislation with crossover votes from both parties, such as the Civil Rights Act, Medicare, and the National Environmental Policy Act. Not anymore. In 2010, Congress passed the ACA through the arcane process of "reconciliation"—and without a single vote from the minority party.[59]

Likewise, in past decades Congress would find a way to come together to make necessary changes to major pieces of legislation. They did so with the Children's Health Insurance Program in 1997, the Immigration Reform and Control Act of 1986, Medicare in 1965, and Social Security in 1935. Not anymore. In the spring of 2013, as the official October start of the ACA was approaching, the parties dug in their heels. Both opponents and supporters of the law wanted to see changes, but Congress was locked. Four months prior to its launch, Senator Max Baucus (D-MT) and Mitch McConnell (R-KY) correctly predicted Congress would make no improvements.[60]

In March 2014, one year later, a Kaiser Family Foundation poll found 49 percent of Americans wanted to see Congress make improvements to the ACA.[61] Just one month later, U.S. Rep. Dennis Ross (R-FL) acknowledged to a town hall of his constituents why that can't happen in the current Congress:

> I think one of the most unfortunate things my party did the last three years was not offer an alternative to health care ... You know what's unfortunate? For the next six months, we're going to go into an election knowing that we're not going to do anything to address health care because we've gone so far for the last three years saying "no," that we don't have an alternative to say "yes" to.[62]

The dysfunction in the House now even affects our leaders' ability to responsibly arrive at national security decisions—an area that used to enjoy some measure of relief from political partisanship. A glaring example of this took place just before the 2014 midterm elections. As President Obama prepared to address the nation about taking military action to confront terrorists in Iraq and Syria, he also announced his intent to have Congress weigh in on the decision. There has always been tension and debate between the power of the president as commander-in-chief of the armed forces to launch military attacks out of urgent need for national defense, and the power and responsibility of Congress to "declare war" as outlined in Article I of the Constitution. The argument seesaws back and forth, but as an institution, Congress usually expresses a desire to be informed and consulted. Making an official decision, however, within the confines of two-year terms? Another story.

On September 9, the day before the president's speech, U.S. Representative Jack Kingston (R-GA) confessed a political truth that plenty of his colleagues realized full well: "A lot of people would like to stay on the sideline and say, 'Just bomb the place and tell us about it later.' It's an election year. A lot of Democrats don't know how it would play in their party, and Republicans don't want to change anything. We like the path we're on now. We can denounce it if it goes bad, and praise it if it goes well and ask what took him so long."[63]

A week later, in mid-September, Congress went home—without taking any vote on the hundreds of air strikes in Iraq and the increasing number of troops the president was sending back in. Congress had already taken five weeks off in August and September. On September 18, after ducking the vote, it announced members would not be coming back to vote on anything until after the midterm elections in November. Five days later the United States launched airstrikes in Syria—without the sanction of the people's representatives.[64]

Of course, this type of political calculation, or cowardice, happens in the Senate as well as the House. But Senators have six years of latitude before voters get a chance to make an evaluation of these policy decisions. On every issue. The frequency of House elections is a forceful influencer.

In various examples on domestic policy earlier in this section, we have seen the power of "partisan asymmetry" through the prism of Republicans' recent control of the House—and the Tea Party's leverage within it. But this by no means absolves Democrats of their role in excessive partisanship. Upon taking control of the House majority in 2006, new Speaker Nancy Pelosi (D-CA) promised to employ a more open legislative process. But a Woodrow Wilson Center study reported that in the next two congressional sessions, the Democrats limited the Republicans' capacity to introduce amendments on 86 percent of bills in 2007–08 and 99 percent in 2009–10. Both proportions of blocking were higher than the 81 percent recorded by the Republicans in 2005-2006.[65] When either political party gets too tight a grip on the steering wheel, the odds rise of creating a collision course—or just plain driving in circles.

At about this point, depending on where a partisan sits on the political spectrum, he or she will cry "false equivalency!" A passionate progressive may say that the conservatives are far more intractable, and then an equally dedicated conservative will rip right back with a counterargument about voting based on principle. Flip on cable news, and you can hear it all day long. But here's the overarching point: Even if one side's story could actually be proven to be thoroughly correct, the rigged nature of our elections makes it far more difficult for any member of Congress to cross the aisle, say the words "I see your point," and work in partnership to negotiate a sensible solution. To do this would require taking a risk, and with the party leadership, cash kings, and base voting blocs waiting to pounce, risk-taking is almost entirely precluded in the skewed system. As the numbers of both swing districts and moderates in Congress continue to dwindle, achieving compromise to pass meaningful legislation becomes even harder.

Blockage in the House stretches far beyond our country's big-ticket economic and health care problems. Whether the issue is transportation, college costs, education policy, planning and resources to repair our dilapidated infrastructure, environmental sustainability, or public safety, the defective congressional process belches out an increasingly poor product. And as we know, the interconnected relationship between all of these issues has an exponential effect on how strong and secure the United States remains as a nation.

We must remember that the bipartisan polling of the "New American Center" revealed that 58 percent of voters often agree with ideas from both Republicans and Democrats. But after seeing how our election system magnifies our polarized map and distorts our votes, it is easy to understand why 49 percent of Americans in that same poll agree that our two-party system is broken and obsolete.[66]

We cannot and should not try to eliminate our opposing political parties. Under rational circumstances, they serve practical purposes. But our system has lost that rational characteristic. Single-member congressional districts, in conjunction with gerrymandering and traditional primary elections, have the effect of distorting the will of the electorate—and pushing members of Congress further apart. Boxed into two-year terms, political pressures shove House members even further into ideological corners. Rational ideas that may not be red enough or blue enough to get one re-elected often get ignored or get shot down. Progress in the House gets halted on issue after issue.

These rules were not etched in marble. They were inked on parchment, right next to additional provisions that allow our citizenry to make changes when we believe they are necessary. The People's House needs some upgrades, and very soon we will be discussing potential solutions.

FILIBUSTER IN PRACTICE

Both political parties in the Senate, to varying degrees, have heightened the abuse of the filibuster over the last two decades. The party in the minority uses the filibuster to block Senate business and doesn't want to get rid of the rule—until it's in the majority and crying foul because now the blocking is at their members' legislative expense. The bickering swings back and forth. We saw statistics in the previous chapter that confirm record high levels of filibuster use. The parties will always disagree about whether a policy that has been prevented should have been prevented. But what is inarguable is that the majority does not rule.

It happens quietly on bill after bill. Awareness that sixty votes will not be attainable means an idea often gets quashed before staff can even begin researching it. Sometimes, though, we do see high profile examples of stoppage even when the parties seem to be coming together. In May 2014, Senator Jeanne Shaheen (D-NH) and Senator Rob Portman (R-OH) worked in a bipartisan fashion to champion the Energy Savings and Industrial Competitiveness Act. They were able to get seven Republicans and six Democrats to co-sponsor the bill, along with support from both the U.S. Chamber of Commerce and the Natural Resource Defense Council. They easily recruited a majority to support the legislation—fifty-six senators. Yet the legislation failed. Recriminations flew back and forth between the Senate leaders about amendments and broken promises. But had it not been for the filibuster rule, a majority of senators, representing a majority of the American people, would have been enough to advance a bipartisan, popularly backed public policy.[67]

A glaring example of how one defect in the D.C. 4-3 prevents efforts to improve or correct another defect occurred twice in the Senate on proposals to mitigate the money flood. The DISCLOSE Act of 2010 was intended to increase disclosure by corporations, unions, and other moneyed interests who financed political ads. The bill was passed through the House, had fifty-seven senators behind it, but was stopped by the Republican minority's filibuster. In 2012, another version of the DISCLOSE Act would have required independent groups to disclose the names of contributors who give more than $10,000 to impact elections. A majority of senators supported this bill, too. The Senate minority killed it as well.[68]

The Senate rules allow the minority to subvert the will of the majority on issue after issue, and not only where legislation is concerned. The record-breaking obstruction over the past several years has also prevented the staffing of federal agencies and courts tasked with executing or adjudicating the nation's laws.

Congressional scholars Norman Ornstein and Thomas Mann label this intentional deterrence "The New Nullification"—harkening back to the period before the Civil War where Southern states believed that "a state could ignore or nullify a federal law it universally viewed as unconstitutional."[69] The authors spell out the difference between the Senate in decades past and its more recent willingness "to use the hold and filibuster to undermine laws on the books from being implemented is an underhanded tactic, one reflecting, in our view, the increasing dysfunction of a parliamentary-style minority party distorting the rules and norms of the Senate to accomplish its ideological and partisan ends."[70]

There are those words again: "dysfunction," caused by a "distortion" of the "rules." Abuse of these rules skews the system and erects a wall against progress. And the abuse has reached a new level. In early 2010, U.S. Senator Richard Shelby (R-AL) single-handedly placed holds on seventy nominations, including posts at the Pentagon and State Department. Shelby's office admitted the holds were to "get the White House's attention" on his demands to have an Air Force refueling tanker and FBI anti-terror facility built in his home state. The day that he finally released most of the holds, Fox News reported what insiders already knew: "A senior member of the Appropriations Committee, Shelby has built his career on steering spending earmarks to Alabama."[71]

It is almost as if James Madison's words from *Federalist 58* were meant for Shelby:

> Were the defensive privilege limited to particular cases, an interested minority might take advantage of it to screen themselves from equitable sacrifices to the general weal (i.e., welfare), or, in particular emergencies, to extort unreasonable indulgences.[72]

The backlog of executive branch nominations now caused by the use of the filibuster is breathtakingly huge. As of May 5, 2014, 258 *nominees* were still waiting for confirmation. Common Cause reported that these included "*over 110 nominees pending on the Senate floor* to executive branch agencies and offices. To put this in perspective, at this point in the George W. Bush Administration, only *thirty-two* executive branch or independent office nominees were pending on the Senate floor. At the same time during the Clinton presidency, only twelve such nominations were pending in the Senate."[73]

In mid-2014, confirmations for ambassadors to more than thirty nations were stalled. The Election Assistance Commission, tasked with ensuring that our elections are run properly, had been left entirely vacant since 2011. Nominations for chief financial officer positions at the VA, EPA, HUD and the Departments of Agriculture, Energy, and Education were also held up in the Senate. These derailments and delays carry the potential to hurt the country in concrete ways.[74]

We saw this paradigm play out publicly as the government worked to implement the new Consumer Financial Protection Bureau (CFPB). The CFPB was a key part of the Dodd-Frank financial regulation passed in response to the 2007–08 economic crash. The Republican minority first blocked the nomination of Elizabeth Warren, who had designed the CFPB. Then they made it clear that the next nominee, former Ohio Attorney General Richard Cordray (D), would be rejected despite acknowledging his impressive background and qualifications. Although the establishment of the CFPB was part of passed law, Senate Republicans made it clear they would block any nominee—unless the law was changed. This kind of "new nullification" weakens the government's ability to respond to challenges that existing legislation is meant to address. Before she left her post as chairwoman of the Federal Deposit Insurance Corporation (FDIC), Sheila Bair articulated this problem in front of the Senate Banking Committee. Due to the Senate's failure to confirm qualified nominees for positions at the CFPB, FDIC, and U.S. Treasury, Bair warned that the financial system was vulnerable.[75] She further emphasized this in a 2011 press conference:

> There are still a lot of uncertainties and challenges in the financial system and a real dangerous risk of overheating. If we don't have a robust regulatory response to that we could find ourselves in the soup again ... I hope desperately the Senate can work with the administration. We have got a lot of issues to deal with now; perhaps more than ever it is important to have strong, smart, quality people in these jobs.[76]

But as we have seen from the sharp incline in filibusters and cloture votes, Senate obstruction of executive branch nominees only increased in the years after that statement. The crisis finally led the Senate to make two reforms to the rules in 2013. In January, it shortened the amount of time necessary for debate after a cloture vote for nominations (not legislation). Later in November, the Senate reduced the number of votes necessary to break a filibuster from sixty to fifty-one for all non-Supreme Court nominations. But even after that measure, the Senate minority has continued to put holds on uncontroversial nominees. The way that we know that these were "uncontroversial" is that in the six months following the change, thirteen judicial nominations were held up by the Republicans—and then all of them were *confirmed by unanimous votes*. In other words, every Senator who blocked one of those nominations *ultimately did not vote against the person he blocked*. Meanwhile, hours and hours of floor time are wasted. The dysfunction in the skewed system has become surreal.[77]

———

In the middle section of this chapter, Halted House, we reviewed instances where the middle two defects in the D.C. 4-3—two-year terms and rigged races—produce an exponentially higher power to freeze Congress. We conclude this section with a high-profile example of how the first and fourth defects—money and the Senate filibuster—have the combined capacity to kill the will of an overwhelming majority.

In Chapter 4, we noted that each year the U.S. records approximately thirty thousand gun-related deaths—by far the largest per-capita average in the world, which only intensifies what has always been a heated debate in our country. Of all issues, it might be most difficult to wring some of the politics out of this one. But we're going to try to examine it logically, in our ongoing effort to understand the role that problematic rules play in the policy process.

Law-abiding American gun owners fight to protect their right to bear arms. That right was first established in the Second Amendment: "A well regulated militia, being necessary to the security of a free state, the right of the people to keep and bear arms, shall not be infringed." The extent of this right has been debated in the public square and in the courts ever since. The right of an individual to own a firearm was upheld by the Supreme Court in 2008. But within the ruling, speaking for the majority, Justice Antonin Scalia also wrote that nothing in the Court's decision "cast doubt on long-standing prohibitions on the possession of firearms by felons and the mentally ill, or laws forbidding the carrying of firearms in sensitive places such as schools and government buildings."[78] Essentially, the Court had affirmed the right while also maintaining Congress's power to pass forms of gun legislation intended to increase public safety.

Americans on the side of stricter gun laws argue that the original constitutional right was specifically intended for state militias. The purpose in establishing this right was for the state to be capable of defending itself against oppression, which made perfect sense after a Revolutionary War had been fought and won to reject such oppression. Although the ultimate goal of some gun control advocates may be to limit the use and ownership of guns back to militias (as former Supreme Court Justice John Paul Stevens favors), the more active efforts are geared toward passing laws that they say will reduce gun violence. Even many gun control advocates will acknowledge that these efforts have not made enough headway in recent years.

Frequent mass shootings in American towns always have the effect of spotlighting anew the gun issue. Discussions usually zero in on efforts to pass laws requiring tougher background checks or to ban assault-style weapons or high-capacity magazines. The familiar scenario played out again in the summer of 2012 when a mentally ill man named James Holmes shot and killed twelve people in a movie theater in Aurora, Colorado. He wounded fifty-eight others. The debate restarted. Only two days later, before any new legislation had even been proposed, U.S. Representative Carolyn McCarthy (D-NY) made this announcement on NBC's *Meet The Press*: "A lot of politicians know it's the right thing to try to fight for something to save lives. They don't have the spine anymore. They pander to who's giving them money."[79]

McCarthy was right in the sense that Congress would end up passing no new laws to increase gun safety in the aftermath of Aurora. The real question is: Was she right about why? Was it because our politicians are "spineless" and "pandering" for the money? Or have our leaders just been representing the will of the people?

A better case for examining those questions came one year later following the mass shooting in Newtown, Connecticut. Twenty-year-old Adam Lanza, another killer with a history of mental illness, walked into the Sandy Hook Elementary School fully armed and took the lives of six adults and twenty children. Even with all of the gun violence we see in the U.S., the murder of so many innocent children in this tragedy brought an even greater level of attention to the gun issue.

It also created enough political will for Congress to at least introduce new legislation. After one Senate bill failed (it would have mandated criminal background checks on all gun sales between private parties), a more modest amendment was proposed with bipartisan co-sponsors, U.S. Senators Joe Manchin (D-WV) and Pat Toomey (R-PA). Manchin explained on Fox News that the measure would merely be a "criminal and mental background check strictly at gun shows and online sales" and that "if you're a law-abiding gun owner, you'll love this bill."[80]

Americans agreed to a great extent with Manchin and Toomey. Two weeks before the vote, a CBS/*New York Times* poll indicated that 90 percent of Americans supported expanded background checks.[81] Moreover, the same poll showed that *85 percent of households with a gun-owning member of the NRA* supported requiring background checks for private sales at gun shows.[82] One comparison of polls sarcastically indicated background checks were more popular than baseball, apple pie, and kittens.[83]

On April 17, 2013, the amendment failed in the Senate. Whether one is for or against the proposed law, the point here is to ask why. If American gun owners (85 percent) were in favor of the amendment, why would our government not respond accordingly? Some believe it is because the NRA and Gun Owners of America are more successful at getting their members to actually voice their opinions to lawmakers. But research released by the Pew Center a month after the vote did not track with that claim. Pew did find another factor, however, stating that "while nearly as many gun control supporters as gun rights supporters report contacting a public official about gun policy in the past six months, more gun rights advocates have contributed money to organizations that take positions on gun policy (12 percent versus 3 percent of gun control supporters)."[84] Ah, the money.

Between the years 2000 and 2014, gun rights groups spent more than $80 million on federal campaigns—with $46 million of it spent by those independent groups given free rein after the *Citizens United* decision. More than $18 million alone was spent during the election cycle preceding Newtown. Of the forty-six senators who voted against the amendment, forty-three of them had received money from gun rights groups since the year 2000 (gun rights groups outspent gun control groups 28–1 in 2000–2010). Despite such strong circumstantial evidence of influence, that does not necessarily constitute a direct causal link. In fact, four Democrats who voted against background checks were likely unswayed by money, as they had received some of the smallest amounts from the NRA.[85]

But influence comes not only from the NRA money that flows *into* lawmakers' coffers. It also comes from the truckloads of cash that loom over incumbents in the form of election-cycle attack ads. In fact, even the mere *threat* of such influence infects political thinking. Lee Drutman, who studies the impact of money on gun policy for the Sunlight Foundation, says lawmakers are plain afraid of the predatory political attacks: "They know what the NRA is capable of doing and the kinds of ads they're capable of running, and especially if you're someone facing a close election, you don't want hundreds of thousands and potentially millions of dollars in advertising to go against you."[86]

Still, if we theoretically assume that gun cash played only a partial role in the defeat, what other possible factor in the D.C. 4-3 could have flexed its muscle to turn back the will of the majority? The vote tally tells the tale. On that Wednesday afternoon, the background check amendment failed in the Senate by a vote of *fifty-four in favor* versus forty-six against. An hour later, another popular amendment to make gun trafficking illegal failed by a vote of *fifty-eight in favor* versus forty-two against. Under the principle of majority rule, both of these majority vote totals would have meant success for the proposed legislation. But as we know, in today's U.S. Senate, without a super-majority to bypass the filibuster, there's just no chance.

Four days after the vote, historian Doris Kearns Goodwin aptly described the connection between these two problems: "That structural Senate, given the sixty votes that are needed, given who they listen to, given the power of special interest—public sentiment cannot penetrate. And we've seen it now for the last decade. That's what the dysfunction is about."[87]

These filibuster rules not only stop progress or slow it down to a crawl, they also violate the principle of majority rule. For both of these reasons, bold action must be taken to restore a measure of order and stability to the U.S. Senate.

TIME TO RISE UP

On issue after issue, the major defects in our congressional system—the D.C. 4-3—impair the policymaking process and lead to an unacceptable product. Americans' general welfare suffers as a result.

Many believe that political shifts in our country are more to blame for the frozen U.S. House—rather than money or the rigged nature of our congressional elections. Others believe that sheer partisan division is more to blame for the Senate standstill than is the overuse of holds and filibusters.

Some say, "we just need to restore some collegiality and dignity back to the Senate. Then the rules won't get so abused."

Are they right? Are they wrong? The answer is "neither" because the causes we are choosing from are *not mutually exclusive*. In fact, they go hand in hand! Nolan McCarty's comprehensive research proves convincingly that the parties have moved farther apart from one another. But the four defects in our skewed congressional system inject steroids into our existing political partisanship.

We've seen how this works. The billions of dollars that wash through the Capitol only reinforce the divide. The cash flood discourages collegiality and cooperation. As Senator Manchin (D-WV) explained: "The money has infiltrated and has driven us apart."[88] And how.

Since the parties have moved so far from each other, the rigged nature of House races caused by winner-take-all elections in single-member districts—many of which are gerrymandered—only *reinforces* the ideological stretch toward the edges. Republican strategist Steve Schmidt sums up the discouraging effect it has on our representatives: "They're absolutely insulated from public opinion, and it's totally collapsed the center of American politics, where people of good faith can use some common sense and get some good stuff done."[89]

Then we have two-year congressional terms that increase the degree to which decision-making is viewed through a short-term political prism, instead of a longer lens better suited to focusing on the common good.

Finally, we know that increased polarization also saturates the U.S. Senate. But the retrograde rules in the Senate permit the partisanship to grind the gears down to a halt. In Lyndon Johnson's six years as Senate Majority Leader between 1953 and 1958, he saw one filibuster. Between 2003 and 2007, Senate Majority Leader Bill Frist (R-TN) faced more than one hundred from the D's. From 2007 to 2014, Senate Majority Leader Harry Reid (D-NV) faced more than four hundred from the R's.[90] The "world's greatest deliberative body" now sees countless cases of the minority overruling the majority, a wholesale reversal of our country's founding principles of representative government through majority rule.

So when some folks understandably bemoan the regional political splits we have seen since the 1960s, and their impact on Congress, they are making an accurate and relevant observation. But if that situation is not likely to change—unless it gets worse—then it is only logical to reform certain rules within the system that are sustaining, prolonging, or worsening the effects of pure partisanship.

The upgrading of long-standing rules is far from a radical idea. In fact, we know from Chapter 3, The Promises and The Powers, that upgrades are precisely what the founders envisioned when they included provisions for change in our Constitution. Recall the words of Thomas Jefferson in 1787:

> Happy for us, that when we find our constitutions defective and insufficient to secure the happiness of our people, we can assemble with all the coolness of philosophers, and set it to rights, while every other nation on earth must have recourse to arms to amend or restore their constitutions.[91]

Jefferson explained that when certain parts of our rule system are "defective," and are working against securing "the happiness of our people," we can rise up to reform the rules. In November 2014, Real Clear Politics reported that its average of polls indicated 66.8 percent of Americans believed that our country is on the wrong track.[92] Considering the defective product we reviewed in Chapter 4, is it any wonder Americans are unhappy? At the same time, Americans blame Congress far more than any other component of our government. And we can clearly see why.

It is easy to wonder in this day and age why even the most patriotic of Americans would choose to sacrifice their privacy, time with their family, maybe even their sanity to serve in the U.S. Congress. But they do. Good citizens still want to be a part of that historic body and create some positive change for their country. But as soon as the D.C. 4-3 positions members of Congress atop that unrelenting political wheel, they come to realize that the process is a white-hot mess.

It doesn't have to be this way. When that car you purchased has a dangerous defect and the manufacturer has violated the terms of its warranty, you bring your car in and they correct the defect. The U.S. Congress, while composed of many well-meaning and hard-working Americans, is failing in an historic fashion. The defect-laden process leads to a defective product. We have a civic relationship with our government, as opposed to a commercial relationship, so the onus is now on us to exercise our civic warranty. Recourse options and practical remedies do exist. The goal now is to get on the same page and start pushing back.

7 The Platform

If we can really understand the problem, the answer will come out of it, because the answer is not separate from the problem.

Jiddu Krishnamurti[1]

Democracy is not something that is going to simply work on its own. You gotta push it, you gotta kick it, you gotta prod it.

Leon Panetta, former defense secretary, CIA director,
federal budget director, U.S. representative[2]

Several decades before Tom Landry set up the rules in his 4-3 defensive system, the sport of football itself was in desperate need of serious changes. Early in the twentieth century, the college game was a lethal display of sheer brutality. Young men crushed each other's necks, broke each other's backs, and sustained deadly concussions. In 1904, the gridiron game was responsible for eighteen deaths and 159 serious injuries to college and prep school players. The following year, *The Washington Post* described the violence this way: "Nearly every death may be traced to 'unnecessary roughness.' Picked up unconscious from beneath a mass of other players, it was generally found that the victim had been kicked in the head or stomach, so as to cause internal injuries or concussion of the brain, which, sooner or later, ended life."[3]

The way the game was played back then, raw strength was required to advance the ball, and players would use their bare heads as battering rams to push the defense down the field and rack up yardage. In 1905, there was a public outcry to ban organized football altogether. Harvard University President Charles Eliot fought to get rid of the game, describing football as "more brutalizing than prizefighting, cockfighting, or bullfighting."[4]

As fate would have it, President Theodore Roosevelt, a Harvard man who loved football and whose son had been injured playing for his alma mater, summoned college coaches to the White House in late 1905 to confront the problem.[5] Soon after, a committee was created to modify the rules of the game. They decided to allow players to make forward passes, which opened up the field and reduced the violent scrums that had been causing so many injuries. The new rules also required that play during a game be halted once a player fell on the ball, in order to decrease the dangerous pile-ons.

The rule changes saved the game of football. And when the rules were modified again to require helmets, first for college players in 1939 and then for the pros in 1943, the leagues were rescued a second time. Football today remains a violent sport and is still controversial for the same reason it was back then. But it survives to the delight of millions of fans. Both the NFL and the college ranks have made many more rules changes over the decades, and logic would suggest that if football continues to survive, the powers that be will continue to make adjustments.

Beyond the quite limited scope of how this principle works in the world of sports, intuitively we know that we change certain rules to enhance our own personal and professional environments all the time. If the by-laws of a company, nonprofit, or educational institution are not effectively serving its end users, eventually something's got to give. When it makes sense to modify the rules, decision makers exercise this power, and then future outcomes are measured and evaluated against the intended goal. We make these kinds of rule changes in our lives all the time—because it is logical to do so.

There may be no greater need for the application of this logic than to our country's ailing system of elections and government. Now that we are aware of the four major structural defects in the D.C. 4-3 that are skewing the process and delivering a poor product, it is only logical to take aim at the causes. We've traveled a good distance in this narrative to define and understand the problem and what's driving it. We are well acquainted with the defects; let's start taking action to correct them. Out of the problems emerge the answers.

Tough political facts exist within the congressional landscape, facts that are less malleable than the D.C. 4-3—asymmetrical partisanship chief among them. We may not be able to correct every single problem causing congressional failure, but that should never be an excuse to ignore those rules that we can *reform* in order to breathe new life into the system.

Much has been written on these pages about the remarkable wisdom of our nation's founders and the fact that relatively few enhancements have been made to our original U.S. Constitution. Since the Bill of Rights was ratified in 1791, we have found it necessary to add only seventeen amendments in twenty-two decades. If we think about all of the changes and challenges our country has confronted since the eighteenth century, it is astonishing that our government framework has held together as well as it has. At the same time, we know that the prescient architects of our system envisioned a future of new frontiers and associated new problems that would most certainly require our government to change. That is why they embedded in the system a process for modifying the rules—to better serve the people. We must never be shy about forcing these changes when circumstances demand them, and now is such a time. In his book *Framed*, Sanford Levinson says that's precisely how it's supposed to work:

> We best honor the founding generation by forthrightly confront-
> ing the "lessons of experience" and accepting Madison's mandate
> to view the national Constitution and its state analogues as works
> in progress. We must therefore use our critical intelligence to
> "improve" them if they are to perpetuate themselves through time
> and, even more importantly, prove friends rather than enemies
> to achieving the great purposes most inspiringly set out in the
> Preamble to the national Constitution.[6]

In that spirit, this chapter will outline a platform of principles and proposed solutions designed to tackle the defects in the D.C. 4-3. Some of these solutions take place at the state level, some at the federal level. Some are already under way; some are not. Some relate to the rules inside the actual government, and some relate to our system of elections. What they all have in common is that they focus on the rules through the dual lenses of logic and fairness.

At each stage along this political odyssey, we have started with the general and then drilled down deeper into the details. Likewise, in this presentation of the platform, each plank will be introduced in headline fashion before we move into specifics of the proposed solutions. We will not obsess here over the degree of difficulty nor the time necessary to achieve these objectives. Those practical concerns will be addressed in the final chapter. Our goal will be to use logic in the service of identifying and understanding answers.

Finally, and perhaps most important, the platform outlined here is a beginning, not an end. This book and the mission to unlock Congress comprise an effort that is first and foremost about education. If the words on these pages serve to inform and educate fellow Americans about the state of the congressional product, some of the major problems driving it, and a sensible platform to upgrade the rules, then we will have successfully launched ourselves off the starting blocks. From that point, we will be in a common place to work together to make these reforms a reality and lift our government back up. So let's start breaking it all down: defect by defect, rule by rule, and solution by solution.

THE UNLOCK CONGRESS PLATFORM

1 EXTEND U.S. HOUSE TERMS TO FOUR YEARS

Increase U.S. Representatives' Capacity
to Function as Effective Public Servants.

Not long after being elected in the Tea Party wave of 2010, freshman U.S. Representative Scott DesJarlais (R-TN) told a journalist: "The two-year cycle is very difficult, and I've never been in politics before. I'm a family physician by trade, so it's an ongoing, I guess necessary part of the job. But I wish there was a better solution."[7]

Of course there is a better solution. It is time to elect all members of the House to four-year terms, on the same day that we elect our U.S. president.

In the last chapter we reviewed the ways in which the pressure of constant campaigning within two-year House terms—combined with a hyper-polarized political environment—can grind Congress's gears down to a halt. The short interval between elections leaves our representatives scant time to manage their wide range of tasks and responsibilities—both official and political. In particular, we have seen how Congress's failure to perform one of the most important of these functions—effective oversight—is dangerous to our country in many ways.

Still, the gridlock that holds back Congress from passing mutually agreed-upon legislation to advance the nation is the primary failure in this equation. Having a thin slice of time available to actually write and pass sound legislation means that short-term electoral consequences deter progress; yet even if opposing party members agreed on a public policy solution to a problem—even if they found compromises that benefited their constituents—two-year terms do not allow for fair assessments of actual legislative products generated in that short time frame. Brookings Institution scholar James L. Sundquist makes the case:

Sometimes a policy that may look like a failure after only two years may appear much more successful after four. Especially when a new government introduces drastic changes, for the electorate to be obliged to render a verdict after only two years may be unfairly, and unwisely, premature. Stability and continuity of a government's policies are sacrificed, along with the opportunity for a sound test of the wisdom of those policies.[8]

A study published in the *Review of Economic Studies* in 2011 reinforces this theory. Researchers Ernesto Dal Bó and Martín Rossi conducted "two natural experiments in the Argentine Congress (where term lengths were assigned randomly) to ascertain which forces are empirically dominant."[9] Legislators were assigned either a two- or four-year term and were interviewed about their experience while also being measured on their legislative production in the overlapping two-year time period. The four-year legislators passed more bills, offered more speeches, and attended more legislative sessions per year than their two-term colleagues. Dal Bó and Rossi concluded that four-year legislators were more productive due to what they term "investment payback logic," which, they explain, is: "when effort yields returns over multiple periods, longer terms yield a higher chance of capturing those returns. A broader implication is that job stability may promote effort despite making individuals less accountable."[10]

But would doubling U.S. representatives' term length really even make them "less accountable"? The irony is that in this day and age, with the current level of partisanship and perpetual clash between the legislative and executive branches, four-year terms could actually make our lawmakers *more* accountable. A sitting U.S. president's political party usually loses House seats during the midterm elections (approximately twenty-five seats on average since the 1940s), sliding the window further shut on cooperation. Sundquist points out: "Unless the president's term is shortened to two years—which no one has proposed—the midterm election cannot result in a clearly defined change in governmental direction anyway. All it can do is deadlock the government, or tighten an existing deadlock."[11]

So if we're trying to unlock the government, and specifically Congress, logic would suggest that extending the two-year term length would align the incentives of the two branches. At the very least it might make House members think twice about the consequences of instantly throwing up a wall against any and all ideas of the opposition party. Traditionalists may fret that such a change may make our government more resemble a parliamentary system (exactly the step many believe we need to take). But the separation of powers among our three government branches, as well as within our bicameral legislature, ensures the retention of plenty of veto points in the system for those concerned about accelerated pace. Domestic policy expert and *Wall Street Journal* columnist William Galston explains how four-year terms would promote more effective governance no matter which side of the aisle is winning elections:

> If the winning presidential candidate and House majority are of the same party, the president would have a better chance of enacting promised legislation, giving the people a chance to judge its consequences. If the electorate instead divides the partisan control of the Oval Office and the House, both the president and the leaders of the House majority would be on notice that neither could outlast the other, forcing them to choose between compromise and a full term of gridlock.[12]

This line of thinking also addresses the question of when to hold elections for four-year terms—whether to offset them from presidential elections by two years (staggering the terms as in the Senate, a third of which is elected every two years), or whether to have them coincide with presidential elections. True, electing half the House every two years would give voters the chance to register their approval or disapproval with more frequency; however, it would also dilute the potential to more closely align the executive and legislative branches. Staggered elections would still permit one party or one segment of the electorate to throw the House back into deadlock—a huge part of the very problem this platform plank seeks to confront. Doing so would create two separate classes in the House, which, as Lyndon Johnson explained, "would create an unnecessary and wholly unfair division in that body."[13]

Some want to combat U.S. representatives' constant campaigning by limiting the number of years in office that members may serve. At face value, the concept of term limits has merit and should not be ruled out as a future option. But the results thus far from individual states where term limits have been instated for elected officeholders present questions about its efficacy.

Michigan and California have passed and been governed by some of the most restrictive term limit reforms for their state legislators. In Michigan's case, a 2012 nonpartisan, comprehensive study by the Michigan Society of Association Executives (MSAE) painted a troubling portrait. The MSAE found that term limits contributed to "declining efficiency and effectiveness, a lack of interest in long-term policy, lack of legislative oversight, and inexperienced committee chairs."[14] The study also reported on the oft-cited concern of decreasing "institutional memory" term limits can cause. Because legislators' time is limited in office, power may shift substantially to staff members whose tenure may continue. More ominously, the study explained, "Legislators may depend more than ever on lobbyists as a source of information."[15]

In California, term limits, first passed in 1990, have had a rocky history as well. In a 2011 piece for *Vanity Fair* analyzing the California political system, journalist Michael Lewis made an observation already familiar to critics of term limits: "No elected official now serves in California government long enough to fully understand it."[16] In 2012, California voters elected to decrease the maximum years allowed in the legislature from fourteen to twelve, but increase the numbers in each chamber (from six to twelve years in the state assembly and eight to twelve in the state senate). Time will tell whether these changes make a difference.

These examples do not completely substantiate the idea that term limits would not benefit the U.S. Congress. However, while the jury is still out, it makes eminent sense to at least give U.S. House members the increased time and latitude to improve their performance before voters decide whether they should be sent back to Washington—or sent packing.

A legitimate question may also be asked about whether four-year terms would help to further protect incumbent officeholders who are already entrenched to the tune of a 90 percent re-election rate.[17] This is a possibility, as members' name recognition increases while in office—as does their ability to raise money and drown out the voices of potential challengers (once again making the case for campaign finance reform). But by the same token, as presented above, four years would also provide a better measurement of the actual job an incumbent member of Congress has done while in office. As a representative's accountability increases, so too does a voter's ability to more rationally judge whether that representative has made a good faith effort to accomplish legislative goals, to exercise congressional oversight in a responsible fashion, and to provide worthy constituent services in her district back home.

So if the U.S. House of Representatives is truly going to function as "The People's House," then our representatives should be permitted to work within a rational window to achieve meaningful results for the citizen consumers of their work product—we, the people. The rule should, as President Johnson expressed in his special message to Congress in 1966, "provide for each member a sufficient period in which he can bring his best judgment to bear on the great questions of national survival, economic growth, and social welfare."[18]

To extend office terms in the U.S. House of Representatives, the nation will need to amend the U.S. Constitution. Amendments require a two-thirds vote from each chamber in Congress, followed by ratification by the legislatures of three-fourths (thirty-eight) of the states.[19]

Fifty years ago, Congress and the country lacked the requisite passion to extend congressional terms as Presidents Johnson and Eisenhower had wished. But as our common history continually reminds us, when it comes to effecting change, even the most reasonable of ideas sometimes takes far too long to come to fruition. Perhaps now is the time. In April 2014, sixteen-year House veteran Representative John Larson (D-CT) introduced a resolution to extend congressional terms to four years. Larson told *The Hill*: "I think this would ease the pressure all the way around, and I think it would also probably create a better climate here of understanding and opportunity for people to better get to know one another ... I'll bet a number of Tea Party members would probably even agree with me as well."[20]

Maybe they would. For this is not about party. It is about country. And logic. Change the rule.

2 UNRIG CONGRESSIONAL RACES

Reform Election Rules to Increase Voter Choice,
Competition, and Fair Representation.

We know our congressional electoral process comprises a harmful defect in the D.C. 4-3. We know that state political parties gerrymander U.S. House districts to maximize their electoral advantage, painting a district Democratic blue or Republican red or taking an already biased canvas and dying it an even darker shade. It is likely that gerrymandering to some degree increases our country's existing partisanship. But what we know empirically from mathematical analysis is that the district-rigging distorts election results, and by extension, the will of the American electorate—not to mention voter trust.

We also know that primary elections serve to limit voters' choices even further—including U.S. Senate races. The activist bases on the left and right end up choosing single nominees on each side who will advance to the general election. Moderate or independent candidates running in these primary races—ones who might potentially appeal to a broader swath of the electorate—have almost no chance of beating their primary opponents who toe the party line. Additionally, "sore loser" laws in more than forty states disallow any candidate who has lost a primary race from entering the general election as an independent.[21]

And then we have the larger, system-wide obstacle of winner-take-all elections in single-member congressional districts, which create stark left-right choices with no in-between. Millions of American votes get wasted or go unrepresented, and members of Congress get pigeonholed into their respective party orthodoxies in D.C. the day they are sworn in. Compromise and negotiation get shoved aside. Stalemate and standstill win the day.

The time has come to unclench the political parties' nasty grip on the process and open up our election system so that our legislative branch may operate as it was intended to—as a representative democracy. To accomplish this plank in the platform, we will need to attack the defect from more than one angle. We'll need to multi-task by simultaneously pursuing three related reforms.

The first two solutions we will examine are geared toward improving the system that operates under the current winner-take-all structure within single-member districts: 1) *Eliminate political gerrymandering,* and 2) *Expand the primary election process.* Both of these reform efforts are underway in various states, and as we make more progress on each, more minds will open up to broader reform.

Learning about these first two reforms will prepare us for the third (and arguably most effective) way to correct this defect: *Replace single-member districts in the U.S. House with proportional representation through multi-seat congressional districts.* We will delve into how this electoral system works and the benefits it can deliver.

These three proposals to unrig congressional elections vary in their extent of potential effects as well as operational difficulty. The common thread they share is the application of logic in an effort to solve the problem. All are geared toward reforming election rules to increase voter choice, electoral competition, and fair representation. We must unrig, in order to unlock.

SLAY THE GERRYMANDER

Our representative democracy is predicated substantially on the principle of every American citizen's vote having an equal value. So how could it be legal to dilute the value of our votes through the practice of gerrymandering? How is it permissible for political parties to intentionally engineer election results so that a ton of our votes are just plain wasted? It is a twisted riddle that we know has concrete electoral consequences.

A number of cases before the Supreme Court have sought to slay the gerrymander by declaring it unconstitutional. For years the Court was more willing to hear gerrymandering cases that dealt with the violation of racial minority rights. In *Davis v. Bandemer* in 1986, the Court ruled that claims of political gerrymandering were justiciable under the Equal Protection Clause, but it upheld the Indiana legislative plan that the plaintiffs had argued was unconstitutional. The Justices could not agree on clear standards regarding whether voters' rights had been substantially diluted.[22] But Justice John Paul Stevens, who dissented in the case, firmly believes that standards can be established without too much difficulty. In fact, Stevens feels so strongly about the unfairness caused by gerrymandering that in 2014 he proposed the following Constitutional Amendment:

> Districts represented by members of Congress, or by members of any state legislative body, shall be compact and composed of contiguous territory. The state shall have the burden of justifying any departures from this requirement by reference to neutral criteria such as natural, political, or historic boundaries or demographic changes. The interest in enhancing or preserving the political power of the party in control of the state government is not such a neutral criterion.[23]

The sticking point of not being able to establish a clear standard of unconstitutional discrimination has persisted for years. But in 2006, in the case of *LULAC v. Perry*, a number of Supreme Court justices, including the frequent swing vote on the Court, Anthony Kennedy, were notably open-minded to the idea of "partisan symmetry" as a potential standard to determine unconstitutionality.[24] In other words, if opponents to political gerrymandering could prove convincingly to the Court that a map was biased to cause one party to systematically win more seats than the other party with the same share of the vote, they might have a case. The Court might strike down such district plans that systematically dilute voting power.

But Justice Kennedy was still concerned that when judging "partisan bias," some of the asymmetry might result from people switching their votes to the other party's candidate—and not being part of the measurement. He also opposed having to rule on redistricting plans where elections had not yet taken place and could not be proven to be unfair. Kennedy cited a third concern that the Court had not yet seen data enabling it to establish "a standard for deciding how much partisan dominance is too much."[25]

This is where the "efficiency gap" metric presented in Chapter 5 comes into play. Its creators, Nick Stephanopoulos and Eric McGhee, believe their approach can be used as a fair and clear standard to determine which gerrymandered plans cross the line into unconstitutionality. The efficiency gap not only measures the votes that are wasted, it also makes vote-switching irrelevant and conducts analyses based on actual election results. These features may well address Justice Kennedy's reservations.

Finally, McGhee and Stephanopoulos are able to designate a *clear standard* in the form of an efficiency gap threshold of *two* congressional seats, above which a gerrymandered plan is understood to be unconstitutional. There is a reason for this number: A threshold of two seats basically translates to the worst 10 percent of all gerrymandered districts—which is in line with the Supreme Court's decisions on the constitutionality of state legislative reapportionments between 1967 and 1975. In other words, the two-seat threshold uses the Court's very own standard from other voting rights cases.

After years of debate and disagreement about how to definitively determine which redistricting plans truly amount to political gerrymanders that violate voters' rights, Stephanopoulos and McGhee believe the efficiency gap provides the answer. They explain that their metric will serve a dual purpose, informing both "lower courts and political actors, in clear quantitative terms, exactly 'how much political ... effect is too much.'"[26]

That last statement provides us an ideal way to segue from the courts to "political actors." Of course, time will tell whether the Court declares any cases of gerrymandering unconstitutional. Such a welcome outcome would hopefully curb the behavior of those politicians who instinctively manipulate district lines to their party's advantage. But outside the courtroom, the onus is on us to exercise our citizen warranty and take the process of redistricting out of the hands of elected officials. We must push every state to form *independent bodies designing congressional districts.*

In more than forty states, legislatures primarily control how congressional districts are drawn (that includes the seven states that possess a single district). We are one of the few democratic countries in the world where politicians have this power. The slightly better news is in six states (all with multiple districts) panels draw district lines with at least some separation from elected officials. Finally, the bright side: four of these states (Arizona, California, Idaho, and Washington) have independent commissions that design both state legislative and U.S. congressional districts (although the legislature must ultimately approve the plan in some cases). Each of these six states also has "regulations limiting direct participation by elected officials."[27]

In Iowa a unique redistricting system has been credited with impressive results in recent years. A nonpartisan body called the Legislative Services Agency (LSA) is tasked with drawing the boundaries. The LSA focuses on making the districts equal in size, compact, and contiguous, while also trying to respect county lines. Justice Stevens would likely approve. Iowa's congressional races have been closer contests than most in other states. Governor Terry Branstad (R-IA) explains why he is proud of the process: "Having a more competitive district encourages somebody to really try to represent not just the ideology of his or her party but to represent the people of the district."[28]

Of course, what works in Iowa's geography may not work as well elsewhere. In fact, states with more racial diversity would likely find it difficult to draw districts that keep county lines intact because the Voting Rights Act mandates that districts meet an appropriate level of minority representation. That qualifier underscores the point that each state will need to craft its own redistricting process individually. States will need to properly train the citizens they appoint to ensure that they will consider competing interests as responsibly as possible. Independent bodies will not be able to take every ounce of partisanship out of redistricting, but enormous room for improvement is evident. Loyola Law School (Los Angeles) Professor Justin Levitt is an expert on this subject, and he carefully explains the potential upsides:

> Though the process will still be political, in the sense that citizen redistricters will need to weigh and balance various conflicting representational values, it is unlikely to be driven by particular politicians' narrow interests in retaining their seats or punishing their opponents. And if the selection process is designed to foster

balance and diversity, the resulting districts may well do a better job at representing the preferences of the whole than does the status quo.[29]

The many differences among our state constitutions can also create roadblocks to the pursuit of redistricting reforms. Former Congressman Mickey Edwards (R-OK), a staunch advocate for independent redistricting, sees good news and bad news: twenty-four states' constitutions allow initiative petitions for citizens to unilaterally put measures on the ballot; twenty-six do not. Edwards candidly explains the challenge:

> In some states it's going to be very hard to do. There's not a constitutional mechanism that makes it easy. But then there are many more states that have some kind of a referendum system so that the legislature can refer something to the voters, and that's where you can really hammer them. Say to them: "Okay, you don't really want to do this, but we're your constituents. Give us the voice. Submit it to the voters." And so in a lot of states you can do that.[30]

We should have no illusions about this part of the solution. Promoting and achieving a more independent process of drawing congressional districts is not a simple fix. Nevertheless, precisely because this reform isn't so easy we must be careful not to allow the perfect to be the enemy of the good. Even when drawn by independent bodies, district lines are tricky to configure, and any expectation of perfectly equitable district designs is utopian. But the goal of making districts *more fair* is not only achievable— it is in alignment with the principles of the U.S. Constitution. Political parties are not necessarily evil entities in and of themselves. But when the parties have the power of the pen over our electoral maps, individual rights get violated.

Therefore, liberate the process. Take it away from the politicians. Entrust it to Americans who actually cast the votes. We should choose our leaders. They should not choose us. Change the rule.

EXPAND THE PRIMARIES—INCREASE THE CHOICES

Working to reform the foul swindle of gerrymandering is a good start. To get rid of even more of the rig, we are going to need to change the rules for how we actually elect our leaders.

In this middle section we focus on the second reform—expanding and increasing choice—that will improve the system while we are still operating under single-member congressional districts. In the upcoming, final section, we will lay out an approach for wholesale change of the winner-take-all system. Each of these proposals is championed by FairVote, a nonpartisan reform organization. Each, in different ways, expands both access to elected office and the range of choices voters will have in primary and general elections. Each is geared toward making all of our votes count, and therefore, making our representatives more accountable.

Primary elections, which tremendously influence electioneering during both House and Senate races, ache to be reformed. Many of these contests are closed party primaries. But even in states where any voter can participate in a single Top Two primary, we still have a serious problem. Because only two candidates advance to the general election—almost always from opposite sides of the political aisle—we are stuck with that same, narrow choice between left and right. And as we observed from our predictably polarized electoral map, we already know who's going to win about 90 percent of these races. So do the candidates! No wonder we hear the same old stale arguments in campaigns. Candidates are not incentivized to consider new ideas and reach out to every district voter—they usually only need to clear that 50 percent hurdle. We need more competition. We need more robust debate. We need more open minds. In a word, we need more *choice*.

States such as California and Washington already have opened up their primaries. Any candidate from any party can place her name on the ballot, and any voter is permitted to vote for any candidate he wishes. The goal is laudable: to provide more open access and choice. And in districts with very high partisan leans, the hope is that the top two candidates who advance turn out to be from the same party, thus compelling each to compete for all of the district's voters in the general election. Ideally, this would incentivize candidates to moderate on some issues and open up to new approaches and solutions.

Unfortunately, because only two candidates advance to the general election, this reform hasn't really achieved much progress in motivating candidates to reach out to the broader electorate. The strength of each party's base voters—who turn out in higher numbers in the primaries— almost always guarantees that two candidates from the opposing major parties will square off in the general. The deeply stained shades of red and blue on the map take care of the rest of the race. The small number of "competitive" districts still results in few competitive elections.

We can see this in the state of Washington. In 2008, 2010, and 2012, Washington used this Top Two system, where voters could vote for anyone they wanted to in the open "preliminary" election. But of twenty-seven congressional elections in those three cycles, twenty-six of them ended up with a general election between a Republican and a Democrat. And in the twenty-seventh race, incumbent Democrat Jim McDermott won 80 percent of the preliminary vote, and then he won 83 percent of the general vote against independent Bob Jeffers-Schroder. In twenty-five of the races, a candidate emerged out of the preliminary election with a majority of the vote. So although these races are more open, which is a good thing, the party bases are still in control of the selections. In 2012, 38 percent of Washington's registered voters participated in the preliminary election, versus 81 percent in the general. Under Top Two, the caboose (the primary) is still driving the train (the general).[31]

So we need to take this to the next level. Changing two rules in the way we elect members of Congress will increase voter choice, participation, and fair representation. First, *advance four candidates* from the preliminary election. Second, use *Ranked Choice Voting* (RCV) to determine which candidate wins the general election and heads to Washington, D.C.

The first rule change is pretty straightforward. If Top Two gives us that same, binary choice between left and right and ends up excluding independent candidates or intra-party (two from the same party) competition in general elections, why not expand it? A far higher number of voters are going to consider candidates and then express their choice in the general election, so why not offer them more choices? Advancing four candidates to a general election is likely to offer a ballot that features two from one party, as well as two others, which frequently will include an independent (basically making "sore loser" laws irrelevant). Now voters will have a wider spectrum of choices. In addition, Top Four will promote more competition, which has the power to broaden the debate.

If we extrapolate what the voting returns from those three Washington election cycles would be under a Top Four system, we see a whole different picture in the general election. In those twenty-seven congressional races, Top Four would have advanced two candidates from the same party in twenty-five instances, versus zero under Top Two (see Figure 7.1). Top Four would advance an independent or a minor party candidate in ten races, as opposed to the one election we saw with McDermott versus Jeffers-Schroder. When we hop over to California and look at their Top Two elections in 2012, if we switch it to Top Four, the number of independent candidates in the general election would have jumped from four to twenty-two.[32]

Figure 7.1 Washington State: Contrasting Top Two and Top Four Systems, U.S. House Races, 2008–2012[33]

	Top Two	Top Four (projected)
Both major parties in general election	26/27	26/27
Intraparty race in general election	0/27	**25**/27
Independent or minor party candidate in general election	1/27	**10**/27

Having a selection of four candidates in general elections may bring up questions about vote-splitting, which occurs when two or more candidates from a party favored by the majority of the electorate take votes away from each other. This development may allow a candidate from a party favored by the minority of voters to win the election. It is the political equivalent of drawing an "inside straight" in a game of poker.

This is why it makes sense to use *Ranked Choice Voting* (RCV) in the general election. By allowing voters to rank their top three choices, and using a formula that takes into account all of the choices, the RCV method allows a more accurate compilation and ordering of everyone's votes. At the same time, potential vote-splitting effects are averted (a sample RCV ballot appears in Figure 7.2). FairVote explains how it works:

> Every ballot initially counts for the candidate marked first. Then, the candidate with the fewest first-choice preferences is eliminated, and any voter that ranked that candidate first will have their vote added to the totals of the next candidate ranked on their ballot. This process then repeats one more time, with the weakest candidate eliminated and their ballots transferred based on voters' preferences, to identify the two candidates with the greatest support. The candidate with the majority of votes in that final round is then elected. Because there will always be four or fewer candidates, voters will have a consistent ballot allowing three choices and a straightforward voter education message of "as easy as 1-2-3."[34]

Figure 7.2 Sample Ballot Illustrating Ranked Choice Voting (RCV)[35]

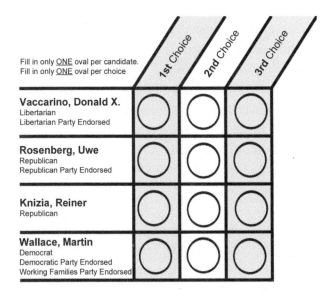

RCV achieves a few big goals in terms of making elections more competitive and more representative. The formula ensures that the winner is preferred by more voters because second and third choices carry value in the tabulation. Candidates will want to receive favorable rankings from their opponents' supporters, so they will be motivated to run broader campaigns that reach out to all voters in a district. Also, because voters can rank their preferences, they don't have to worry about "wasting" their votes on a longer shot candidate, or worry about any potential "spoiler effect" that could occur from voting their consciences. Those fears are valid in a plurality voting system, where voters are often forced to think strategically instead of asserting their true preferences. With RCV, voters can leave the booth knowing that the value of their choices will resonate in the determination of the winner.

Other democracies use RCV, namely the City of London, Australia, Ireland, and Scotland. A number of U.S. cities do so as well, including Oakland, Minneapolis, and San Francisco. The mayor of Portland, Maine, Mike Brennan (D), says that RCV drove him to run a far more inclusive race in 2011. Moreover, Mayor Brennan's local newspaper editorial board explained that RCV had a positive impact on the entire election campaign:

> A candidate with a hot-button neighborhood issue could have run away with the election without ever meeting a voter from another part of town. Under the ranked-choice system, candidates were forced to engage with each other and talk to each other's voters. The result was an interesting conversation about Portland and its future that would not have happened in a "turn-out-your-base" election. That debate helped clarify the job description for Portland's mayor, and it will make life easier for Brennan when he shows up for work.[36]

In 2013, Betsy Hodges (D) was elected mayor of Minneapolis under the RCV system. Hodges says that RCV not only incentivized her to reach out to more voters and listen to a wider array of opinions—it has also helped to guide her in office:

> On second choice votes, there's a whole sector of folks where I may not have been their first choice, but I knew what they were voting

for and where their values were. And I had a sense of why I might be their second choice. And that's been really useful information to have as I govern. That is the gift that Ranked Choice Voting gives to the people it elects that we would not have otherwise. And frankly, it's a gift to the voters ... It deepens people's experience of democracy. It gives us more choice. It gets us away from the negative and to the issues. And at the end of the day you have a better read on where people are at and what the community is thinking.[37]

Imagine that.

Within our current structure of winner-take-all, single-member congressional races, we need to advocate for these upgrades to the rules. We need to convert party primaries into *integrated preliminary elections that advance four candidates,* and then elect a winner through *Ranked Choice Voting.* Doing so will increase choice, competition, and therefore the breadth and substance of election campaigns. Through these changes, the political center has a greater chance to be represented.

Thus far in this section, we've reviewed ways to eliminate gerrymandering and to reform the traditional two-candidate, winner-take-all general election process. Having a firm understanding of how these reforms work provides a good base as we transition to the most ambitious solution in our effort to unrig the races.

PROPORTIONAL REPRESENTATION

The previous two solutions in this effort to unrig congressional races are necessary steps to improve the status quo. Our third and final proposal takes dead aim at the root cause of the defect: winner-take-all elections in single-member House districts.

We have seen how our polarized national map combined with winner-take-all has drastically reduced the number of competitive races, thereby thinning the number of moderates in the House, and increasing the political division between the two opposing teams. We have also seen how the rigging has landed control of the House with a majority party whose winning candidates received a *minority* of the total national vote. On top of that, the makeup of the House of Representatives does not accurately reflect the wide range of political views in the United States, which we form based on our life experiences, gender, ethnicity, and other factors that shape our philosophical backgrounds. It all adds up to an ugly electoral equation: distorted representation + heightened partisanship = deterrence to congressional productivity.

Each of these problems ultimately stems from the distortions created when we elect just one person to represent the diversity of views and opinions in each district—but there is a solution. *Multi-seat districts,* in which several people are elected to represent a constituency, allow for an accurate reflection of all voters when combined with a proportional voting system. Multi-seat districts have been used before to elect members of Congress, and they are still used in some state legislatures and local U.S. governments.

The systems of *proportional representation* (PR) that multi-seat districts would make possible are used in most developed democracies in the world and in a growing number of American cities. The electoral method of PR operates just the way it sounds. Groups of like-minded voters can come together to elect a number of preferred candidates that is proportionate to their share of the electorate. It is based firmly in logic and fairness. Right now, 49 percent of a single-member district's constituents can vote for a candidate and end up having no one represent their vote. Under PR, every vote counts, and everyone who votes receives a degree of representation.

Unlike certain European-style PR systems that depend on parties being elected, in the U.S. under the plan proposed by FairVote we would still vote for individual candidates. In fact, we already do this in ten of our state legislatures.[38] And for our nation's first fifty years, nearly 25 percent of our congressional seats were elected in multi-member districts. In 1967, Congress passed a law mandating single-member congressional districts, which was triggered by the 1964 Supreme Court ruling that cited the "one person, one vote" principle.[39]

But the ideal of every vote being equal under that law has turned out to be more farce than history under a single-member, winner-take-all structure. Under our current system, any voter who chooses a losing candidate is essentially unrepresented. At the same time, voters who select a candidate who wins by a landslide do not gain any extra influence. In each case, the participation of these voters in the election was essentially meaningless. By solving both of those problems, PR brings to the House a broader and more accurate reflection of the country's preferences. Proportional representation would also deliver practical political results. Let's break down how this system would work and specifically how it would change the complexion of Congress.

Using the RCV process (also known as the "single transferable vote" when used in multi-seat districts), voters would be free to rank as many or as few of the candidates running in their districts as they please. The FairVote plan calls for multi-member districts of between three and five seats, which would be created by combining current House districts (the total number of 435 representatives would remain constant). A candidate is elected if he or she receives one more vote than a total percentage that is calculated by taking 100 percent and dividing it by the number of seats available plus one. So if a district had three seats, then a candidate would have to clear a threshold of 25 percent of voter support in order to win a seat (100 percent divided by 3+1). Twenty-five percent is the bar because once it is eclipsed, it becomes mathematically impossible for three other candidates to each earn a larger share of the vote. Once a candidate has reached 25 percent of voter support, all of that candidate's "surplus ballots beyond the threshold are transferred to remaining candidates according to voters' next-choice preferences."[40]

The Ranked Choice Voting system would work in a similar fashion politically as it does in single-member contests, motivating candidates to reach out to as many voters as possible. Because the minimum thresholds in these three to five-seat "superdistricts" would be between 25 percent and 16.7 percent, any blocs of voters larger than these respective thresholds would be able to elect a preferred candidate. Substantial political minorities would have the chance to be represented, or, at the very least, to have their votes more directly influence the overall election. Independents and third-party candidates would have better chances of winning seats due to the lower victory threshold. This is in stark contrast to single-member districts, where minority voting blocs are effectively voiceless in the overwhelming number of geographical regions with a partisan lean that is prohibitively red or blue.

Again, we have seen PR work before in state legislative elections. After the Civil War, Illinois was gripped by severe polarization with high concentrations of Democrats in the South and Republicans in the North. In 1870, through a Constitutional Convention, the state house structure was changed to three-member districts, elected proportionally—a system that lasted for more than a century before the size of the House was reduced. A 2001 Commission chaired by former Illinois Governor Jim Edgar (R) and former U.S. Representative Abner Mikva (D-IL) extolled the virtues of the multi-member system that had existed in the House. The Commission reported that under three-member districts, party representation was more proportional, candidate independence increased, and efforts toward achieving statewide consensus improved.[41]

Let's take a look at how the FairVote multi-member district plan, if implemented nationally, would diversify the political landscape in Congress. Using a breakdown of our own self-described political ideologies in America, we can see the political spectrum of Congress in 2013–2014; note the tiny slice of centrists in contrast to the hard partisan leans to the left and the right (see Figure 7.3). But when we use proportional representation across that same divided electorate, we see a breakdown where the percentage of centrist seats is nearly quintupled: from 3 percent to 14 percent. There's the missing political center, a force we know we need in Congress to build bridges between the two parties. The chart also portrays a more accurate representation of American voters, 19 percent of whom classify themselves as centrists.

We also see that under PR, liberal or moderately liberal candidates make gains versus conservatives or moderate conservatives, but overall the candidates who are right of center still hold control of a slight majority of seats.

Figure 7.3 Political Spectrums of the U.S. Electorate, the 113th U.S. Congress, and Congress under Fair Voting[42]

Spectrum of the U. S. Electorate

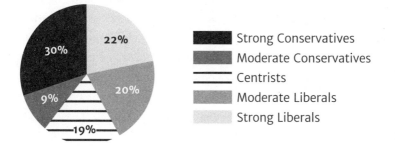

Spectrum of the 113th Congress

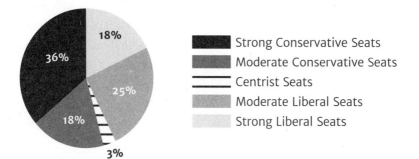

Spectrum of Congress Under Fair Voting

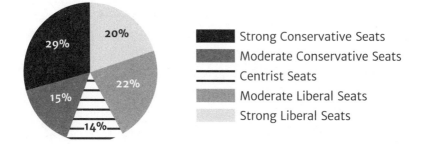

Now let's consider how PR would change the national map. In the first map at right (see Figure 7.4), we see the recent, stark geographic division where districts lean more than 53 percent for either party. As districts outside of this threshold are rarely competitive, the map illustrates the degree to which representation across the vast majority of the country is frozen to a single, predetermined partisan outcome. We also know from statistics in Chapter 5 that these partisan leans currently favor Republicans due to the geographical concentrations of Democratic votes in our congressional district structure. So in an election where the national vote is an even 50/50 for each party (not taking incumbency into account), the R's would be favored to win 213 seats to the D's 175 (with the remainder of the seats being swing seats).

In the second map, we can see how the divisive, predictable red–blue split across single-member districts is replaced by a "shared representation" shade suffusing most of the nation. Every multi-member district within that wide swath would have at least one Democrat and one Republican serving the district. (The smaller shaded areas reflect smaller districts containing just one or two seats that are likely to be won by one party.) Shared representation would allow millions of Republicans in Massachusetts, Democrats in Oklahoma, and other unrepresented groups around the country to finally have a voice in Congress. Instead of votes being wasted, they are represented. Because a lower threshold of votes is required to get elected, a more diverse delegation of officeholders will represent their districts in Congress. Because proportional representation more accurately reflects the voters in each district, the likely seat share between Republicans and Democrats in an even election under this system moves much closer to a fair representation of Americans' overall voting preferences—with the R's still holding the advantage, 203–200.

Under PR, women and minority candidates increase their chances of gaining seats.[43] And beyond the new voting coalitions that would enjoy representation, campaigns for Congress would also be conducted with more robust public policy discussion. A wider outreach to a wider electorate would necessitate a wider—and less divisive—discussion of the issues. These are the kinds of political processes that lead to more open minds, more honest communication, and more compromise. These are sensibilities that we know are desperately missing in the U.S. House.

Figure 7.4 Success: Shared Representation and Partisan Fairness Nationwide[44]

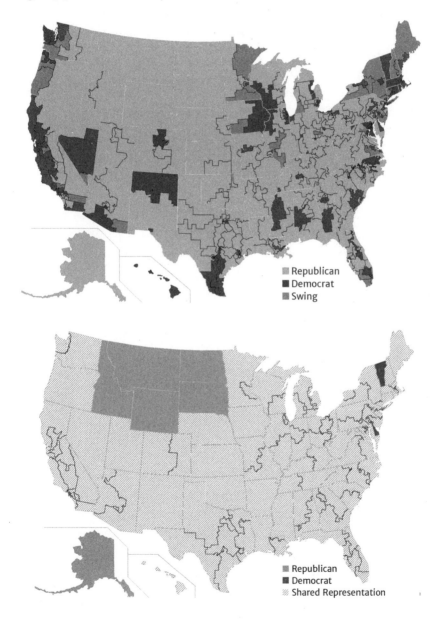

Some may worry that under a PR system the House might become too fractured, as is sometimes the case in countries that have "national list systems" where voters vote for parties, or other systems with very low electoral thresholds. But political scientists find this very unlikely in a PR system with RCV in districts of no more than five seats. More likely, the two major political parties would need to run more diverse arrays of candidates who appeal to more voters. Atypical groups that often go un-represented—for example, libertarian or urban Republicans, or rural or fiscally conservative Democrats—would have the chance to be represent-ed. In a system like ours, whose polarization and stalemate have reached record levels, the moderation and new perspectives that PR would bring are exactly what Congress needs. FairVote's executive director, Rob Richie, articulates why the mix is so important:

> That's what we actually used to get twenty-five years ago, when you had these members winning in other parties' districts. So when you were a Republican winning a Democratic district or vice versa, you were attuned to potential opportunities to work with the other party, because you actually needed to win in a district where that party was a majority. And the fact that we have almost no members like that today is a big reason why we see such lit-tle cooperation. But if you had these multi-seat district systems, you'd have a lot more members who had won based on the votes of people who want them to be solution-oriented members—while still having the left and the right.[45]

More than any other body in our federal government, the U.S. House of Representatives was designed to accurately reflect the will of the American people. But it doesn't. Rules requiring winner-take-all in single-member congressional districts, combined with our self-sorted political divide, have given disproportional seat share and power to the Republicans in recent years. Some may worry that this reality will demotivate some citi-zens on the right from wanting to adopt reforms. This is a logical concern. Still, the argument to unrig our House elections and achieve fairness for

American voters is not a partisan pursuit. It is about protecting the system, ultimately for everyone. Conservative author Reihan Salam reinforced this point in a column he wrote in *Slate* magazine promoting multi-member districts:

> It should appeal to Republicans, too. Yes, it would deny the GOP
> an edge over Democrats in the short term. But at the same time,
> it would help stranded conservatives like myself, and it would
> guarantee that some political reversal of fortune wouldn't one day
> result in Republican underrepresentation.[46]

Moving to proportional representation makes good sense, both in terms of the fairness it will produce and the pragmatism it can increase. So many other advanced democracies use proportional systems for good reason. When more citizens are actually represented in their legislature, elected leaders can be held more accountable for their performances. If we truly want "one person = one vote," then we need to instate the correct method of elections for achieving it.

Proportional representation is constitutional, and logical. The only thing preventing it in the U.S. is a 1967 apportionment law that can be repealed. The FairVote organization, at the vanguard of this reform effort, is working to present legislation that would allow multi-seat districts in the states and to eventually mandate a process of proportional representation. More details on how the FairVote plan works can be found in its online report: *Monopoly Politics 2014 and the Fair Voting Solution.*[47]

Clearly, the ways in which our rigged election system sends candidates to Congress serve neither the country nor our founding principles. We can draw the districts more fairly. We can convert party primaries into more expansive preliminary elections that provide voters a real set of choices in general elections. And we can ensure through proportional representation that every one of our votes matters. We have reviewed reform proposals here to ensure a more fair and productive method for electing members of Congress who can work on behalf of the country as a whole. Let's change some rules.

3 ABOLISH THE FILIBUSTER

Restore Majority Rule to the U.S. Senate.

In 1806, a Scottish writer started working on the poem *Marmion,* which came to include these famous words: "Oh, what a tangled web we weave, when first we practice to deceive."[48]

Coincidentally, these words were written the very same year that Aaron Burr successfully pushed the U.S. Senate to eliminate the "previous question motion"—which eventually led to the Senate filibuster rule. Two centuries later, both the history and the meaning of the poem have parallels to the current dilemma presented by the filibuster—and to our path to abolishing it.

First, to this day many people think William Shakespeare authored *Marmion.* Actually Sir Walter Scott penned the famous poem, recounting a fifteenth century battle between England and his home country of Scotland. The Senate filibuster has experienced a similar brand of mistaken identity, as many Americans believe our country's founders designed it and codified it in the U.S. Constitution. But this is wrong as well. As we learned in Chapter 5, the filibuster is nothing more than a historical accident. A rule the Senate created to clean up another rule, it has brought unintended consequences and tightly gummed up a major gear in our legislative engine.

Second, its meaning. This, too, shares a life with the famous words from Scott's poem. Over the years, the U.S. Senate has woven a wacky web of rules so tangled and convoluted that even incumbent senators *cannot agree on whether their own rules allow them to change the rules.* The result? A state of affairs so confused and controversial that in 2014 a Supreme Court case was filed to declare the filibuster unconstitutional.

"It's almost impossible to predict. But if it matters that we're right, then we'll win."[49]

Constitutional lawyer Emmet Bondurant spoke those words regarding *Common Cause v. Biden,* the lawsuit he first filed as lead counsel in 2012 and then appealed to the U.S. Supreme Court in 2014.[50] The suit sought a judgment from the Court that would declare the filibuster unconstitutional (due to its requirement of sixty votes—a violation of majority rule). But because of that tangled web in the Senate, the Common Cause lawsuit actually had to make the case that *two Senate rules,* working in concert, were unconstitutional. We're going to dip our toe into legal waters just a tad so that we may arrive at a shared understanding of just how meticulously ridiculous the Senate rules system has become. Beyond the damage we have seen it do to the congressional process, the filibuster also violates bedrock principles of American democracy. The better we understand this defect, the better equipped we will be to *apply pressure to our leaders to abolish it.*

Our nation's founders, both in the *Federalist Papers* and in our U.S. Constitution, outlined the principle of majority rule as the activator in each chamber of Congress to conduct business and pass legislation. This seems simple enough, and it should be. But Article I, Section 5 of the Constitution also allows each chamber to write its own rules, every two years at the beginning of each congressional session. Here we find the constitutional loophole that the U.S. Senate has driven a truck through, inventing two blocking rules—Rule V and Rule XXII—that have sustained the filibuster and also added great confusion to efforts aimed at a solution.

When the Senate created Rule V in 1959, it dictated that all Senate rules of one session must continue into the next session. It further established, through Rule XXII, that the only way it could amend these rules was by clearing a cloture hurdle of two-thirds of a Senate quorum (this would equal sixty-seven out of one hundred senators on the floor). After Rule XXII was changed in 1975, the Senate required three-fifths support from Senators (sixty out of one hundred) to achieve cloture and get a vote on proposed legislation and nominations. This became the filibuster rule of the modern era. As the Common Cause lawsuit explained: "The combination of Rule V and Rule XXII has made it virtually impossible for the majority in the Senate to amend the rules of the Senate to prevent the minority in the Senate from obstructing the business of the Senate by filibustering."[51] That's right—*the Senate's own filibuster rule, followed to the letter, stops the Senate from getting rid of its own filibuster rule!*

The legal argument Common Cause presented in its suit against the Senate first asserted that the Senate's rulemaking power is *not unlimited* and cannot conflict with other provisions in the Constitution. In Count

One, Bondurant and his team argued that Rule XXII, the filibuster, is unconstitutional for the following reasons:

> The rule conflicts with the fundamental principle of majority rule
> embedded in the Constitution and on which the Constitution was
> founded ... the rule also upsets the carefully crafted checks and
> balances between the three branches of government by giving a
> dissident *minority in only one house of one branch* (the legislative
> branch) the power to create gridlock ... The rule gives the minority
> in the Senate the power to nullify the votes cast by members of the
> House of Representatives in favor of bills that passed the House
> that have the support of a majority of senators, and would have
> been passed in the Senate and become law but for filibusters; and
> the rule, in combination with Rule V, deprives the majority in the
> Senate of the power granted by Art. I, § 5, cl. 2 to amend the rule of
> the Senate by majority vote.[52]

The lawsuit based its contention that the sixty-vote rule is unconstitutional on two clauses in Article I of the Constitution. First, Common Cause argued that the Quorum Clause in Section 5 "provides that only the presence of a simple majority of senators is necessary to 'do Business' in the Senate. Rule XXII conflicts with the Quorum Clause because under Rule XXII, the Senate cannot 'do Business' as a practical matter without the *presence* of at least sixty senators to vote in favor of a motion for cloture."[53]

The second constitutional clause that the suit argued has been violated is the Presentment Clause in Section 7, which "provides that only the vote of a simple majority of a quorum is required to 'pass' a bill or a resolution prior to its being sent to the House of Representatives or presented to the President." Further confirming the meaning of this clause, Common Cause cited the Supreme Court case *United States v. Ballin,* which affirmed that: "[W]hen a quorum is present, the act of a majority of the quorum is the act of the body."[54]

The suit also claimed that the filibuster "has significantly increased the under-representation in the Senate of people living in the more populous states well beyond that dictated by the Great Compromise." We remember from Chapter 5 the imbalance Sanford Levinson explained, where roughly a quarter of our senators are elected by "less than 5 percent of the population."[55] The plaintiffs defined what this can mean when the filibuster is brandished by the smaller states: "Rule XXII gives senators elected from 21 states that may contain as little as 11 percent of the U.S. population an absolute veto power over bills, resolutions and presidential appointments supported by senators who represent [89] percent of the people of the United States."[56]

Finally, the plaintiffs addressed how the two rules work in concert with one another to prevent their own repeal:

> Rule V, in combination with Rule XXII, also violates the fundamental constitutional principle that prohibits one Congress (or one house of Congress) from binding its successors. The effect of the two rules is to make rules that were adopted by long-dead senators binding on successive generations of senators without their consent, and prevent the Senate from exercising the power granted by Art. I, § 5, c. 2 to amend its rules by a majority vote.[57]

To break all of that down to bare bones, the lawsuit argued that the Senate has exceeded its rule-making authority. It also has violated the principle of majority rule in order to retain the arcane web of rules that allows for the survival of the defective filibuster—and all of the congressional deterrence that comes with it. The remedy? The plaintiffs beseeched the Court to declare the relevant sections of Rule V and Rule XXII unconstitutional. Bondurant explained what would follow if the justices provided these declaratory judgments: "At that point, the general rule of all parliamentary bodies, recognized by the Supreme Court in *United States v. Ballin*, would be that when the rules don't specify otherwise, it's by majority vote."[58]

On September 3, 2014, Common Cause filed the case with the Supreme Court. When the lawyers opposing the suit argued against it, they did not in any way defend the constitutionality of the filibuster. Instead, counsel claimed that the plaintiffs did not have proper legal standing to be heard, and that the question was political in nature and therefore not a suitable one for the judiciary.[59] On November 3, 2014, the day before the midterm elections, the Supreme Court announced it would not hear the case. It made no further comment. And so now it is up to us.

THE "NUCLEAR OPTION"

The irony in all of this is that in November 2013, the Democratic majority in the Senate actually did reform part of the filibuster by lowering the number of votes to fifty-one to approve presidential nominations—but they had to break their own Senate rules to do so! This is known in the Senate as exercising the "nuclear option." To vote to reduce the threshold to fifty-one votes, *they had to break the Senate filibuster rule that would have required sixty votes.* That's why it is labeled "nuclear" and generally used only as a threat. The Senate has become akin to a kindergarten sandbox where kids can declare a new rule by Crayola-decree. So where does the real authority lie? Strangely, this is tricky, because the U.S. Senate has traditionally operated according to its own precedents and a sense of collegiality. But in a constitutional system, it would certainly be far more logical, and truer to the spirit of the founders, to have the operation of the Senate governed according to the principles in our original Constitution, as well as the Court's interpretation of those principles.

In the time that has passed since the Senate did change the rules on nominations, we do know that it has made a difference. After the rule change in the 113th Congress, the Senate confirmed roughly double the number of circuit judges in approximately the same time period.[60] But we cannot allow the progress on nominations to be used as an excuse to take our foot off the pedal on eliminating the filibuster when it comes to blocking legislation. The most important function our legislature performs is to pass laws or repeal laws in the interest of the American people. Emmet Bondurant explains that as long as our senators have to work under the daily threat of the filibuster, our democracy is not operating correctly:

> The Senate basically is exercising a veto power over the entire legislative process. It frustrates all the work of the House of Representatives in passing bills by majority vote and then sending them over there and then have a minority of Senators veto it. So it stops

Congress. It stops the administration's legislative package. And it entrenches bad legislation against repeal.[61]

That stoppage causes much of the damage we examined in the previous two chapters. It is the reason the filibuster must be purged, and the sooner the better. The most clear and straightforward way to do so would have been for the Court to declare the filibuster unconstitutional. But even without that legal sanction, we may not be too far away from a wholesale elimination of the rule. Stephen Spaulding, who serves as policy counsel for Common Cause, explains why:

> I was shocked that the Senate did what they did. I thought this was just going to play out as another threat. Now that that precedent has been set, I think within the decade, if not earlier, we're very likely to see the sixty-vote rule thrown out altogether, including for legislation. I think the likely route is through exactly the way they did it with the nuclear option.[62]

But Spaulding quickly adds that we the people have got to push it. So despite the Supreme Court's refusal to consider the case, the suit's argument is of great value in our effort to abolish the filibuster. A majority of Americans (61 percent) have said they want to see the Senate reform its rules to unfreeze the system, and a plurality of voters (44 percent) have said the filibuster should be jettisoned altogether.[63] We need to keep spreading the word about why this defect must be corrected. We need to increase those numbers and keep applying pressure to the U.S. Senate. The filibuster was an accident. It is counterproductive to promoting our general welfare, and counter to the principles in our U.S. Constitution. Change the rule.

4   REBALANCE CAMPAIGN FINANCE RULES

Decrease the Money Flood's Disproportionate Influence on Congress.

Finally, we confront the challenge of reforming the granddaddy of the D.C. 4-3. It is a gigantic defect that leaders have been trying to correct for decades. But they need our help. Good people in office are trying to turn back the money tide, but they simply cannot do it without us. We're going to start this last section with a brief refresher on the current landscape, because the rules surrounding the money are not getting better. In fact, they are getting worse. We need to understand the imbalance if we are to rebalance.

In 2010 the court cases *Citizens United v. FEC* and *SpeechNOW.org v. FEC* gave Super PACs license to spend hundreds of millions of dollars on electing and reelecting members of Congress. These decisions have effectively allowed individuals and formal organizations to invest huge sums of money into independent political communications. But it didn't stop there.

In April 2014, in *McCutcheon v. FEC*, the Supreme Court struck down the overall limits on how much any one person could contribute to multiple campaigns and political committees over a two-year period. Justice Steven Breyer wrote in his dissent, "If *Citizens United* opened a door, today's decision, we fear, will open a floodgate." Breyer also explained that the ruling "overturns key precedent, creates serious loopholes in the law, and undermines, perhaps devastates, what remains of campaign finance reform."[64]

Hours after the decision, Senator John McCain (R-AZ) echoed Breyer: "I am concerned that today's ruling may represent the latest step in an effort by a majority of the Court to dismantle entirely the longstanding structure of campaign finance law erected to limit the undue influence of special interests on American politics."[65]

One of the only meaningful limitations that remains within current campaign finance rules is that individuals cannot give more than $2,600 to a single congressional candidate per two-year cycle (the Federal Election Commission indexes these limits for inflation in odd-numbered years). But the rules that permit all of the other dollars to slosh around the system still give massively disproportionate power to the thin sliver of folks who can afford it. Before the McCutcheon decision, a person's total contributions to candidates were limited to $48,600 per cycle, and the limit for giving to political parties was $74,600. Those aggregate limits are now history. Justice Breyer explained how the loopholes now allow one wealthy contributor to inject a total of *$3.6 million directly into the treasuries of candidates and political parties* in a single election cycle to advance his political interests.[66]

And at the end of the 113th Congress in 2014, Congress sneaked a provision into a bill at the eleventh hour that increased the amount an individual can give to party committees during an election cycle—from $259,200 to more than $1.5 million.[67]

These individual contributors are the people Martin Gilens was talking about when he concluded from his research that "actual policy outcomes strongly reflect the preferences of the most affluent but bear virtually no relationship to the preferences of poor or middle income Americans." *The percentage of people in America who give $10,000 or more in an election cycle is less than 0.01 percent.*[68]

Justice Breyer emphasized that principle in his dissenting view in the *McCutcheon* case, pushing back against the argument that the First Amendment should allow unlimited political speech for this tiny affluent minority—even if it drowns out all those who don't have the big money to be heard. Breyer asserted, "The First Amendment advances not only the individual's right to engage in political speech, but also the public's interest in preserving a democratic order in which collective speech *matters.*"[69]

It's what the money flood defect is all about—disproportionate influence. Undemocratic representation. A skewing and distorting of the system in favor of the very few who can afford to pay the toll. We know this, and now we need to change this.

When we consider the big cash sums above and recall all of those hefty totals we reviewed in Chapter 5, as well as all of the shady loopholes through which wealthy interests funnel money into the system, it might seem as though solving this problem will require an equally intricate set of solutions. But it won't. There is a straightforward way to start evening the odds. The challenge, as is the case with each plank in the Unlock Congress platform, will be in mustering up the public will to get it done. We need to empower the voices and votes of the great masses of American citizens. We need to recover the founders' vision of electing representatives who are dependent upon the people—versus indebted to those few purchasers with deep enough pockets to protect their vested interests.

The first of two solutions is a reform effort that is already in its early stages: *publicly financed congressional elections—either through matched contributions or tax-rebate vouchers.* Both of these public financing options strengthen the power of the people by using small dollar contributions. We will outline a system here that deleverages the influence of the wealthy at the top and shifts leverage to ordinary Americans who have been shut out of the game. In the process, candidates for Congress all across the political spectrum will be incentivized to appeal to as many voters as possible and spend less time dialing up the cash kings. Again, even though the rule change itself is not all that complicated, achieving the reform will require a new kind of Congress, and that is where we all come in.

The second solution focuses on *constitutionally protecting new laws and rules* that we push Congress to put in place. It should be acknowledged that it does not make sense, nor is it possible, to eliminate fundraising altogether from the system. As we have seen, the Supreme Court has repeatedly upheld the practice, citing First Amendment rights to freedom of speech. The Court's interpretations of laws that govern campaign finance comprise an important piece of what will be our effort to reverse the flow of the money flood. We will soon go over what is necessary at the Supreme Court and U.S. Constitution levels to validate and secure reforms that would even the playing field. But first we need to start evening that playing field.

A PUBLIC MATCH MADE IN HEAVEN

Earlier, we read the words of the Apostle Paul, who described money as "a root to all kinds of evil." Of course, even if money is the "root," we really know that it is human intent in the acquisition or use of money that truly determines actual "evil." Using money to pay your child's admission fee to an amusement park is not evil. Contributing to a politician with the intent to persuade an oversight agency to go easy on safety inspections for a faulty ride at your amusement park—that is evil. The problem of the money flood is that the well-resourced park owner can afford to purchase influence, while most of the parents who are customers at the park cannot. It's a hell of a problem.

If we know we will never entirely eliminate money from the system, it does not make sense to try to yank this defect out straight from the root. Instead, we want to grow the garden. We want more Americans to be able to afford to financially express support for candidates. We want to reduce the leverage of the cash kings by bringing in more cash from the rest of the country. Ideally, we would want *everyone* to participate in this process. But at the very least, we need to empower them with the ability to do so.

Professional sports leagues use this principle in determining the draft selection process for players each year. The teams with the weaker win-loss records, ostensibly with inferior resources in terms of talent, are among the first teams permitted to make choices for new players. Of course, every team owner would like to have the top pick, even if his team is already league champion. But the collective members of a larger entity—the league itself—know that without a system that ensures a measure of fairness, the league would not be very competitive. Leveling the playing field for the entire league helps increase the chances that the league will flourish in the future, and by extension, each team organization will too.

The best way to even the unbalanced odds in congressional elections is by publicly financing campaigns in a way that empowers and incentivizes all Americans to engage in the process. Even the term "publicly finance" gives some people pause when it comes to politics. But as we shall see when we look at the potential costs and benefits of this type of reform, it's a steal. The good kind.

The first of two pragmatic proposals to rebalance the way congressional races are financed is through the *public matching of small dollar campaign contributions.* A form of this already exists in some states, and U.S. Representative John Sarbanes (D-MD) introduced federal legislation in 2014 to apply it nationally. The general concept is that Americans who decide to contribute a relatively small donation (generally in the range of $25 to $200) will have their money matched with public funds at an exponentially higher level. Sarbanes's "Government by the People Act" calls for a match of 6-1 for donations under $150, and a 9-1 match if a candidate agrees to exclusively accept small dollar contributions. Also, as a preemptive provision to help defend against the deluge of Super PAC funds that cascade into the final days of campaigns, the proposed law would provide additional resources for candidates who raise more than $50,000 from small donors in the sixty days prior to an election. Advocating for his bill, Sarbanes explained:

To be eligible for these matching funds, a candidate would have to agree to a limit on large donations and demonstrate broad-based support from a network of small-dollar contributors ... The funding for these changes should come from closing tax and regulatory loopholes that are the decades-old legacy of special-interest influence in Congress. It's only fair that those responsible for breaking the policymaking machinery in Washington should bear the cost of fixing it.[70]

Sarbanes spells out the goal. And it is not dissimilar from the reform principles discussed earlier in creating multi-member districts: to compel candidates to reach out to more of the electorate and to empower more Americans to participate meaningfully in our representative democracy. We cannot fully quarantine the cash kings who pay for results in Congress, but we can cut down their leverage. So that is one big way—by increasing the power the rest of us have to affect elections and policy. And a key by-product of such a matching system is that more voters become personally engaged in the process. When citizens are incentivized to make an investment in a candidate, they are then more likely to stay involved and increase their participation. We know from Chapter 2, The Public Opinion, that many of us are in dire need of such motivating factors.

The second option for publicly financing congressional elections is a *tax-rebate voucher system* where every American over the age of 18 would receive a small amount from the government for the express and sole purpose of contributing it toward a political campaign. A system of this kind has been favored both by Harvard Law Professor Lawrence Lessig and by Richard Painter, former chief White House ethics officer under President George W. Bush.

In *Republic Lost,* Lessig describes a system where everyone receives a $50 voucher to give to the candidate of his or her choice. Voters who make no selection would see the $50 allocated by default to their registered political parties or toward running elections. On top of this, an individual could give an additional $100 of her own money, but candidates could receive it only if they agreed to receive *only* these kinds of donations—cash from PACs and political parties would not be allowed.[71]

Lessig estimates the annual cost of this kind of voucher program to be $3 billion. To some Americans, especially those who favor smaller government and reduced federal spending, this figure might elevate an eyebrow, or worse. But here is where the egregious shortcomings of the congressional product we examined in Chapter 4 come back into play in a big way. If up to 93 percent of Americans disapprove of Congress, certainly part of our discontent must be about the ways it spends our money in the federal budget (trillions of our tax dollars). We know it is. We lamented the ridiculously high sums we pay for prescription drugs versus other developed countries. We reviewed the trillions of dollars Congress has approved to prosecute foreign wars over the last decade, wars which a substantial percentage of Americans have found to be questionable judgments with questionable returns. We have seen how Americans have suffered in an economy where legal loopholes and lax oversight led to massive profits for corporate interests and played a role in the onset of a severe recession. We have seen so much more.

In advancing this type of system, which he calls "Taxation Only with Representation," Richard Painter argues that not only are we entitled to a tax-rebate voucher to fund candidates, it is also a prudent investment:

> This is not about the government paying for anything with "its" money. This is about the government allowing us to use a portion of *our money* that would otherwise go to taxes for the purpose of choosing the public officials who spend the rest ... The cost of financing political campaigns with taxpayer money would be substantial but is small in comparison to the economic loss caused by ineffective regulation and wasteful government spending that often occurs when campaign contributors get the quid pro quos they want. On the merits, taxpayer financing of political campaigns would probably save money in the long run.[72]

A citizens' movement is working to pass fundamental reforms like these through Congress, an enterprise we will meet in the conclusion of this section. In both of these publicly financed systems, participation is increased. Our representatives' dependency on the tiny private club of wealthy donors is reduced. Candidates have the opportunity, indeed the motivation, to expand their reach and be competitive in campaigns; meanwhile, they will feel less pressure to accede to the wishes of moneyed interests. These solutions do not get rid of money. Instead, they bring more money from more participants, and in the process, they help to *rebalance* the power structure between the wealthy few and the majority of American citizens.

To be clear, although these reforms can substantially improve the status quo through a rebalancing, alone they cannot completely solve the money flood problem. Lobbyists and big money interests still will have legal avenues to inject large sums into the system. While the two reforms above do not require more than for a law to be passed, additional efforts to restrict gobs of money from flowing into the flood will be subject to a higher legal power.

CONSTITUTIONAL INTERPRETATION AND AMENDMENT

It is part of our system's brilliance: Congress passes laws. Frequently the Supreme Court is called on to render an interpretation on whether a law is constitutional—that is, legally permissible. The Court's ruling serves as the final word on the issue—unless we the people, through our state legislatures and representatives in Congress, ratify an amendment to the U.S. Constitution. Unless repealed, the Constitution is the authority we are bound by. Thus the heading above. Our final attack on the money flood problem will deal with the Supreme Court's rulings on campaign finance and what may be necessary for us to do to override these decisions.

Fortunately, we do not need to comprehensively review the history of Supreme Court campaign finance decisions to understand the current landscape. Unfortunately, that's because a handful of rulings permit a ton of special interest money to course through election campaigns. We know that *Citizens United* allows the Super PACs to raise huge sums from corporations and unions for "independent expenditures." No matter what such expenditures are called, they are used to get candidates elected. And they also could mean that candidates may claim they have opted into genuine "clean election" reforms even as they are angling to get the big PACs to "independently" invest in their campaigns.[73]

The companion case to *Citizens United* was *SpeechNOW.org v. FEC,* where the D.C. Circuit Court of Appeals allowed individuals to contribute as much as they want to the Super PACs.[74] We also know that *McCutcheon v. FEC* struck down aggregate limits for individual giving to multiple candidates in a campaign cycle. It's the wild west. And long ago, in the 1976 case *Buckley v. Valeo,* the Court upheld candidates' and committees' rights to spend as much as they like on campaign activities, and for individuals to shell out as much as they like on independent expenditures.[75]

Much of the reasoning behind these decisions rests on First Amendment rights to free speech. These Supreme Court cases and opinions matter a great deal not only because of what they allow, but also because of what they *might allow in the future* with regard to campaign finance law. It is still possible that the high court could limit contributions to Super PACs. But the Court's track record on other reasonable limits set in place by Congress does not bode well for new reform efforts. We are not just talking about cash limits. We are talking about legislation to improve transparency, to regulate lobbying practices, and of course to uphold the kinds of public financing reforms presented above. And this is why the long-term effort to unlock Congress will require a *constitutional amendment permitting Congress to regulate campaign finance.*

Americans are not opposed to taking that big a step, at least not when asked. A 2012 poll conducted by Democracy Corps in twelve battleground states found 73 percent of Americans favor a constitutional amendment to overturn the *Citizens United* decision.[76]

In September 2014, U.S. Senator Tom Udall (D-NM) introduced a resolution (with forty-eight co-sponsors) to create such a constitutional amendment. The Democracy for All Amendment includes the following text: "To advance democratic self-government and political equality, and to protect the integrity of government and the electoral process, Congress and the States may regulate and set reasonable limits on the raising and spending of money by candidates and others to influence elections."[77]

It sounds good. And if adopted, the amendment would prohibit the courts from interfering in congressional reforms that curb or regulate how much money makes its way into campaigns—as well as the ways in which it gets scooped up and spent. The only problem is that, as of right now, the amendment doesn't have a prayer. Here we have another issue that breaks down along partisan lines. Every one of Senator Udall's co-sponsors was a Democrat, and that is certainly not going to move the resolution anywhere, especially under current rules in the Senate.

The party split on campaign finance reform is a major obstacle, but that's nothing new in this effort to unlock Congress. To make any of these reforms happen, we will have to push the system by applying pressure to incumbents on each side of the divide—and by electing new representatives who share a passion for reforming the rules and restoring the system.

We have the collective power to get those results, and we will go into that soon. But when it comes to tackling the money flood, a bipartisan effort is already afoot. The Mayday project is dedicated to electing new members of Congress who will pledge to support fundamental reforms along the lines of publicly financed congressional elections.

Mayday, a political action committee, was co-founded in 2014 by author and Harvard Law Professor Lawrence Lessig, and Mark McKinnon, a Republican strategist and former advisor to President George W. Bush. Lessig has been cited several times in these pages, and his book, *Republic Lost,* is an excellent resource for those looking to learn more about the money flood. The contradiction of creating a Super PAC to reform the rules so that we can eliminate Super PACs is not lost on Lessig, who urges contributors to "embrace the irony."

McKinnon is well aware that Republicans do not traditionally support changing the way money flows into the system. Nevertheless, he sees a path: "Conservatives are realizing that we don't really have a free public policy market, and the reason for that is directly tied to money. The whole idea of crony capitalism is getting a lot of equity in the party right now."[78]

Mayday set out a four-step plan to: 1) financially support a small number of candidates in the 2014 elections who pledged to support campaign finance reform (Mayday raised and spent more than $7 million in that cycle, winning two of eight races it engaged in); 2) learn lessons from 2014 and work in future elections to win a majority of like-minded representatives; 3) push for legislation that adopts a form of publicly financed congressional campaigns; and 4) advocate for a constitutional amendment that would give Congress the power to keep in place any reforms that it passes.

Mayday is one of several organizations pounding the drum for campaign finance reform, and it is certainly among the most ambitious.

The effort to ratify a constitutional amendment is last on the list for a reason—and not just because it is difficult. All of this stuff is hard. But as Lessig and McKinnon will be the first to reiterate, it all starts with us. Americans consistently voice their collective preference to rein in all the money that pulses through our system, but voting on that issue—or volunteering to work to push it up to a higher position on the public agenda—is quite another thing. We need to back up our beliefs, by taking action.

Using public financing to rebalance the power equation is straightforward and makes good sense. The time has come to give everyday Americans—not just the millionaires and billionaires—a real way to express in political campaigns their First Amendment rights. It is about fairness. And when you stop and think about it, it is also about logic.

PUSHING THE PLATFORM

We have reviewed several proposals in this chapter that would surely strengthen our currently defective legislative branch. Achieving these rule changes in our system of elections and governance will most certainly not result in perfection. What they will do, appropriate to language in our very own Declaration of Independence, is make our Congress "more perfect." Closer to perfect. In a word: better.

SUMMARIZING THE UNLOCK CONGRESS PLATFORM

1. **Extend U.S. House Terms to Four Years:** Increase U.S. Representatives' Capacity to Function As Effective Public Servants.
2. **Unrig Congressional Races:** Reform Election Rules to Increase Voter Choice, Competition, and Fair Representation.
3. **Abolish the "Filibuster":** Restore Majority Rule to the U.S. Senate.
4. **Rebalance Campaign Finance Rules:** Decrease the Money Flood's Disproportionate Influence on Congress.

As we have noted, accomplishing some of these goals will require new laws and, therefore, new members of Congress. We as Americans will need to push these new candidates and representatives to support the platform. Other proposals will be achieved through statewide ballot initiatives or referenda that will require us to advocate within our individual states. Still others can only be achieved by amending our U.S. Constitution, which will ultimately require us to push our legislators at both the state and federal levels.

Whether it's starting a petition drive in a state, applying pressure to our candidates running for office, or actually putting one's name on the ballot to champion these proposals, we all have an opportunity to push the platform together and reform the rules. It will take a combination of association, perspiration, and inspiration. It will take citizenship. It will take us, we the people, to make it all possible.

8 The Possibility

All things are possible until they are proven impossible.

Pearl S. Buck[1]

With willing hearts and skillful hands, the difficult we do at once. The impossible takes a bit longer.

motto of the U.S. Navy Seabees during World War II[2]

E ven small slices of history remind us that there is an enormous difference between a goal that is difficult to accomplish and one that might understandably be classified as "impossible." And even many of those eventually become possible. It just takes time and passion.

During our country's passionate fight for independence, an inexperienced Continental Army beat back the vaunted British Redcoats in what looked like an impossible victory. The United States was born. Over the next two centuries, America would achieve epic successes in world wars, in the advancement of civil rights, in the race to outer space. These victories, and so many other American milestones, were uphill battles from the start. But very often, the challenges with the steepest inclines tend to provide the most satisfying and meaningful rewards. And we the people—each and every one of us—have the power to make history.

THE POWER OF ONE

Gregory Watson decided to take his long shot more than thirty years ago. He was just a college student in 1982. Was he interested in politics? Yes. Did he have any inkling that he was going to have the kind of impact once reserved for the likes of Jefferson and Madison? Not in a million years.

But it only took a decade.

Watson was a sophomore majoring in economics at the University of Texas. While searching for a topic to write about in his class on government, he discovered an unratified constitutional amendment from 1789 regarding congressional compensation. The amendment would have disallowed members of Congress from receiving any pay raise they had voted for themselves—until after their next election.

Watson argued in his paper that although only six states had originally ratified it, the proposed amendment was a live issue that could still be considered by the states. His professor disagreed, and handed him back his grade on the assignment. It was a C. Far from deterred, Watson remembers being spurred on instead.

"I knew that the amendment was technically still pending before the state legislatures, and I also knew that Congress was still abusing its privilege to establish its own rate of pay. And so when I got the C on my paper from the professor, I decided that I was going to prove her wrong.[3]

"I remembered that in December of 1981, just four months before I had discovered the amendment, Congress had given itself a sneaky, backdoor pay raise in the form of a special tax break. A tax break, I would point out, only applicable to members of Congress, not to any other category of tax-payer. And they hid this tax break in a bill where they thought no one would look for it. The black lung benefits bill. And of course somebody did find it and reported it in the media. It ended up being just another embarrassing incident for Congress where they were caught with their hand in the cookie jar. So that was very fresh in my mind. And now it's March of 1982, and I'm thinking this is something that could put a stop to those kinds of abuses on Capitol Hill."

No longer just an assignment in a college course for Gregory Watson, his project now had larger goals—the pursuit of which he believed was possible. Long before the advent of email, this college student had to put in the hard work of personally reaching out to state legislators across the country—one by one. He called, he faxed, he wrote, and then he dialed them up again.

"I knew that all I had to do was show this to the state legislatures and convince them that it had no deadline. And therefore, because it had no deadline, it was technically still pending business. And they could still take it up—even though it was 192 or 193 years later. And sure enough, that's what happened. The very next year I was able to get Maine to ap-prove it. And once I got a state to approve it, the momentum took off. The year after that, 1984, I got Colorado to pass it. It really took off in 1985. Five states passed it. I knew it was just a simple matter of clearly presenting this issue to the state legislatures, and that they would act appropriately. And they did."

In 1992, ten years after turning in that class paper, Michigan became the thirty-eighth and pivotal state to ratify what would become the Twen-ty-seventh Amendment to the U.S. Constitution: "No law, varying the compensation for the services of the Senators and Representatives, shall take effect, until an election of Representatives shall have intervened."[4]

Gregory Watson is still involved. He works as a Republican policy aide in the Texas state legislature. And he highly recommends political participation, in whatever form one chooses.

"You must remember the wisdom of the very old saying: When the cat's away, the mice will play. If the public does not constantly monitor and communicate with their elected officials, guess what? Their elected officials are going to play, and they're going to engage in sleazy behavior. There are some good elected officials in this world. And the only way to keep them honest is by constantly monitoring them and constantly communicating with them."

Of course, a big part of monitoring our leaders—and holding them accountable—comes right back to the rules. It makes perfect sense that the original author of the proposed rule that became the Twenty-seventh Amendment, James Madison, is the very same founder whom we recall writing, "The aim of every political constitution is, or ought to be, first to obtain for rulers men who possess most wisdom to discern, and most virtue to pursue, the common good of the society; and in the next place, to take the most effectual precautions for keeping them virtuous whilst they continue to hold their public trust."

Looking back, Watson notes that achieving meaningful changes to the rules takes time. The keys, he says, are patience, tenacity, and dedication. He remembers what fueled him in the beginning, as well as each step of the way as he progressed toward his and our victory:

"It was passion from day one. And to be very candid and honest with you, even if the professor had given me an A, I still would have gone for it anyway, because I believe in trying to get things accomplished. Even if she'd given me an A, I'd have still gone and tried to get the amendment ratified. It was just a question of when."

THE POWER OF THOUSANDS

As a kid, Melissa Bean was loaded with energy and loved to read. She attended public schools and her parents expected and rewarded a strong work ethic. Her father, a Marine Raider in World War II, returned to work at various canning companies before starting his own engineering and manufacturing firm. Although government was a subject rarely discussed in her home, Bean had an early interest in the economic debates of the seventies. But a business career was her goal.

After graduation, she enrolled at a local community college to pursue an associate's degree in business, which her mother assured her could be transferred to a four-college. And she immediately started working: "I took a part-time job while I was taking full-time classes, and it happened to be at a computer company that was one of the Inc. 500 fastest growing companies, Data Access Systems, Inc. This was right when the computer industry was really taking off. There was tremendous opportunity in the company, and they wanted me to come on full time. When I told them that I hadn't finished school, they said, 'We have tuition reimbursement, you can go at night and we'll pay for it.' It took much longer to get the degree, but it worked out for me because I kept getting great opportunities in sales and management. I was hiring all these people with four-year degrees—and I still hadn't even finished my own bachelor's degree! But, I had enough work experience and industry knowledge, at that point, to be running the branch."[5] Her success led to her being recruited to other management roles at high tech firms.

Bean kept working, kept learning, and kept growing. After completing her associate's degree at Oakton Community College, she pursued a bachelor's degree in political science at Chicago's Roosevelt University at night. By this time, Bean had gotten married and was raising two young daughters. Both parents worked, and soon she started thinking more about family balance: "I think we both have always been really ambitious about our careers. But once you have kids, they are your top priority. So I would say that one of the reasons I started my own business, after a vice president of sales job at a national company, was because I wasn't having the quality of life and the availability for my kids that I wanted at that point in my life."

Years later, as her children grew up, Melissa Bean felt she had reached a turning point. "I had a choice to make: did I really want to scale this business up, or did I want to license my product, keep my work flexibility, and instead of devoting it all to my kids who needed me less, I could make myself available for other things I cared about." She chose the latter.

For years, prompted by Bean's political views, which she readily shared with friends and colleagues, people were often telling her she should run for office. But Bean remembers saying, "I would never do that. You'd have to be a little crazy to do that. Less money, more scrutiny, who needs that? I just wasn't interested."

As a parent of young children, however, her concerns led her to have even firmer convictions about the role of government in protecting the re-sources and opportunities American children count on. Bean had come to care more about the issues affecting her community—and her family. "It was sort of this gradual thing. I began to observe an erosion of the things we value most in this country—a shrinking middle class, which to me is the engine of our economy, and opportunity for all. Lack of commitment to educational excellence. And attacks on separation of church and state. It didn't just seem extreme, it seemed like we were regressing. And that made me fearful for the future of the country, and for my kids and grand-kids. Those were the things that made me say, 'We all have to care about this. We've got to get involved. We've got to pay attention.'

"I was also very concerned about the environment. Air quality. Water quality. EPA regulations that had been on the books since I was a kid were suddenly being messed with. That frightened me for everybody, my kids included. I felt like if the moms don't get involved and start stomping our feet and waving our hands and saying, 'This isn't okay,' then who will?"

A self-described centrist, she became more actively involved in poli-tics. As she was helping other candidates, people began urging her to run as a moderate Democrat in Illinois's Eighth Congressional District. Bean initially resisted, even as a part of her felt incredibly frustrated by what she was watching. But once the seed was planted, encouragement from friends, strangers, and her husband got her to seriously consider it. A meeting with senior U.S. Senator Richard Durbin (D-IL) finally convinced her: "When I sat with him, I expected him to say, 'It's really great for you to consider, but you don't have a shot.' Instead, he encouraged me. He said, 'I think you have the right profile, the right attitude. I think you represent your district, and I think if you're willing to work hard at it, you definitely should do it.' And I was absolutely shocked. And he said, 'But be prepared. It took President Lincoln three times to get elected to Congress, it took me three times to get elected, and it could take you that long.' Well, it took me two attempts."

In 2004, Melissa Bean was elected to the U.S. Congress. She had unseated the longest-serving Republican in the House at the time, thirty-five-year veteran Phil Crane. In the six years she represented the conservative-leaning Eighth District, Bean was a member of the Blue Dog Coalition ("created in 1995 to represent the common-sense middle of the Democratic Party") and the New Democrat Coalition ("pro-growth, fiscally responsible wing of the Democratic Party").[6] Bean's participation in both coalitions and her voting record in the House earned her a reputation as a genuine moderate.[7]

In 2010, Bean lost her third re-election bid by the razor-thin margin of 290 votes. But she doesn't have a single regret: "I thought being in Congress was the best job in the world. It was crazy hours. You were away from your family. It was a huge sacrifice. I've always been a type-A workaholic. In my sales background, the more you worked, the better you did. You see the results. But Congress took it to an exponentially higher level—I didn't know I could get into that gear. But it fuels you, and it's exciting. It's ambitious. It's the best thing I ever did. It's a great honor, yet it's extremely humbling. If you are a problem solver by nature, Congress lets you tackle *any* issue that needs to be addressed. I loved it. I would recommend this experience to anybody who is willing to work really hard in the short term for potential long-term benefit to the country."

If Melissa Bean's story sounds a bit unremarkable in some ways, that's because it is. We have had more than twelve thousand Americans serve in Congress since 1789, and so many of them, like Bean, never had a clue early on that they would wind up walking the halls of the U.S. Capitol. Former schoolteachers, NFL football players, car dealers, tax attorneys, veterans, farmers, novelists, veterinarians, actors, nurses, parents—there is no uniform resume required to apply for the job. Thousands of U.S. citizens representing different regions, professions, ethnic backgrounds, and political philosophies have stepped up to the plate. Americans' continuing desire to serve our country in public office rests at the very heart of our democracy.

Based on her own years in office, Melissa Bean is confident when she says that anyone can run and serve in the U.S. Congress—if they have the passion and the willingness to work for it. But setting aside running for office, she also says that as Americans, the very least we can do is tune in. Pay attention. Create the change we want.

THE POWER OF MILLIONS

We can do this. But it's going to take a whole lot of us. As Americans we possess not only the power of our votes, but the power of our voices. We're going to need to use both in order to *apply pressure* to the system and reform the rules.

Politics is a brutal business. The stakes are monumental because they apply directly to what kind of country we are going to live in and how we're going to hand it off to future generations. The laws Congress passes can sometimes seem like distant, abstract concepts. But even the least politically involved among us know that is not the case. Every law and every rule in some way sets limitations and permissions on our daily activities, no matter what we are striving for in our individual lives.

This book has tried to demonstrate how the combination of the four defects in the D.C. 4-3 skew the system into delivering a faulty product to us, the American people. In the big picture, the United States remains a rich and powerful nation. But in the smaller frames of our experiences as individuals, as families, as communities, we see a different story. The quality of life for far too many hard-working, law-abiding Americans is not moving in the direction that we desire. Our economic well-being, our health care *non-system,* our crumbling infrastructure, our education gap, our immigration mess, our college unaffordability, our long-term unfunded liabilities and national debt ...

Creating and enacting legislation that will govern a nation, as well as conducting effective oversight over the execution of these laws, is no easy assignment. The job of Congress would be difficult even under the best of circumstances. Think about it: 535 disparate people with diverse backgrounds, representing vast constituencies with differing opinions about how the country should move forward. Small families sitting at their dinner tables have dramatic disagreements about far less consequential subjects. That's why having the capacity to communicate honestly and arrive at sensible compromise is imperative to having a well-functioning Congress. Not all of the decisions made and deals struck by our representatives will be optimal, but in a world that moves exponentially faster than the one faced by our nation's founders, our legislative branch must be able to take decisive action, measure the results, and then proceed accordingly.

Obviously, we as individuals have a personal responsibility to work toward making our lives better. But so does our government. Each and every member of Congress takes an oath to uphold the U.S. Constitution. Each legislator is tasked with working to promote our general welfare. Political ideology and partisanship will always be a part of our system. But when we allow hostile division and political competition to prevent Congress from finding areas of common ground to advance the country, we are insulting the founders' vision of how our system was meant to operate. The irony of this story is that *Congress's own rules* permit and cultivate a system so skewed that it cannot create the *rules and policies* necessary to positively impact the country!

We know that billions of dollars, contributed disproportionately by the few, flood through our congressional system every day of every election cycle. We know that this money is not given for the sake of generosity; the cash kings drive decision-making on public policy. We have seen how money drives outcomes that are at cross-purposes with the general welfare of the American people. We need reform.

We know that U.S. House races are rigged in a fashion that guarantees predictable and optimally partisan results. We know from the Cook Partisan Voter Index and from FairVote research that winner-take-all elections in single-member congressional districts limit voters' choices and extinguish the threadbare political center. We have reviewed studies that mathematically show how the effects of gerrymandering make the problem worse. Yes, partisanship and regional political divides are inherently embedded in our politics, but the rigging of election races pushes the parties' intractability to the next level.

We know that before the Constitution was ratified there was debate about the length of House terms; James Madison and others favored three years due to the rigors and requirements of the job. More than two centuries later, congressional districts are more than twenty times larger, and the nation's domestic and international challenges are far more complicated. The money flood, combined with new media technologies, creates a constant campaign in which members of Congress must keep their feet shuffling atop that greasy political wheel. It never stops spinning, and representatives never stop thinking about their next election—each one occurring just twenty-two months after they are sworn in.

We know that the filibuster is a rule that was never a part of our Constitution and was instead a historical accident, one conceptually contrary to our country's founding principles of republican government based on majority rule. We know that both political parties have increasingly used filibusters and holds to bottleneck the nation's business over the last two decades. And record amounts of obstruction have occurred in the most recent congressional sessions. The abuse of these blocking tactics has cornered the Senate into a state of inertia.

We know all of this. And we know what it adds up to. As citizen consumers of our legislative branch's defective product, we have a breach of contract on our hands. But unlike exercising a warranty in a business exchange, we are going to have to put in some work to correct this product's defects. We cannot just show up on the steps of the Capitol with a copy of the Constitution and demand that Congress start delivering better results. We do not get an automatic refund of our tax dollars from the government for its poor performance. We have to look at the recourse options our U.S. Constitution actually affords us, and then we have to choose.

The obvious option available to us is to elect new people. We have tried this. We have listened to candidates' promises and positions on the issues. We have voted in new people. It hasn't worked. Americans have been dissatisfied with the congressional product in recent decades under alternating party control and where both higher and lower numbers of laws were being passed. NBC political director and moderator of "Meet the Press" Chuck Todd summed this up in 2014: "…'06, '08, '10, you could argue that we've been voting a lot of change. Three of the last four cycles, there's been a change. And nothing happened."[8]

Because it is not just the people, *it's the system.* The rules in the system take the good folks who go to Washington and place them right up on that perpetual wheel. Fortunately, a second option afforded to us in our U.S.

Constitution, and in our state constitutions, is to pressure our leaders to reform the rules. Through ballot initiatives, referenda, new legislation, and constitutional amendments, we can change some of these wrongheaded rules and restore logic and the potential for pragmatism to the system.

Yes, this effort will require us to elect new members of Congress, but based on a new calculus for our votes. A new conversation pushed by the people. To get involved and stay up to date about this reform mission, sign up at **www.unlockcongress.com**. For we should be under no illusions: Changing the subject from the same tired old political tropes to a fresh focus on the rules will be enormously challenging. None of it will happen without *participation*. Us.

It will be a step-by-step process, and it may not happen quickly. Gregory Watson spent a decade working toward his goal, which is why he emphasizes that patience is essential to any movement to reform long-standing rules. Melissa Bean, like so many other neophyte candidates, was cautioned that she might have to run more than once and sacrifice years of her life just to get elected to a first term in Congress. Like so many other well-intentioned candidates for public office, she was patient, too. The same patience and persistence is required, on a collective level, when the goal is to dramatically restructure old processes that have become entrenched.

We are well aware that much of the partisanship on Capitol Hill has occurred naturally and that our politically divided electorate often makes it difficult for our representatives to achieve effective, meaningful results. But again, this impediment should not stop us from taking the necessary steps to *reform the rules and restore the system.* There is no perfect product to be found in this living equation. Rather, our goal is to find the places where the rules engender harmful defects and dysfunction, and then update and improve them to the point where the system encourages a more rational and constructive legislative process. Every single one of our lives and those of whom we care about are affected by it. At the same time, every single one of us has the power to shake it up. Gregory Watson learned this fact first hand:

"The ratification of the Twenty-seventh Amendment showed me that if a person will persistently nag, cajole, pester, and badger, that person will ultimately be able to move the wheels of government and make government respond."

Imagine the power of a huge cross-section—millions of Americans—coming together to move those wheels in a new direction. Our elected leaders on Capitol Hill *need us* to assemble on their behalf and push as one to rework the rulebook. It is an oft-spoken cliché, but nonetheless true: This is *our* country. And we can make the choice to exercise our constitutionally granted civic warranty to free a Congress that has become imprisoned within its own clumsily evolved system. In that spirit, we look back at one final film scene, this one from the 1994 prison classic, *The Shawshank Redemption.* The main character in the movie, innocent convict Andy Dufresne, uses a tiny rock hammer to burrow out a narrow escape tunnel from his jail cell. When he finally finishes building the long hatch and then crawls through five hundred yards of raw sewage to his freedom, we hear narration from his best friend "Red," played by Morgan Freeman:

> I remember thinking it would take a man six hundred years to tunnel through the wall with it. Old Andy did it in less than twenty. Oh, Andy loved geology. I imagine it appealed to his meticulous nature. An ice age here, a million years of mountain building there. Geology is the study of pressure and time ... That's all it takes, really—pressure and time.[9]

We have every reason to feel "mad as hell" about the poor product that the U.S. Congress generates. But we do possess the power to give our representatives a better opportunity to achieve the worthwhile goals that they went to Washington to work on in the first place. It will take passion. It will take pressure. And it will take time. If we push back together, we can make these changes a reality. We can rock the rules back into balance—and unlock the U.S. Congress.

Postscript

I n early 1994, on my first day working as a local reporter for CBS-TV in Rock Island, Illinois, I was assigned to cover a press conference for Congressman Lane Evans (D-IL). The story was about an agricultural bill and its consequences for farmers throughout the Quad Cities. I remember thinking I would settle quietly into the background, listen, and try to learn something. Instead, Representative Evans approached me directly, warmly introduced himself, and gave me the sincere and unmistakable impression that he cared deeply about his job. Congressman Evans, a U.S. veteran first elected in 1982, was forced to retire several years ago due to his battle with Parkinson's disease. Three weeks before the completion of this book, I received news of his passing. He was a good man.

Public servants like Lane Evans are not the exception in Congress. I believe there are a great many dedicated women and men serving our country in Washington, D.C. I believe this because I have been a witness to it. In the years since that early memory in western Illinois, I've worked as a broadcast journalist, political campaign strategist, and higher education advocate. These experiences afforded me the unique opportunity to view candidates and elected officeholders through three prisms. I covered them as a member of the media, worked alongside them managing their U.S. House and Senate races, and then collaborated with members of each party to provide resources and programming for American students.

Through the years, I always carried and continue to hold a great deal of respect for elected officials. I believe that the politicians with whom I have worked, as well as the vast majority of lawmakers, are in it for the right reasons. Although the job requires them to play rough and make trade-offs, most representatives do so to position themselves to accomplish a greater good. The fact that there are rules in the congressional system that now work in stark opposition to rational discussion and cooperation has frustrated me to the point of exasperation. I finally felt compelled to write it all down.

Searching for the problem's causes—and trying to find solutions—has been a fascinating and humbling experience. The workings of America's government and the large-scale challenges we face as a nation are extraordinarily complex subjects. Naturally, I hope that the arguments presented here about Congress's structural ills and potential cures will be persuasive, or at the very least, enlightening. That said, I am certain that keeping an open mind about our ongoing dilemma in Congress will be absolutely essential to reforming it. If history is any guide, it will be an organic process featuring unforeseen twists and turns.

In addition to flexibility, a successful effort to unlock Congress will take a civic army. This is the hard part. As strongly as I feel about the defects in our first branch of government, I am well aware that a relatively small proportion of Americans share a similarly intense interest. This is understandable. We all have so much going on in our lives, and we have to prioritize. Changing the rules in our government structure doesn't sound like a whole lot of fun, and there are never any guarantees that sweat equity poured into such an effort will actually pay off. Long before I wrote the first word on the first page, I well understood that motivating a critical mass of Americans to feel passionate enough to start pushing back on the system was more than a bit pie-in-the-sky. Still, it can happen.

The encouraging news is that many expert leaders are already fighting on the front lines of congressional reform. Many of these passionate people and proud organizations have been cited on these pages (and are noted in Acknowledgments). If one or more of the solutions in the Unlock Congress platform strike a chord, I encourage you to learn more about the activist champions behind each ongoing effort. They are easy to find, and they need our help. And if you are interested in being kept up to date about future reform activities and ways you can get involved, please do sign up at **www.unlockcongress.com**.

Finally, an important note regarding an incredibly valuable segment of the American population: the Millennial generation. More than *85 million* of these young Americans have proven their power to shake up obsolete, inefficient structures through disruptive technologies and innovative problem solving. They are committed to community service and volunteer at a higher level when compared to recent generations.[1] There are a ton of civic-minded, whip-smart young professionals who want to play a serious role in strengthening our country.

At the same time, many Millennials are increasingly turned off by the thought of public service within government. A 2013 poll conducted by the Institute on Politics revealed that 47 percent of Millennials believe our politics are "no longer able to meet the challenges our country is facing," and an increasing number do not believe that being active in the process yields worthwhile results.[2]

Based on some of this research, an *Atlantic* article in 2013 concluded: "The only way Millennials might engage Washington is if they first radically change it."[3] Whether the set of reforms that have been outlined in this book amount to "radical change" is subject to interpretation. Certainly all of these ideas and arguments are intended for the widest possible American audience. But one thing is certain: A successful campaign for national reform will require active and passionate leadership from America's Millennials. Our country cries out for a new Greatest Generation to help us rewire the rules and reenergize our government. A gigantic civic opportunity sits waiting. If they choose to, America's young leaders have the talent, knowledge, and conviction to step in and drive a movement to make political history.

In the fall of 2014, after intruders had breached White House security twice in two weeks, Jon Stewart joked on *The Daily Show*, "Here's how dysfunctional the Secret Service is at this point: Congress had to help them come up with solutions!" His live audience—which includes a great many Millennials—roared.[4] Everyone gets the joke. But in so many ways, it's just not funny anymore.

We all have good reason to be urgently concerned about our defective Congress. We all have the capacity to comprehend why this has happened. And we all have the power to reform the problematic elements within the D.C. 4-3—and lift our country back up again. *It is possible.*

Acknowledgments

I t is fitting that I am writing this on the morning of Thanksgiving, as it is my best attempt at expressing gratitude to all those who joined this authentic team effort. I am more than just thankful for the generous contributions of so many good people. More accurately, this book simply would not have come to exist without their immensely valuable time and assistance.

Early on in this process, author and congressional scholar Norman Ornstein of the American Enterprise Institute was kind enough to meet with me, discuss ideas, and offer sage advice. The extensive body of work on Congress that he and his co-author Thomas Mann have contributed made a huge impact on my research long before I wrote the first word. I am particularly grateful to Norm for keeping in touch along the way.

As I moved deeper into the research process, a broad range of legal and political scholars, as well as public servants and reform activists, graciously shared with me their expertise and experience. Finding Eric Petersen, a specialist in American national government at the Congressional Research Service, was a stroke of luck. Eric's candid feedback and wise counsel kept me grounded throughout.

Additional critical review, exhaustive fact-checking, and personal interviews were generously afforded to me by Sanford Levinson at the University of Texas, Lawrence Lessig at Harvard University (and Mayday PAC), Nolan McCarty and Sam Wang at Princeton University, Nicholas Stephanopoulos at the University of Chicago Law School, Justin Levitt at Loyola University Law School in Los Angeles, Whitney Burns, Dave Bradlee, Nathan Fenstermacher, Harry Stein, Russ Choma, Joshua Tauberer, and Ira Shapiro.

The indispensable trio of Rob Richie, Andrew Douglas, and Drew Spencer at FairVote played a substantial role by providing both research and design resources to make the case for election reform. Their proficiency and dedicated advocacy are nothing short of inspirational.

Former U.S. Representatives Mickey Edwards and Melissa Bean offered their time, experience, and intellect in personal interviews for this book, and I greatly appreciate their cooperation. I offer similar thanks to Gregory Watson, who proudly shared with me, in detail, his historic story about the ratification of the Twenty-seventh Amendment.

Emmet Bondurant and Stephen Spaulding of Common Cause could not possibly have been more helpful on the subject of the standstill in the U.S. Senate. The multiple interviews they provided, as well as critical review of both research and content, were a godsend.

It is a satisfying feeling to thank by name all of the preceding folks whose collective expertise provided a guiding hand along this journey. At the same time, I am mindful of a constellation of additional authors, scholars, justices, members of Congress, official staff, and reform advocates whose work played a less visible yet profoundly substantial role in this composition. A great number of these folks are included in the endnotes that follow. Although I do not speak for them, many of their voices helped to inform mine. For this, I am humbled and appreciative.

Down the home stretch, John Deever and Tessa Avila each made wonderful contributions in their respective copyediting and design efforts. Their patience, guidance, and attention to detail shine on every page. As well, my friend Scott Weisman and his crew at LaunchPad Lab put their heart and talent into designing a terrific website: **www.unlockcongress.com**.

The work on this book was a fairly solitary experience, and it just might have become a maddening one without the steadfast support of an extraordinary group of family and dear friends. They listened, read, motivated, and then listened some more. Enormous thanks to Bridget Samburg, Jenny Wittner, Eric Adelstein, Jon Callahan, David Scherer, J.D. Grom, Connie Mixon, Nicole Robinson, Rhonda Keaveney, Elory Rozner, Carolyn Golden, Dana Cohen, Bud Elliot, Marva Paull, and Alicia and Aaron Oberman.

Finally, I take great pride in celebrating the "Big Three." Amy and Brad Herzog of Why Not Books have gone beyond the call in their roles as publisher, editors, counselors, and ultimately dear friends. This book simply would not have come together in the fashion it did without them. Equal praise is due to Steve Rhodes, who served as my editor and researcher in Chicago from the get go. His passion for this project, along with the brainpower he put into every paragraph, has made all the difference.

How fortunate I am to have had the chance to work with all of these excellent people. How inadequate the above words are in communicating how genuinely grateful I am to each and every one of them. Nevertheless, and from the most sincere place I know: *Thank you.*

Appendix: Priorities Polling

CBS News Poll, July 29–August 4, 2014. N = 1,344 adults nationwide

http://www.cbsnews.com/news/americans-views-of-obama-congress-gloomy/

What do you think is the most important problem facing this country today?
(open-ended)

Economy/jobs	22
Immigration/illegal immigrants	13
Health care/health insurance	5
Partisan politics	4

Gallup Poll, January 5–8, 2014. N = 1,018 adults nationwide

http://www.gallup.com/poll/166844/government-itself-cited-top-problem.aspx

What do you think is the most important problem facing this country today?
(open-ended)

Dissatisfaction with government/Congress/politicians; poor leadership/corruption/abuse of power	21
Economy in general	18
Unemployment/jobs	16
Poor health care/hospitals/high costs of health care	16
Federal budget deficit/federal debt	8

CBS News Poll, October 18–21, 2013. N = 1,007 adults nationwide
http://www.cbsnews.com/8301-250_162-57608707/poll-post-shutdown-congress
-disapproval-at-all-time-high/?pageNum=2

What do you think is the most important problem facing this country today?
(open-ended)

Economy	26
Budget	12
Health care	8
Partisan politics	8
Immigration	3

CNN/ORC Poll, September 6–8, 2013. N = 1,022 adults nationwide
http://i2.cdn.turner.com/cnn/2013/images/09/11/rel8g.pdf

Which of the following is the most important issue facing the country today?
(random order)

Economy	41
Health care	16
Situation in Syria	15
Federal budget	13
Environment	5
Gun policy	5
Immigration	3

Gallup Poll, June 20–24, 2013. N = 2,048 adults nationwide
http://www.gallup.com/poll/163298/americans-say-economy-top-worry-nation
-future.aspx

Looking ahead, what is your greatest worry or concern about the future of the
United States?(open-ended)

Economy	17
Debt/deficit/nation's finances	11
Employment/jobs	6
Wars/conflicts in other countries	5
Health care	4
Government not working for the betterment of the people	4
Losing freedom/civil liberties	4

New York Times/CBS Poll, September 8–12, 2012. N = 1,301 adults
http://www.nytimes.com/interactive/2012/09/15/us/politics/New-York-Times-CBS
-Poll-Results.html?_r=0

What is the most important issue to you in deciding how you will vote for president this year? (open-ended)

Economy/jobs/unemployment (commingled)	41
Health care/Medicare/Medicaid	14
Politicians/government	6
Budget/deficit	4
Education	2
Taxes	2

CBS News Poll, November 7–10, 2010. N = 1,137 adults nationwide
http://www.cbsnews.com/stories/2010/11/11/politics/main7045964.shtml

Of all of the problems facing the country today, which one do you want the new Congress to concentrate on first when it begins in January? (open-ended)

Economy and jobs	56
Health care	14
Budget deficit/national debt	4
Education	2
Immigration	2
Taxes	2
Wars/Afghanistan/Iraq	2

CNN Poll, March 19–21, 2010. N = 1,030 adults nationwide
http://i2.cdn.turner.com/cnn/2010/images/03/23/rel5f.pdf

Which of the following will be the most important issue when you decide how to vote for Congress this year? (random order)

Economy	43
Health care	23
Education	11
Federal budget deficit	8
The wars/Iraq and Afghanistan	7

Bloomberg Poll, September 10–14, 2009. N = 1,004 adults nationwide
http://media.bloomberg.com/bb/avfile/r7m6GlwsDwNE

Which of the following do you see as the most important issue facing the country right now?

Economy	46
Health care	23
Federal budget deficit	16
The wars in Iraq and Afghanistan	10
Climate change	2

NBC/*Wall Street Journal*, August 15–18, 2008. N = 1,005 adults
http://s.wsj.net/public/resources/documents/WSJ_NBCPoll_prtl_082108.pdf

Please tell me which of these items you think should be the top priority for the federal government:

Job creation and economic growth	27
Energy and the cost of gas	18
Health care	14
The war in Iraq	13
Terrorism	9
Illegal immigration	8

Gallup Poll, April 23–26, 2007. N = 1,007 adults nationwide
http://www.gallup.com/poll/27433/all-major-groups-agree-iraq-should
-governments-top-focus.aspx

In your view, what one or two issues should be the top priorities for the President and Congress to deal with at this time? (open-ended)

Situation in Iraq/war	66
Poor health care/cost of health care	20
Economy in general	14
Immigration/illegal aliens	14
Fuel/oil crisis	7
Environment	5

ABC News/*Washington Post* **Poll, November 1–4, 2006. N = 1,205 adults**
http://www.washingtonpost.com/wp-srv/politics/polls/postpoll_110406.htm

Which of the following will be/was the single most important issue in your vote
for Congress this year? *(items rotated)*

Iraq	31
Economy	21
Health care	12
Terrorism	11
Immigration	9

Fox News/Opinion Dynamics Poll, August 29–30, 2006.
N = 900 registered voters nationwide
http://www.foxnews.com/projects/pdf/FOX_231_rls_web.pdf

As of today, which one of the following issues will be the most important in
deciding your vote for Congress this fall? *(items rotated)*

Economy	23
Iraq	14
Terrorism	12
Health care	11
Immigration	9
Gas prices	8

Associated Press/Ipsos Poll, September 16–18, 2005.
N = 500 registered voters nationwide
http://surveys.ap.org/data/Ipsos/national/2005/2005-09-18%20AP%20Topline%20results.pdf

I'm going to read you a list of ***eight*** *issues. Please tell me which ONE should be the highest*
priority for President Bush and the U.S. Congress in the next few months?

The economy and jobs	25
The situation in Iraq	19
Energy and gas prices	17
Terrorism	11
Health care	10
Education	7

NBC/*Wall Street Journal* Poll, June 25–28, 2004. N = 1,025 adults nationwide
http://www.pollingreport.com/prioriti4.htm

Please tell me which one of the following issues will be most important to you personally in your voting for Congress and President this year? (read list)

The war in Iraq	25
Terrorism and homeland security	22
Jobs and unemployment	21
Health care and prescription drug coverage	11
The federal budget deficit	9

Note: For poll results no longer available at a pollster's or news organization's original URL, survey data is also available at http://www.pollingreport.com/prioriti.htm

Notes

PREAMBLE

1. Patrick Marley, "Pocan Compares Congress to Kindergarten," *Milwaukee Journal Sentinel,* October 1, 2013 http://www.jsonline.com/blogs/news /225971441.html (accessed October 15, 2014).
2. Daniel Newhauser, "Steven LaTourette: Congress Doesn't Function," *Roll Call,* August 1, 2012. http://www.rollcall.com/issues/58_15/Steven -LaTourette-Says-Congress-Does-Not-Function-216623-1.html (accessed October 15, 2014).
3. Adam Ashton, "The Last Moments of Jennifer Moreno, an Army Nurse Killed in Afghanistan," *Army Times,* April 29, 2014. http://www.armytimes.com /article/20140429/NEWS/304290068/The-last-moments-Jennifer-Moreno -an-Army-nurse-killed-Afghanistan (accessed November 5, 2014).
4. Cheryl K. Chumley, "Shutdown Outrage: Military Death Benefits Denied to Families of Fallen Troops," *The Washington Times,* October 8, 2013. http:// www.washingtontimes.com/news/2013/oct/8/shutdown-leaves-families -killed-soldiers-no-funera/ (accessed November 5, 2014).
5. Tony Dokoupil, "'I Won't Ever Understand It': Kin of Fallen Express Grief, Anger over Death Benefits," NBC News, October 9, 2013. http://www .nbcnews.com/news/other/i-wont-ever-understand-it-kin-fallen -express-grief-anger-f8C11359442 (accessed November 5, 2014).
6. Sarah Muller, "John McCain: 'I'm Ashamed … All of Us Should Be,'" *The Last Word,* MSNBC, October 8, 2013. http://www.msnbc.com/the-last-word /john-mccain-im-ashamedall-us-should-be (accessed November 5, 2014).
7. Elizabeth Mendes and Joy Wilke, "Americans Confidence in Congress Falls to Lowest on Record," *Gallup Politics,* June 13, 2013. http://www.gallup.com /poll/163052/americans-confidence-congress-falls-lowest-record.aspx (accessed October 15, 2014).
8. Rebecca Riffkin, "Public Faith in Congress Falls Again, Hits Historic Low," *Gallup Politics,* June 19, 2014. http://www.gallup.com/poll/171710/public -faith-congress-falls-again-hits-historic-low.aspx (accessed October 15, 2014).
9. The Center on Congress, November 2012 Public Opinion Survey. http://www .centeroncongress.org/november-2012-public-opinion-survey (accessed October 15, 2014).
10. Thomas E. Mann and Norman J. Ornstein, *It's Even Worse Than It Looks* (New York: Basic Books, 2012), 101.
11. Mickey Edwards, *The Parties Versus The People* (New Haven: Yale University Press, 2012), xi.

275

12. Adam Nagourney, "Democrats Reel as Senator Says No To 3rd Term," *The New York Times*, February 15, 2010. http://www.nytimes.com/2010/02/16/us/politics/16bayh .html (accessed October 15, 2014).

13. "Too-Big-to-Fail Is Still Too Dangerous," Bloomberg View, July 31, 2014. http://www. bloombergview.com/articles/2014-07-31/too-big-to-fail-is-still-too -dangerous (accessed December 16, 2014); Erika Eichelberger, "Feds Say Big Banks Are Still Too Big to Fail," Mother Jones, July 31, 2014. http://www.motherjones.com /mojo/2014/07/gao-report-too-big-to-fail-brown-vitter (accessed December 16, 2014).

14. Neil Irwin, "The Benefits of Economic Expansions Are Increasingly Going to the Richest Americans," *The New York Times*, September 26, 2014. http://www.nytimes .com/2014/09/27/upshot/the-benefits-of-economic-expansions-are-increasingly -going-to-the-richest-americans.html?abt=0002&abg=0 (accessed October 15, 2014).

15. Patrick O'Connor, "Poll Finds Widespread Economic Anxiety," *The Wall Street Journal*, August 5, 2014. http://online.wsj.com/articles/wsj-nbc-poll-finds -widespread-economic-anxiety-1407277801?tesla=y&$HeadlineQueryString$ (accessed October 15, 2014).

16. U.S. Social Security Administration, *A Summary of the 2014 Annual Reports.* http://www.ssa.gov/oact/trsum/ (accessed October 15, 2014).

17. Pew Research Social and Demographic Trends. *Millennials in Adulthood: Detached from Institutions, Networked with Friends.* http://www.pewsocialtrends.org/2014/03/07 /millennials-in-adulthood/ (accessed October 15, 2014).

18. "A Growth Opening," *The Wall Street Journal*, December 5, 2014. http://www.wsj.com /articles/a-growth-opening-1417823921 (accessed December 9, 2014); Nelson D. Schwartz, "Big Job Gains and Rising Pay in Labor Data," *The New York Times*, December 5, 2014. http://www.nytimes.com/2014/12/06/business/economy /november-jobs-unemployment-figures.html?_r=0 (accessed December 9, 2014).

19. James Hamblin, "How Is U.S. Health Care Bad?" *The Atlantic*, September 4, 2013. http://www.theatlantic.com/health/archive/2013/09/how-is-us-health-care -bad-chart/279334/ (accessed October 15, 2014).

20. Mark Blumenthal, "Government Shutdown: Polls Show Voters Blamed GOP For 1995 Crisis," *Huffington Post*, May 30, 2012. http://www.huffingtonpost.com/2011/03/30 /voters-blamed-gop-for-1995-shutdown_n_842769.html (accessed November 30, 2014); Neil King Jr., "Poll Finds GOP Blamed More for Shutdown," *The Wall Street Journal*, October 13, 2013. http://online.wsj.com/news/articles/SB10001424052702303 3820045791275719759128 10 (accessed October 15, 2014).

21. Russ Choma, "Money Won on Tuesday, but Rules of the Game Changed," *Open Secrets Blog*, Center for Responsive Politics, November 5, 2014. http://www .opensecrets.org/news/2014/11/money-won-on-tuesday-but-rules-of-the-game -changed/ (accessed November 8, 2014).

22. Tim Wirth, "Congress for Sale," *Anderson Cooper 360 Degrees*, CNN, February, 27, 2014. http://edition.cnn.com/TRANSCRIPTS/1402/27/acd.01.html (accessed October 15, 2014).

23. Dwight D. Eisenhower, *The White House Years: Mandate for Change 1953–1956* (New York: Doubleday, 1963).

24. Rahm Emanuel, *The Lead*, CNN, October 30, 2013. http://www.politico.com/story /2013/10/rahm-emanuel-hillary-clinton-99129.html (accessed October 15, 2014).

25. James E. Clyburn, "'Cumulative Voting' Would Enhance Fairness in Charleston County," *Charleston Gazette Post and Courier*, March 5, 2001. http://archive.fairvote .org/op_eds/clyburn.htm (accessed October 15, 2014).

26. Robert Dole, "Filibuster Reform Finds an Unlikely Ally," *The Rachel Maddow Show*, MSNBC, October 7, 2013. http://www.msnbc.com/rachel-maddow-show/filibuster -reform-finds-unlikely-ally (accessed October 15, 2014).

27. James Madison, "The Alleged Tendency of the New Plan to Elevate the Few at the Expense of the Many Considered in Connection with Representation," *Federalist 57*, February 19, 1788. http://thomas.loc.gov/home/histdox/fed_57.html (accessed October 15, 2014).

28. Tony Dokoupil, "Why Our Nation Isn't As Divided As We Think," NBC News, October 15, 2013. http://www.nbcnews.com/politics/politics-news/new-american -center-why-our-nation-isnt-divided-we-think-v20960588 (accessed October 15, 2014).

29. "13 Things That Define the New American Center," *Esquire*, October 15, 2013. http:// www.esquire.com/blogs/politics/new-american-center-1113 (accessed October 15, 2014).

CHAPTER ONE: THE PASSION

1. Devin Henry, "Do Members of Congress Work Hard?" *MinnPost*, January 1, 2013. http://www.minnpost.com/dc-dispatches/2013/01/do-members-congress-work -hard (accessed October 16, 2014).

2. "Browse Public Laws 113th Congress," Library of Congress, http://thomas.loc.gov /home/LegislativeData.php?&n=PublicLaws&c=113 (accessed January 3, 2015).

3. Polly DeFrank and Erich Bartlebaugh, "Our 'Do Nothing Congress,' By The Numbers," NBC News, July 31, 2014. http://www.nbcnews.com/politics/congress /our-do-nothing-congress-numbers-n169526 (accessed October 16, 2014).

4. Mark Murray, "Poll: 74 Percent of Voters Say Congress Has Been Unproductive," NBC News, August 3, 2014. http://www.nbcnews.com/politics/first-read/poll-74 -percent-voters-say-congress-has-been-unproductive-n170896 (accessed October 16, 2014).

5. James Madison, "The Senate," *Federalist 62*. http://thomas.loc.gov/home/histdox /fed_62.html (accessed October 16, 2014).

6. Howard Beale Rant: *Network*. https://www.youtube.com/watch?v=AS4aiA17YsM (accessed December 3, 2014).

7. Marshall Smelser, "The Federalist Period as an Age of Passion," *American Quarterly*, 10 (1958): 391.

8. President Jimmy Carter, "Crisis of Confidence," *Jimmy Carter: American Experience Presidents Series*, PBS. http://www.pbs.org/wgbh/americanexperience/features /primary-resources/carter-crisis/ (accessed October 16, 2014).

9. "Confidence in Institutions," Gallup. http://www.gallup.com/poll/1597/confidence -institutions.aspx#2 (accessed October 16, 2014).

10. David Brooks, *Meet the Press*, NBC News, December 30, 2012. http://www.nbcnews .com/id/50314590/ns/meet_the_press-transcripts/t/december-president-barack- obama-tom-brokaw-jon-meacham-doris-kearns-goodwin-david-brooks-chuck- todd/#.VEBXpb5wVQ8 (accessed October 16, 2014).

11. Carole Carlson, "Civil Rights Advocate Hilbert Bradley Had Passion for Justice," *The Post-Tribune*, October 14, 2013. http://posttrib.suntimes.com/news/lake/23150352 -418/civil-rights-advocate-hilbert-bradley-had-passion-for-justice.html #.U1QTnsZijok (accessed October 16, 2014).

12. Ibid.

CHAPTER TWO: THE PUBLIC OPINION

1. 156 Cong. Rec. 29 S973–S1013 (daily ed. March 3, 2010) (statement of Michael G. Bennet). http://www.gpo.gov/fdsys/pkg/CREC-2010-03-03/html/CREC-2010-03 -03-pt1-PgS973-8.htm (accessed October 16, 2014).
2. Tom Coburn, "Sixty Minutes," CBS News, December 21, 2014. http://www.cbsnews .com/news/senator-tom-coburn-60-minutes/ (accessed December 23, 2014).
3. Chris Cillizza, "Congress's Approval Problem in One Chart," *Washington Post,* November 15, 2011. http://www.washingtonpost.com/blogs/the-fix/post/congress -approval-problem-in-one-chart/2011/11/15/gIQAkHmtON_blog.html (accessed December 18, 2014). To watch Bennet's presentation, visit https://www.youtube .com/watch?v=awXdkKgF3Qw (accessed December 18, 2014).
4. Elizabeth Mendes and Joy Wilke, "Americans Confidence in Congress Falls to Lowest on Record," *Gallup Politics,* June 13, 2013. http://www.gallup.com /poll/163052/americans-confidence-congress-falls-lowest-record.aspx (accessed October 1, 2014).
5. Paul Steinhauser, "Congress, Tea Party Hit All-time Low in CNN Polling," *CNN Politics,* CNN, October 1, 2013. http://www.cnn.com/2013/09/30/politics/cnn-poll -congress-approval/ (accessed October 16, 2014).
6. Holly Yan, "Government Shutdown: Get Up to Speed in Twenty Questions," *CNN Politics,* CNN, October 1, 2013. http://www.cnn.com/2013/09/30/politics/government -shutdown-up-to-speed/index.html?c=&page=0 (accessed October 16, 2014).
7. Rebecca Riffkin, "Public Faith in Congress Falls Again, Hits Historic Low," *Gallup Politics,* June 19, 2014. http://www.gallup.com/poll/171710/public-faith-congress -falls-again-hits-historic-low.aspx (accessed October 16, 2014).
8. CNN/ORC Poll, August 2, 2011. http://i2.cdn.turner.com/cnn/2011/images/08/02 /rel12a.pdf (accessed October 16, 2014).
9. "CNN Poll: Two-thirds Say Fiscal Cliff Poses Major Problem," *Political Ticker,* CNN, November 26, 2014. http://politicalticker.blogs.cnn.com/2012/11/26/cnn-poll-two -thirds-say-fiscal-cliff-poses-major-problem/ (accessed October 16, 2014).
10. Jill Lawrence, "Business Tries to Tame Tea Party Conservatives It Helped Elect," *National Journal,* August 19, 2013. http://www.nationaljournal.com/domesticpolicy /business-tries-to-tame-tea-party-conservatives-it-helped-elect-20130819 (accessed October 16, 2014).
11. "Broken Government: A Special Report," *CNN,* Feb. 26, 2010.
12. Peter Beinart, "Why Washington Is Frozen," *Time,* March 1, 2010, 20.
13. James Fallows, "After the Crash: How America Can Rise Again," *The Atlantic,* Jan./Feb. 2010, 48.
14. "Elections Make the Government Pay Attention," ANES. http://electionstudies.org /nesguide/toptable/tab5c_2.htm (accessed October 16, 2014).
15. FairVote, "Turnout of U.S. Eligible Voting Population, 1948–2012." http://www .fairvote.org/voter-turnout#.Uh-OEhbj7ol (accessed October 16, 2014).
16. "2010 November General Election Turnout Rates," United States Election Project. http://www.electproject.org/2010g (accessed October 16, 2014).
17. U.S. Census Bureau, "Table 399. Voting-Age Population—Reported Registration and Voting by Selected Characteristics," *Statistical Abstract of the United States.* http://www. census.gov/compendia/statab/2012/tables/12s0399.pdf (accessed October 16, 2014).
18. United States Election Project.
19. "Who Votes, Who Doesn't, and Why," Pew Research Center for the People and the Press, October 18, 2006. http://www.people-press.org/2006/10/18/who-votes -who-doesnt-and-why/ (accessed October 16, 2014).

20. "2012 Election Turnout Dips below 2008 and 2004 Levels: Number of Eligible Voters Increases by Eight Million, Five Million Fewer Votes Cast," Bipartisan Policy Center, November 8, 2012. http://bipartisanpolicy.org/library/2012-voter -turnout/ (accessed October 16, 2014).
21. Susan Page, "Why 90 Million Americans Won't Vote in October," *USA Today,* August 15, 2012. http://usatoday30.usatoday.com/news/politics/story/2012-08-15 /non-voters-obama-romney/57055184/1 (accessed October 16, 2014).
22. Jeffrey M. Jones, "Disapproval of Congress Linked to Higher Voter Turnout," Gallup, August 25, 2014. http://www.gallup.com/poll/175442/disapproval -congress-linked-higher-voter-turnout.aspx (accessed November 12, 2014).
23. Charlotte Alter, "Voter Turnout in Midterm Election Hits 72-Year Low," *Time,* November 10, 2014. http://time.com/3576090/midterm-elections-turnout-world -war-two/ (accessed November 12, 2014).
24. Elizabeth Mendes, "Americans Down on Congress, OK with Own Representative," Gallup Politics, May 9, 2013. http://www.gallup.com/poll/162362 /americans-down-congress-own-representative.aspx (accessed October 16, 2014).
25. Center on Congress. November 2012 Public Opinion Survey. http://www .centeroncongress.org/november-2012-public-opinion-survey (accessed October 16, 2014).

CHAPTER THREE: THE PROMISES AND THE POWERS
1. Lee H. Hamilton, "How a Former Member Should View the Congress," Center on Congress, April 22, 2004. http://www.centeroncongress.org/how-former -member-should-view-congress (accessed October 16, 2014); U.S. Constitution Article 1. http://www.senate.gov/civics/constitution_item/constitution.htm (accessed November 15, 2014).
2. Letter to C.W.F. Dumas, Sept 19, 1787. The National Historical Publications and Records Commission "Founders Online" Database of the U.S. National Archives. http://founders.archives.gov/documents/Jefferson/01-12-02-0108 (accessed November 17, 2014).
3. Ida A. Brudnick, "Congressional Salaries and Allowances," Congressional Research Service, January 15, 2013. http://library.clerk.house.gov/reference-files/113 _20130124_Salary.pdf (accessed October 16, 2014).
4. Ida A. Brudnick, "Legislative Branch: FY2014 Appropriations," Washington: Congressional Research Service, 2014, 9.
5. Jesse Rifkin, "Members of Congress Haven't Had a Raise in Years," *USA Today,* August 15, 2013. http://www.usatoday.com/story/news/politics/2013/08/15 /congress-pay-salaries/2660545/ (accessed October 16, 2014).
6. Congressional Budget Office, "Monthly Budget Review for September of 2014," October 8, 2014. https://www.cbo.gov/publication/49450 (accessed October 16, 2014).
7. Federal Trade Commission (FTC), "Consumer Information: Warranties." http://www. consumer.ftc.gov/articles/0252-warranties (accessed October 16, 2014).
8. "Ratification of the U.S. Constitution: The 13th State: Rhode Island," James P. Adams Library, Rhode Island College. http://ric.libguides.com/content .php?pid=133950&sid=1240751 (accessed October 16, 2014).
9. Richard B. Morris, *The Forging of the Union: 1781–1789,* (New York: Harper & Row, 1987), 309.
10. James Madison, *Federalist 10,* November 23, 1787. http://thomas.loc.gov/home /histdox/fed_10.html (accessed October 16, 2014).
11. Ibid.
12. Ibid.

13. Lee H. Hamilton, *How Congress Works and Why You Should Care,* (Bloomington: Indiana University Press, 2004), 55. Italics in original.

14. Alexander Hamilton, *Federalist 22,* December 14, 1787. http://thomas.loc.gov/home /histdox/fed_22.html (accessed October 16, 2014).

15. *How Congress Works,* 87.

16. U.S. Senate, "Oath of Office." http://www.senate.gov/artandhistory/history /common/briefing/Oath_Office.htm (accessed October 16, 2014).

17. *How Congress Works,* 6.

18. U.S. Department of State, Office of the Historian. http://history.state.gov /milestones/1776-1783/Articles (accessed October 16, 2014,).

19. *The Constitution of the United States,* http://www.archives.gov/exhibits/charters /constitution_transcript.html (accessed October 20, 2014).

20. Sanford Levinson, *Our Undemocratic Constitution: Where the Constitution Goes Wrong (and How We the People Can Correct It),* (New York: Oxford University Press, 2006), 13. Italics in original.

21. *The Constitution of the United States.*

22. *How Congress Works,* 16.

23. Johnny H. Killian, George A. Costello, and Kenneth R. Thomas, eds., *The Constitution of the United States of America—Analysis and Interpretation* (Washington, D.C.: U.S. Government Printing Office, 2004), 161. http://www.gpo.gov/fdsys/pkg/CDOC -108sdoc17/pdf/CDOC-108sdoc17.pdf (accessed December 18, 2014).

24. *Jacobson v. Massachusetts,* 197 U.S. 11 (1905). http://supreme.justia.com/cases/federal /us/197/11/case.html (accessed December 10, 2014).

25. Killian et al., 163.

26. *United States v. Butler,* 297 U.S. 1 (1936) at 65–66.

27. *Helvering v. Davis,* 301 U.S. 619, 640, 645 (1937).

28. FTC.

29. Elise Stevens Wilson, The Gilder Lehman Institute of American History, "The Battle over the Bank: Hamilton v. Jefferson," http://www.gilderlehrman.org /history-by-era/age-jefferson-and-madison/resources/battle-over-bank- hamilton-v-jefferson (accessed December 11, 2014).

30. *McCulloch v. Maryland,* 17 U.S. 316 (1819).

31. *The Supreme Court,* "The Court and Democracy," PBS. http://www.pbs.org/wnet /supremecourt/democracy/landmark_marbury.html (accessed October 16, 2014).

32. *McCulloch v. Maryland.*

33. L. Elaine Halchin and Frederick M. Kaiser, "Congressional Oversight," Congressional Research Service, October 17, 2012. http://www.fas.org/sgp/crs/misc/97-936.pdf (accessed October 16, 2014).

34. Killian et al., 94, 98–99, 177, 184, 199.

35. Peter H. Schuck, *Why Government Fails So Often: And How It Can Do Better,* (New Jersey: Princeton University Press, 2014), 372.

36. *How Congress Works,* 30.

37. *How Congress Works,* 31, 32.

CHAPTER FOUR: THE PRODUCT

1. Alexander Hamilton, "Other Defects of the Present Confederation," *Federalist 21.* http://thomas.loc.gov/home/histdox/fed_21.html (accessed October 20, 2014).

2. Ramsey Cox, "Manchin Introduces Bill to 'Soften the Landing' If Nation Goes over 'Fiscal Cliff,'" *The Hill,* December 30, 2012. http://thehill.com/blogs/floor-action /senate/274923-manchin-introduces-bill-to-soften-the-fall-from-the-fiscal-cliff (accessed October 20, 2014).

3. "Direction of the Country," Pollingreport.com. http://www.pollingreport.com /right.htm (accessed November 5, 2014).
4. "Most Important Problem," *Gallup.com*. http://www.gallup.com/poll/1675/most -important-problem.aspx (accessed December 17, 2014).
5. Jeffrey M. Jones, "Americans Want Next President to Prioritize Jobs, Corruption," *Gallup*, July 30, 2012. http://www.gallup.com/poll/156347/americans-next -president-prioritize-jobs-corruption.aspx (accessed October 20, 2014).
6. Lydia Saad, "Government Itself Still Cited as Top U.S. Problem," *Gallup*, January 15, 2014. http://www.gallup.com/poll/166844/government-itself-cited-top-problem .aspx (accessed October 20, 2014).
7. Frank Newport and Joy Wilke, "Americans Rank Economy as Top Priority for Government," *Gallup*, January 16, 2014. http://www.gallup.com/poll/166880 /americans-rate-economy-top-priority-government.aspx (accessed October 20, 2014).
8. James Truslow Adams, *The Epic of America*, (Westport: Greenwood Press, 1933), 405; see Columbia University Libraries Archival Collections at http://www.columbia.edu /cu/lweb/archival/collections/ldpd_4078384/ (accessed October 20, 2014).
9. Testimony of John Cox, "The State of the American Dream—Economic Policy and the Future of the Middle Class," Senate Banking Committee, June 5, 2013. http://www. banking.senate.gov/public/index.cfm?FuseAction=Files.View&FileStore _id=d3699006-d874-4730-94c2-5f68f82f7a05 (accessed October 20, 2014).
10. Joe and Harry Gantz, *American Winter*, 2013.
11. John Cox Testimony.
12. Lawrence Mishel and Kar-Fai Gee, "Why Aren't Workers Benefiting from Labour Productivity Growth in the United States?" *International Productivity Monitor* 23, Spring (2012): 31-43. http://www.csls.ca/ipm/23/ipm-23-mishel-gee.pdf (accessed December 9, 2014).
13. Jacob S. Hacker and Paul Pierson, *Winner-Take-All Politics: How Washington Made the Rich Richer—and Turned Its Back on the Middle Class*, (New York: Simon & Schuster, 2011), 22.
14. Hacker and Pierson, *Winner-Take-All Politics*, 36.
15. U.S. Department of Education, "College Affordability and Completion: Ensuring a Pathway to Opportunity." http://www.ed.gov/college (accessed October 20, 2014).
16. Pew Research Center, "Most Parents Expect Their Children to Attend College," February 27, 2012. http://www.pewresearch.org/daily-number/most-parents -expect-their-children-to-attend-college/ (accessed October 15, 2014).
17. Steven Greenhouse, "Our Economic Pickle," *The New York Times*, January 12, 2013, http://www.nytimes.com/2013/01/13/sunday-review/americas-productivity -climbs-but-wages-stagnate.html (accessed October 20, 2014).
18. Sentier Research, "Household Income Down by 4.4 Percent Overall Post Recession— Many Groups with Larger Income Declines." http://www.sentierresearch.com /pressreleases/Sentier_PressRelease_PostRecessionaryHouseholdIncomeChange _June2009toJune2013_08_21_13.pdf (accessed October 20, 2014).
19. Pew Research Center, "Five Years after Market Crash, Economy Seen as 'No More Secure,'" September 12, 2013. http://www.people-press.org/2013/09/12/five-years -after-market-crash-u-s-economy-seen-as-no-more-secure/ (accessed October 20, 2014).
20. Ibid.
21. Ibid.
22. Ibid.

23. Rebecca Riffkin, "In U.S., 67% Dissatisfied with Income, Wealth Distribution," *Gallup*, January 20, 2014. http://www.gallup.com/poll/166904/dissatisfied -income-wealth-distribution.aspx (accessed October 20, 2014).

24. Ibid.

25. NBC News/*Wall Street Journal*, Study #14643, August 2014. http://online.wsj.com/ public/resources/documents/WSJNBCpoll08062014.pdf (accessed October 20, 2014).

26. Emmanuel Saez, "Striking It Richer: The Evolution of Top Incomes in the United States," Econometrics Laboratory of the Institute of Business and Economic Research, Department of Economics, University of California, Berkeley, September 3, 2013. http://elsa.berkeley.edu/~saez/saez-UStopincomes-2012.pdf (accessed October 20, 2014).

27. Pavlina R. Tcherneva, "Reorienting Fiscal Policy: A Bottom-Up Approach," *Journal of Post Keynesian Economics* 37(1), 43–66, as cited by Matthew Yglesias, Vox.com, September 25, 2014. http://www.vox.com/xpress/2014/9/25/6843509/income -distribution-recoveries-pavlina-tcherneva (accessed October 8, 2014).

28. Steve Rattner, "Inequality, Unbelievably, Gets Worse," *The New York Times*, November 16, 2014. http://www.nytimes.com/2014/11/17/opinion/inequality -unbelievably-gets-worse.html?_r=0 (accessed November 20, 2014).

29. Hacker and Pierson, *Winner-Take-All Politics*, 44.

30. Miles Corak, *Chasing the Same Dream, Climbing Different Ladders: Economic Mobility in the United States and Canada*, Economic Mobility Initiative: An Initiative of the Pew Charitable Trusts (January 2009), 7. https://milescorak.files.wordpress. com/2014/07/pew-charitable-trusts-economic-mobility-project-corak- chasing-the-same-dream-climbing-different-ladders-economic-mobility -in-the-united-states-and-canada.pdf (accessed December 11, 2014).

31. Families USA: The Voice for Health Care Consumers, "Federal Poverty Guidelines," February 2014. http://www.familiesusa.org/resources/tools-for-advocates/guides /federal-poverty-guidelines.html (accessed October 20, 2014).

32. U.S. Census, *Income, Poverty, and Health Insurance Coverage in the United States: 2012*, September 2013, 13. http://www.census.gov/prod/2013pubs/p60-245.pdf (accessed December 12, 2014).

33. Valerie Strauss, "Record Number of Homeless Children Enrolled in Public Schools, New Data Show," *The Washington Post*, October 24, 2013. http://www.washingtonpost .com/blogs/answer-sheet/wp/2013/10/24/record-number-of-homeless-children -enrolled-in-public-schools-new-data-show/ (accessed October 20, 2014).

34. Hope Yen, "Exclusive: Signs of Declining Economic Security," *Associated Press*, July 28, 2013. http://bigstory.ap.org/article/exclusive-4-5-us-face-near-poverty-no -work-0 (accessed October 20, 2014).

35. Andrea Ford, Heather Jones, Claire Manibog and Lon Tweeten, "What Makes Health Care So Expensive?" *Time Magazine*, February 20, 2013. http://healthland.time.com /2013/02/20/what-makes-health-care-so-expensive/ (accessed October 20, 2014).

36. U.S. Social Security Administration, "Historical Background and Development of Social Security." http://www.ssa.gov/history/briefhistory3.html (accessed October 20, 2014).

37. U.S. Social Security Administration, "Social Security Basic Facts," April 2, 2014. http://www.ssa.gov/news/press/basicfact.html (accessed November 18, 2014).

38. U.S. Social Security Administration, "A Summary of the 2014 Annual Reports." http://www.ssa.gov/oact/trsum/ (accessed October 20, 2014).

39. U.S. Social Security Administration, "Operations of the Combined OASI and DI Trust Funds, in Current Dollars, 2014 OASDI Trustees Report," http://www.ssa.gov/oact /tr/2014/lr6f8.html (accessed November 15, 2014).

40. U.S. SSA, "Summary of 2014 Annual Reports."

41. Ibid.
42. Gary Kind and Samir S. Soneji, "Social Security: It's Worse Than You Think," *The New York Times,* January 5, 2013. http://www.nytimes.com/2013/01/06/opinion /sunday/social-security-its-worse-than-you-think.html (accessed October 20, 2014).
43. Centers for Medicare and Medicaid Services, "National Health Expenditures 2013 Highlights," http://www.cms.gov/Research-Statistics-Data-and-Systems/Statistics -Trends-and-Reports/NationalHealthExpendData/Downloads/highlights.pdf (accessed October 20, 2014).
44. Centers for Medicare and Medicaid Services, "Medicare Stable but Requires Strengthening," April 23, 2012. http://www.cms.gov/Newsroom /MediaReleaseDatabase/Press-Releases/2012-Press-Releases-Items /2012-04-232.html (accessed December 12, 2014).
45. U.S. SSA, "Summary of the 2014 Annual Reports."
46. *Gallup,* "Medicare," http://www.gallup.com/poll/14596/medicare.aspx (accessed October 20, 2014).
47. Congressional Budget Office, "Monthly Budget Review: Summary for Fiscal Year 2014," November 10, 2014. http://www.cbo.gov/publication/49759 (accessed November 15, 2014).
48. Ibid.
49. Treasury Direct, "The Debt to the Penny and Who Holds It." http://www .treasurydirect.gov/NP/debt/current (accessed January 3, 2015).
50. Maya MacGuineas, "The Budget Gap Is Too Big for Small Solutions," *The New York Times,* January 11, 2013. http://www.nytimes.com/roomfordebate/2012/08/29 /is-the-deficit-urgent-or-a-distraction/the-budget-gap-is-too-big-for-small -solutions (accessed October 20, 2014,).
51. Josh Boak, "Five Things You Need to Know about National Debt," *Business Insider,* April 8, 2013. http://www.businessinsider.com/5-things-must-know-about -national-debt-2013-4 (accessed October 20, 2014).
52. Treasury Direct, "Historical Debt Outstanding, Annual, 2000–2014." http://www .treasurydirect.gov/govt/reports/pd/histdebt/histdebt_histo5.htm (accessed October 20, 2014).
53. Congressional Budget Office, "The 2014 Long-Term Budget Outlook," July 15, 2014. http://www.cbo.gov/publication/45471 (accessed November 15, 2014).
54. Suzy Khimm, "Congress Is Addicted to Stop-gap Budgets," *The Washington Post,* September 30, 2011. http://www.washingtonpost.com/blogs/wonkblog/post /congress-is-addicted-to-stop-gap-budgets/2011/09/30/gIQAXa1dAL_blog.html (accessed November 15, 2014).
55. John Noseworthy, *Meet The Press,* NBC News, January 15, 2013. http://www.nbcnews .com/id/53985963/ns/meet_the_press-transcripts/t/january-janet-napolitano -gene-sperling-jim-cramer-delos-cosgrove-john-noseworthy-steve-schmidt -donna-edwards-judy-woodruff-chuck-todd/#.VHEQ6b5wXEg (accessed November 21, 2014).
56. Ibid.
57. Toby Cosgrove, *Meet The Press,* NBC News, January 15, 2013.
58. Cathy Schoen, Robin Osborn, David Squires, and Michelle M. Doty, "Access, Affordability, and Insurance Complexity Are Often Worse in the United States Compared to Ten Other Countries," The Commonwealth Fund, November 13, 2013. http://www.commonwealthfund.org/Publications/In-the-Literature/2013/Nov /Access-Affordability-and-Insurance.aspx (accessed October 20, 2014).
59. Ibid.

60. James Hamblin, "How Is U.S. Health Care Bad?" *The Atlantic,* September 4, 2013. http://www.theatlantic.com/health/archive/2013/09/how-is-us-health-care-bad-chart/279334/ (accessed October 20, 2014).

61. Ford, Jones, Manibog, and Tweeten, "What Makes Health Care So Expensive"; Elizabeth Rosenthal, "The $2.7 Trillion Medical Bill," *The New York Times,* June 1, 2013. http://www.nytimes.com/2013/06/02/health/colonoscopies-explain-why-us-leads-the-world-in-health-expenditures.html (accessed October 20, 2014).

62. "The Cost of Cancer Drugs," *60 Minutes,* CBS News, October 15, 2014. http://www.cbsnews.com/news/the-cost-of-cancer-drugs/ (accessed October 20, 2014).

63. Hacker and Pierson, *Winner-Take-All Politics,* 31.

64. The National Academies, "Americans Have Worse Health Than People in Other High-Income Countries; Health Disadvantage is Pervasive Across Age and Socio-Economic Groups," January 9, 2013. http://www8.nationalacademies.org/onpinews/newsitem.aspx?RecordID=13497 (accessed October 20, 2014).

65. Ibid.

66. Toby Cosgrove, *Meet The Press.*

67. Charles Roehrig, "U.S. Health Spending as a Share of GDP: Where Are We Headed?," Altarum Institute, July 16, 2013. http://altarum.org/health-policy-blog/u-s-health-spending-as-a-share-of-gdp-where-are-we-headed (accessed October 20, 2014).

68. John Noseworthy, *Meet The Press.*

69. Alexander Hamilton, "Concerning the Militia," *Federalist 29,* January 10, 1788, http://thomas.loc.gov/home/histdox/fed_29.html (accessed October 20, 2014).

70. *The Constitution of the United States,* http://www.archives.gov/exhibits/charters/constitution_transcript.html (accessed October 20, 2014).

71. Kay King, *Congress and National Security,* (New York: Council on Foreign Relations, 2012), 6,7.

72. Robert Higgs, "U.S. Military Spending in the Cold War Era: Opportunity Costs, Foreign Crises, and Domestic Constraints," Table 1, November 29, 1988. http://www.cato.org/pubs/pas/pa114.html (accessed December 18, 2014).

73. Robert David Johnson, "Congress and U.S. Foreign Policy Before 9/11," in *Congress and the Politics of National Security,* ed. David P. Auerswald and Colton C. Campbell, (Cambridge: University Press, 2012), 37; James Lindsay, "Congress and Defense Policy, 1961 to 1986," *Armed Forces & Society,* Vol. 13, No. 4 (Fall 1987).

74. Mark J. Oleszek and Walter J. Oleszek, "Institutional Challenges Confronting Congress after 9/11: Partisan Polarization and Effective Oversight," in *Congress and the Politics of National Security,* ed. David P. Auerswald and Colton C. Campbell, (Cambridge: University Press, 2012), 65; Frank Oliveri, "Gates' Budget Cuts Make GOP Squirm," *CQ Weekly,* January 10, 2011, 123.

75. Josh Sweigart, Congress Pushes for Weapons Pentagon Didn't Want," *Dayton Daily News,* August 18, 2012. http://www.daytondailynews.com/news/news/congress-pushes-for-weapons-pentagon-didnt-want/nRC7w/ (accessed October 20, 2014).

76. Mark Koba, "U.S. Military Spending Dwarfs Rest of World," *NBC News,* February 24, 2014. http://www.nbcnews.com/storyline/military-spending-cuts/u-s-military-spending-dwarfs-rest-world-n37461 (accessed October 20, 2014).

77. Josh Gerstein, "Obama: 'History Will Judge' Iraq War," *Politico,* December 12, 2011. http://www.politico.com/news/stories/1211/70303.html (accessed October 20, 2014); John King, "Bush 43: "History Will Ultimately Judge... I'm a Content Man,'" *CNN Politics,* April 25, 2013. http://www.cnn.com/2013/04/24/politics/bush-interview-king/index.html (accessed October 20, 2014); Thomas C. Frohlich and Alexander Kent, "Countries spending the most on the military," *USA Today,*

July 12, 2014. http://www.usatoday.com/story/money/business/2014/07/12
/countries-spending-most-on-military/12491639/ (accessed November 25, 2014).

78. Iraq Coalition Casualty Count, www.icasualties.org (accessed October 20, 2014).

79. Linda J. Bilmes, *The Financial Legacy of Iraq and Afghanistan: How Wartime Spending Decisions Will Constrain Future National Security Budgets,* (Cambridge: Harvard, 2013), 1. https://research.hks.harvard.edu/publications/workingpapers/citation .aspx?PubId=8956 (accessed October 20, 2014).

80. "Libya and the Iraq Syndrome," *The Economist,* May 3, 2011. http://www.economist .com/node/18284079 (accessed October 20, 2014).

81. Andrew Dugan, "On Tenth Anniversary, 53 Percent in U.S. See Iraq War as Mistake," *Gallup,* March 13, 2013. http://www.gallup.com/poll/161399/10th -anniversary-iraq-war-mistake.aspx

82. Kay King, *Congress and National Security.* (accessed October 20, 2014).

83. Thomas H. Kean and Lee H. Hamilton, *The 9/11 Commission Report: Final Report of the National Commission on Terrorist Attacks Upon the United States,* (New York: W.W. Norton, 2003), 107.

84. Alexander Bolton, "9/11 Panel Rips Congress on ISIS," *The Hill,* September 9, 2014. http://thehill.com/homenews/news/217054-9-11-commission-rips-congress-on -isis (accessed October 20, 2014).

85. Philip Ewing, "9/11 Panel Chairs Slam Hill 'Dysfunction,'" *Politico,* July 22, 2014. http://www.politico.com/story/2014/07/911-panel-tom-kean-lee-hamilton -109189.html (accessed October 20, 2014).

86. Loch K. Johnson, "Congress and Intelligence," in *Congress and the Politics of National Security,* ed. David P. Auerswald and Colton C. Campbell, (Cambridge: University Press, 2012), 129.

87. John McCain, *Meet the Press,* NBC News, November 21, 2004. http://www.nbcnews .com/id/6531547/ns/meet_the_press/t/transcript-nov/#.UyBu5P3t_ok (accessed October 20, 2014).

88. Mark J. Oleszek and Walter J. Oleszek, "Institutional Challenges Confronting Congress after 9/11: Partisan Polarization and Effective Oversight," in *Congress and the Politics of National Security,* ed. David P. Auerswald and Colton C. Campbell, (Cambridge: University Press, 2012), 62; *Workshop on Congressional Oversight and Investigations,* H. Doc. No. 96–117 (Washington: GPO, 1979), 3.

89. Lee H. Hamilton, *Strengthening Congress,* (Bloomington: Indiana University Press, 2009), 30.

90. L. Elaine Halchin and Frederick M. Kaiser, *Congressional Oversight and Intelligence: Current Structure and Alternatives,* (Congressional Research Service, 2012). http://www. fas.org/sgp/crs/intel/RL32525.pdf (accessed October 20, 2014).

91. NSA Memo, "Communications Intelligence Activities," October 24, 1952. "http:// www.nsa.gov/public_info/_files/truman/truman_memo.pdf (accessed October 20, 2014).

92. James Comey, "FBI Director on Threat of ISIS, Cybercrime," *60 Minutes, CBS News,* October 5, 2014. http://www.cbsnews.com/news/fbi-director-james-comey-on -privacy-and-surveillance/ (accessed December 14, 2014).

93. Ibid.

94. Carl Bernstein and Bob Woodward, "FBI Finds Nixon Aides Sabotaged Democrats," *The Washington Post,* October 10, 1972. http://www.washingtonpost.com/politics /fbi-finds-nixon-aides-sabotaged-democrats/2012/06/06/gJQAoHIJJV_story.html (accessed October 20, 2014).

95. Loch K. Johnson, "Congress and Intelligence," 127.

96. James Risen and Eric Lichtblau, "Bush Lets U.S. Spy on Callers Without Courts," *The New York Times,* December 16, 2005. http://www.nytimes.com/2005/12/16 /politics/16program.html?pagewanted=all (accessed October 20, 2014).

97. Louis Fisher, "National Security Surveillance," in *Congress and the Politics of National Security,* ed. David P. Auerswald and Colton C. Campbell, (Cambridge: University Press, 2012), 213.

98. Bernard Horowitz and Harvey Rishikof, "Enemy Combatant Detainees," in *Congress and the Politics of National Security,* ed. David P. Auerswald and Colton C. Campbell, (Cambridge: University Press, 2012), 180.

99. Dana Priest and William M. Arkin, "Top Secret America: National Security Inc.", *The Washington Post,* July 20, 2010. http://projects.washingtonpost.com/top-secret -america/articles/national-security-inc/ (accessed October 20, 2014).

100. Dana Priest and William M. Arkin, "Top Secret America: A Hidden World, Growing Beyond Control," *The Washington Post,* July 19, 2010. http://projects.washingtonpost .com/top-secret-america/articles/a-hidden-world-growing-beyond-control/ (accessed October 20, 2014).

101. Dana Priest and William M. Arkin, "Top Secret America: National Security Inc."

102. Barton Gellman and Laura Poitras, "U.S., British Intelligence Mining Data from Nine U.S. Internet Companies in Broad Secret Program," *The Washington Post,* June 7, 2013. http://www.washingtonpost.com/investigations/us-intelligence-mining -data-from-nine-us-internet-companies-in-broad-secret-program/2013/06/06 /3a0c0da8-cebf-11e2-8845-d970ccb04497_story.html (accessed October 20, 2014).

103. John E. Sununu, "Surveillance State," *The Boston Globe,* July 22, 2013. http://www. bostonglobe.com/opinion/2013/07/21/edward-snowden-case-reveals-lax-oversight -congress-surveillance-state/Ldav8iIMta7XERVUbE1K5K/story.html (accessed October 20, 2014).

104. U.S. Department of Veterans Affairs, "The Origin of the VA Motto: Lincoln's Second Inaugural Address." http://www.va.gov/opa/publications/celebrate/vamotto.pdf (accessed October 20, 2014).

105. U.S. Department of Veterans Affairs, "America's Wars." http://www.va.gov/opa /publications/factsheets/fs_americas_wars.pdf (accessed October 20, 2014).

106. U.S. Department of Veterans Affairs, "Office of Public and Intergovernmental Affairs: New to VA." http://www.va.gov/opa/newtova.asp (accessed September 20, 2014).

107. The U.S. Department of Housing and Urban Development, "The 2013 Annual Homeless Assessment Report to Congress," https://www.onecpd.info/resources /documents/AHAR-2013-Part1.pdf (accessed November 30, 2014).

108. Jake Miller, "GOP Senator: Veterans' Disability Claims Backlog a 'National Embarrassment,'" *CBS News,* February 8, 2014. http://www.cbsnews.com/news /gop-sen-veterans-disability-claims-backlog-a-national-embarrassment/ (accessed October 20, 2014).

109. Michael M. Phillips and Ben Kesling, "Congress is Getting Tougher on the VA," *The Wall Street Journal,* February 10, 2014. http://online.wsj.com/news/articles /SB10001424052702304450904579371382766771434 (accessed September 20, 2014).

110. Paul Rieckhoff, "Congress Lets Down Military Members and Vets," CNN, March 4, 2014. http://www.cnn.com/2014/03/04/opinion/rieckhoff-congress-military-vets/ (accessed October 20, 2014).

111. Ibid.

112. U.S. Department of Veterans Affairs, "VA 2013 Budget Fast Facts." http://www .amvets.org/pdfs/legislative_pdfs/2012/Fy2013_Fast_Facts_VAs_Budget _Highlights.pdf (accessed October 20, 2014).

113. Jon Campbell, "Twenty-two Veterans Commit Suicide Daily," August 12, 2014. http://www.tbbf.org/22-veterans-commit-suicide-daily/08-2014 (accessed December 13, 2014).
114. Interaction, "What Our Leaders Think About Foreign Assistance." http://www .interaction.org/what-thought-leaders-think-about-us-foreign-assistance (accessed October 20, 2014).
115. Ibid.
116. Susan Epstein, "Foreign Aid Oversight Challenges for Congress," in *Congress and the Politics of National Security,* ed. David P. Auerswald and Colton C. Campbell, (Cambridge: University Press, 2012), 154–155.
117. The Ely and Edythe Broad Foundation, "The Education Crisis: Statistics," http:// broadeducation.org/about/crisis_stats.html (accessed October 20, 2014)
118. Ibid.
119. Ibid.
120. Ibid.
121. The Conference Board, Partnership for 21st Century Skills, Corporate Voice for Working Families, and the Society for Human Resource Management, "Are They Really Ready To Work?" http://www.p21.org/storage/documents/key_findings _joint.pdf (accessed October 20, 2014).
122. Ibid.
123. Jason Amos, "Dropouts, Diplomas, and Dollars: U.S. High Schools and the Nation's Economy," Alliance for Excellent Education, September 17, 2008. http://all4ed.org /press/alliance-for-excellent-education-urges-congressional-candidates-to -invest-in-nations-economic-future-by-addressing-dropout-crisis/ (accessed October 20, 2014).
124. Clive R. Belfield, Henry M. Levin, Rachel Rosen, "The Economic Value of Opportunity Youth," January 2012. http://knowledgecenter.completionbydesign.org/sites /default/files/307%20Belfield%202012.pdf(accessed October 20, 2014).
125. Ibid.
126. Joel I. Klein, Condoleezza Rice, *U.S. Education Reform and National Security,* (New York: Council on Foreign Relations, 2012), xiii.
127. Ibid.
128. Mission Readiness: Military Leaders for Kids, "Ready, Willing and Unable to Serve," 2009. http://cdn.missionreadiness.org/NATEE1109.pdf (accessed October 20, 2014).
129. National Science Board, "Science and Engineering Indicators 2010," 10–01 (Arlington, VA: National Science Foundation, 2010), table 2–36. http://www.nsf .gov/statistics/seind10/pdf/seind1-.pdf (accessed April 16, 2014).
130. Interview with Timothy McKnight, chief information security officer of Northrop Grumman Corporation, in "The Stand: Cybersecurity," 1105 Government Information Group, http://washingtontechnology.com/pages/custom/stand-cybersecurity .aspx (accessed March 7, 2012).
131. Jeb Bush and Clint Bolick, *Immigration Wars,* (New York: Simon & Schuster, 2013), 70.
132. Peter Muller, "Immigration Problems Only Get Worse," *National Journal,* December 18, 2013. http://www.nationaljournal.com/next-america/workforce/immigration -problems-only-get-worse-20131218 (accessed October 20, 2014).
133. President George W. Bush's Council of Economic Advisers, "Immigration's Economic Impact," June 20, 2007. http://georgewbush-whitehouse.archives.gov /cea/cea_immigration_062007.html (accessed October 20, 2014).
134. Julia Preston, "Number of Illegal Immigrants in U.S. May Be on Rise Again, Estimates Say," *The New York Times,* September 13, 2013. http://www.nytimes.com /2013/09/24/us/immigrant-population-shows-signs-of-growth-estimates-show .html?_r=0&pagewanted=print (accessed October 20, 2014).

135. Frank Newport and Joy Wilke, "Immigration Reform Proposals Garner Broad Support in U.S.," *Gallup*, June 19, 2013. http://www.gallup.com/poll/163169 /immigration-reform-proposals-garner-broad-support.aspx (accessed October 20, 2014).

136. President Barack Obama's National Economic Council, "The Economic Benefits of Fixing Our Broken Immigration System," July, 2013. http://www.whitehouse.gov /sites/default/files/docs/report.pdf (accessed October 20, 2014).

137. Tim Kane and Kirk A. Johnson, "The Real Problem with Immigration... and the Real Solution," The Heritage Foundation, March 1, 2006. http://www.heritage .org/research/reports/2006/03/the-real-problem-with-immigration-and-the -real-solution (accessed January 3, 2015).

138. Immigration Policy Center, "From Anecdotes to Evidence: Setting the Record Straight on Immigrants and Crime," July 25, 2013. http://www.immigrationpolicy .org/just-facts/anecdotes-evidence-setting-record-straight-immigrants-and -crime-0 (accessed October 20, 2014).

139. U.S. Senate. Hearing 108-925. "The 9/11 Commission and Recommendations for the Future of Federal Law Enforcement and Border Security," August 19, 2004. http:// www.gpo.gov/fdsys/pkg/CHRG-108shrg96459/html/CHRG-108shrg96459.htm (accessed October 20, 2014).

140. Michael Ciric, "Illegal Immigration Costs U.S. Taxpayers $113 Billion Annually," *Chicago Now,* April 12, 2011. http://www.chicagonow.com/chicago-political -commentary/2011/04/illegal-immigration-costs-u-s-taxpayers-113-billion -annually/#.VHNnRL5wXEh (accessed November 24, 2014).

141. Center for Disease Control and Prevention, "Firearm Deaths and Death Rates." http://www.cdc.gov/nchs/pressroom/FIREARM_DEATHS_AND_DEATH_RATES .pdf (accessed October 20, 2014).

142. Sripal Bangalore and Franz H. Messerli, "Gun Ownership and Firearm-related Deaths," *The American Journal of Medicine,* 126 (2013): 873–876. http://www.amjmed .com/article/S0002-9343(13)00444-0/fulltext (accessed October 20, 2014).

143. Ibid.

144. *The Constitution of the United States,* Legal Information Institute, Cornell University Law School. http://www.law.cornell.edu/constitution/preamble (accessed October 20, 2014).

145. Paul C. Light, "Government's Greatest Achievements of the Past Half Century," The Brookings Institute, December 2000. http://www.brookings.edu/research /papers/2000/12/11governance-light (accessed October 20, 2014)

146. American Society of Civil Engineers, "2013 Report Card for America's Infrastructure," http://www.infrastructurereportcard.org/a/#p/overview/executive-summary (accessed October 20, 2014).

147. Ibid.

148. U.S. Social Security Administration, http://www.ssa.gov/history/tally65.html (accessed October 20, 2014).

CHAPTER FIVE: THE PROBLEM

1. David Walker, *AC360 Later,* CNN, October 14, 2014.

2. Upton Sinclair, *I, Candidate for Governor: And How I Got Licked,* 1935. Reprinted by University of California Press, 1994.

3. Mark Ribowsky, *The Last Cowboy: A Life of Tom Landry,* (New York: Liveright Publishing Corporation, 2013), 235.

4. Mickey Edwards, *The Parties Versus the People : How to Turn Republicans and Democrats into Americans,* (New Haven: Yale University Press, 2012), 7–8.

5. Lee H. Hamilton, "Why Isn't Congress More Efficient?" The Center on Congress, October 1, 2007. http://congress.indiana.edu/why-isnt-congress-more-efficient (accessed October 20, 2014).

6. Nolan McCarty, "Hate Our Polarized Politics? Why You Can't Blame Gerrymandering," *The Washington Post,* October 26, 2012. http://www.washingtonpost.com /opinions/hate-our-polarized-politics-why-you-cant-blame-gerrymandering /2012/10/26/c2794552-1d80-11e2-9cd5-b55c38388962_story.html (accessed October 20, 2014).

7. Keith Poole, Nolan McCarty, and Howard Rosenthal, "An Update on Political Polarization through the 112th Congress," January 16, 2013. http://voteview.com /blog/?p=726 (accessed September 5, 2014); Poole, McCarty, and Rosenthal, "Polarization is Real (and Asymmetric)," May 16, 2012. http://voteview.com/blog/?p=494 (accessed September 5, 2014).

8. Warren Beatty and Jeremy Pikser, *Bulworth.* Excerpt published by Jim Kirwan at "Bulworth in 2013," April 6, 2013, at http://www.rense.com/general95/bulworth .html (accessed December 15, 2014).

9. Jack Abramoff, "Jack Abramoff: The Lobbyists' Playbook," *60 Minutes,* CBS News, November 7, 2011. http://www.cbsnews.com/8301-18560_162-57459874 /jack-abramoff-the-lobbyists-playbook/?pageNum=4 (accessed October 20, 2014).

10. Jeffrey H. Birnbaum, "Cost of Congressional Campaigns Skyrockets," *The Washington Post,* October 3, 2014. http://www.washingtonpost.com/wp-dyn/articles /A2935-2004Oct2.html (accessed October 20, 2014).

11. Paul Steinhauser and Robert Yoon, "Cost to Win Congressional Election Skyrockets," *CNN Politics,* July 11, 2013. http://www.cnn.com/2013/07/11/politics/congress-election -costs/ (accessed October 20, 2014).

12. Jay Costa, "What's the Cost of a Seat in Congress?" Maplight, March 10, 2013. http:// maplight.org/content/73190 (accessed November 8, 2014).

13. Ron Facheux, "The Only Way to Fix Campaign-Finance Regulation Is to Destroy It," *The Atlantic,* July 30, 2012. http://www.theatlantic.com/politics/archive/2012/07/the -only-way-to-fix-campaign-finance-regulation-is-to-destroy-it/260426/ (accessed October 20, 2014).

14. Federal Election Commission, "FEC Summarizes Campaign Activity of the 2011–2012 Election Cycle," April 19, 2013. http://www.fec.gov/press/press2013 /20130419_2012-24m-Summary.shtml (accessed October 20, 2014).

15. Campaign Finance Institute, "PAC Contributions to Congressional Candidates 1978–2012 (in $ millions)," http://www.cfinst.org/pdf/vital/VitalStats_t10.pdf (accessed October 20, 2014)

16. Lee Fang, "Where Have All the Lobbyists Gone?" *The Nation,* February 19, 2014. http://www.thenation.com/article/178460/shadow-lobbying-complex (accessed October 20, 2014).

17. Lawrence Lessig, *Republic Lost,* (New York: Hachette Book Group, 2011), 235; Brian Kelleher Richter, Krislert Samphantharak, and Jeffrey H. Timmons, "Lobbying and Taxes," *American Journal of Political Science* 53 (2009): 893, 907.

18. Jeffrey H. Birnbaum, "Hill a Stepping Stone to K Street for Some," *The Washington Post,* July 27, 2005. http://www.washingtonpost.com/wp-dyn/content/article/2005 /07/26/AR2005072601562.html (accessed October 20, 2014).

19. Lawrence Lessig, *Republic Lost,* 123.

20. Eliza Newlin Carney, "Money Dominates Committee and Leadership Races—Rules of the Game," Roll Call, November 19, 2014. http://blogs.rollcall.com/beltway -insiders/money-dominates-committee-and-leadership-races-rules-of-the-game/ (accessed November 20, 2014).

21. Mickey Edwards, *The Parties Versus the People*, 93–94.
22. Ryan Grim and Sabrina Siddiqui, "Call Time For Congress Shows How Fundraising Dominates," *Huffington Post*, January 8, 2013. http://www.huffingtonpost.com /2013/01/08/call-time-congressional-fundraising_n_2427291.html (accessed October 20, 2014).
23. James Madison, "The Alleged Tendency of the New Plan to Elevate the Few at the Expense of the Many Considered in Connection with Representation," *Federalist* 57, February 19, 1788. http://thomas.loc.gov/home/histdox/fed_57.html (accessed October 20, 2014).
24. Lawrence Lessig, *Republic Lost*, 235.
25. John Hofmeister, AC360, CNN, January 22, 2014. http://edition.cnn.com /TRANSCRIPTS/1401/22/acd.01.html (accessed October 20, 2014).
26. Martin Gilens, "Inequality and Democratic Responsiveness: Who Gets What They Want from Government?" Princeton University, August, 2004. http://www .princeton.edu/~mgilens/idr.pdf (accessed October 20, 2014).
27. Ibid.
28. Martin Gilens and Benjamin I. Page, "Testing Theories of American Politics: Elites, Interest Groups, and Average Citizens," *Perspectives on American Politics* 12, no. 3 (September 2014): 564–581. http://www.princeton.edu/~mgilens/Gilens%20home page%20materials/Gilens%20and%20Page/Gilens%20and%20Page%202014-Testing %20Theories%203-7-14.pdf (accessed October 20, 2014).
29. John Dunbar, "The 'Citizens United' Decision and Why It Matters," The Center for Public Integrity, October 18, 2012. http://www.publicintegrity.org/2012/10/18/11527 /citizens-united-decision-and-why-it-matters (accessed November 29, 2014).
30. *Citizens United v. Federal Election Commission* 558 U.S. 310 (2010). http://www .supremecourt.gov/opinions/09pdf/08-205.pdf (accessed December 15, 2014).
31. Washington Post–ABC News Poll, *The Washington Post*, February 8, 2010. http:// www.washingtonpost.com/wp-srv/politics/polls/postpoll_021010 .html?sid=ST2010021702073 (accessed October 20, 2014).
32. Norman J. Ornstein, *Dan Rather Reports*, HDNET, July 5, 2012. http://www.google .com/url?sa=t&rct=j&q=&esrc=s&source=web&cd=4&ved=0CDQQFjAD&url =http%3A%2F%2Fwww.axs.tv%2Fui%2Finc%2Fshow_transcripts.php%3Fami %3DA8958%26t%3DDan_Rather_Reports%26en%3D720&ei=4SZ7VP --LNTGsQSA24LwBA&usg=AFQjCNHboMwNM3t4IoXiN9IgahXtnSDX7w&sig2 =NGdBYLnWREpkc__Qxf-iuw&bvm=bv.80642063,d.cWc (accessed November 30, 2014).
33. Russ Choma, "Money Won on Tuesday, but Rules of the Game Changed," Center for Responsive Politics, November 5, 2014. http://www.opensecrets.org/news/2014/11 /money-won-on-tuesday-but-rules-of-the-game-changed/ (accessed November 8, 2014); Center for Responsive Politics, "CRP 2014 Pre-Election Press Kit," http:// tinyurl.com/l725bg8 (accessed November 21, 2014).
34. Nicholas Confessore, "Secret Money Fueling a Flood of Political Ads," *The New York Times*, October 10, 2014. http://www.nytimes.com/2014/10/11/us/politics /ads-paid-for-by-secret-money-flood-the-midterm-elections.html?_r=0 (accessed November 8, 2014).
35. Mark Warren, "Help, We're In A Living Hell And Don't Know How To Get Out," *Esquire*, October 15, 2014. http://www.esquire.com/blogs/politics/congress -living-hell-1114 (accessed October 20, 2014).
36. Andrew Romano, "*House of Cards* Season Two Review: Even More Bingeworthy Than the First," *The Daily Beast*, February 14, 2014. http://www.thedailybeast.com /articles/2014/02/14/house-of-cards-season-two-review-even-more-bingeworthy -than-the-first.html (accessed November 30, 2014).

37. Bill Bishop, *The Big Sort: Why the Clustering of Like-Minded America is Tearing Us Apart*, (New York: Houghton Mifflin Company, 2008), 5.

38. *Reynolds v. Sims*, 377 U.S. 533, 84 S. Ct. 1362, 12 L. Ed. 2d 506 (1964.)

39. Rob Richie and Andrew Spencer, "The Right Choice for Elections: How Choice Voting Will End Gerrymandering and Expand Minority Voting Rights, from City Councils to Congress," *University of Richmond Law Review* 47, no. 3 (March 28, 2013): 966–967. http://lawreview.richmond.edu/wp/wp-content/uploads/2013/03/Richie-473.pdf (accessed October 20, 2014).

40. Mickey Edwards, *The Parties Versus The People*, 42.

41. Barry C. Burden, Michael S. Kang, and Bradley Jones, "Sore Loser Laws and Congressional Polarization," *Legislative Studies Quarterly* 39, Issue 3, (August 2014): 299–325. http://papers.ssrn.com/sol3/papers.cfm?abstract_id=2354168 (accessed October 20, 2014).

42. David Wasserman, "Introducing the 2014 Cook Political Report Partisan Voter Index," *The Cook Political Report*, April 4, 2013. http://cookpolitical.com/story/5604 (accessed October 20, 2014).

43. Ibid.

44. Ibid.

45. FairVote, "The Dominance of Partisanship in Winner-Take-All Elections," November 2013. http://www.fairvote.org/assets/PowerofPartisanship2014.pdf (accessed October 20, 2014).

46. Rob Richie and Andrew Spencer, "Choice Voting," 972.

47. John G. Matsusaka, *For the Many or the Few*, (Chicago: University of Chicago Press, 2004), 3, ix.

48. FairVote, "Winner-Take-All Elections."

49. Keith Poole, Nolan McCarty, and Howard Rosenthal, "Political Polarization."

50. FairVote, "The Polarization Crisis in Congress: The Decline of Crossover Representatives and Crossover Voting in the U.S. House," November 2013. http://www.fairvote.org/assets/CrossoverVoting2014.pdf (accessed October 20, 2014).

51. Ibid.

52. George Washington, Farewell Address, 1796. http://www.ourdocuments.gov/doc.php?doc=15&page=transcript (accessed December 15, 2014).

53. Phil Foglia, "Nineteenth Century Mass. Gov. Elbridge Gerry Knew All About Gerrymandering of Political Districts—He Invented It!" *New York Daily News*, March 14, 2012. http://www.nydailynews.com/new-york/19th-century-mass-gov-elbridge-gerry-knew-gerrymandering-political-districts-invented-article-1.1038276 (accessed October 20, 2014).

54. Elmer Cummings Griffith, *The Rise and Development of the Gerrymander*, (Chicago: Scott, Foresman and Company, 1907), 73.

55. "The Gerrymander. A New Species of Monster." *Boston Gazette*, March 26, 1812. See http://www.loc.gov/exhibits/treasures/trr113.html (accessed June 18, 2014).

56. Lois Beckett, "Is Partisan Gerrymandering Unconstitutional?" *Propublica*, November 7, 2011. http://www.propublica.org/article/is-partisan-gerrymandering-unconstitutional (accessed October 20, 2014).

57. Election Results, 2010, *The New York Times*, November 2010, http://elections.nytimes.com/2010/results/illinois (accessed October 20, 2014); 2012 Illinois House Results, *Politico*, November 19, 2012. http://www.politico.com/2012-election/results/house/illinois/ (accessed October 20, 2014); Peter Bell, "Modern Gerrymanders: 10 Most Contorted Congressional Districts—MAPS," *National Journal*, March 30, 2012. http://www.nationaljournal.com/hotline/redistricting/modern-gerrymanders-10-most-contorted-congressional-districts-maps-20120330 (accessed October 20, 2014).

58. GIS shapefile data created by the United States Department of the Interior. http:// commons.wikimedia.org/wiki/File:Illinois_US_Congressional_District_4 _(since_2013).tif and http://commons.wikimedia.org/wiki/File:Illinois_US _Congressional_District_7_(since_2013).tif (accessed December 20, 2014).

59. Jennifer Steinhauer, "Weighing the Effect of an Exit of Centrists," *The New York Times,* October 8, 2012. http://www.nytimes.com/2012/10/09/us/politics/pool -of-moderates-in-congress-is-shrinking.html?pagewanted=all&_r=0 (accessed October 20, 2014).

60. U.S. Representative Scott Rigell, *The Rachel Maddow Show,* MSNBC, October 1, 2013. http://votesmart.org/public-statement/815773/msnbc-the-rachel-maddow-show -transcript-government-shutdown-and-aca (accessed October 20, 2014,).

61. Judd Gregg, *Charlie Rose Show,* October 8, 2013.

62. Charles E. Schumer, "End Partisan Primaries—Save America," *The New York Times,* July 21, 2014. http://www.nytimes.com/2014/07/22/opinion/charles-schumer-adopt -the-open-primary.html (accessed October 20, 2014); George Mitchell, AC360, CNN December 4, 2012.

63. John Paul Stevens, *Six Amendments: How and Why We Should Change the Constitution,* (Little, Brown and Company, 2014), Kindle Edition p. 55.

64. Nolan McCarty, Keith T. Poole, Howard Rosenthal, "Does Gerrymandering Cause Polarization?" *American Journal of Political Science* 53, Issue 3, (July 2009): 666–680. http://voteview.com/ajps_393.pdf (accessed October 20, 2014).

65. Nolan McCarty, "Hate Our Polarized Politics? Why You Can't Blame Gerrymander-ing," *The Washington Post,* October 26, 2012. http://www.washingtonpost.com /opinions/hate-our-polarized-politics-why-you-cant-blame-gerrymandering /2012/10/26/c2794552-1d80-11e2-9cd5-b55c38388962_story.html (accessed October 20, 2014).

66. "2012 REDMAP Summary Report," The Redistricting Majority Project, January 4, 2013. http://www.redistrictingmajorityproject.com (accessed October 20, 2014).

67. Olga Pierce, Jeff Larson, and Lois Beckett, "The Hidden Hands in Redistricting: Corporations and Other Powerful Interests," *ProPublica,* September 23, 2011. http:// www.propublica.org/article/hidden-hands-in-redistricting-corporations-special -interests (accessed October 20, 2014).

68. Sundeep Iyer, "Redistricting and Congressional Control Following the 2012 Election," Brennan Center for Justice, November 28, 2012. http://www.brennancenter .org/analysis/redistricting-and-congressional-control-following-2012-election (accessed October 20, 2014).

69. Sam Wang, "Gerrymanders, Part 1: Busting the Both-Sides-Do-It Myth," Princeton Election Consortium, December 30, 2012. http://election.princeton.edu/2012/12/30 /gerrymanders-part-1-busting-the-both-sides-do-it-myth/ (accessed October 20, 2014).

70. Ibid.

71. *LULAC v. Perry,* 548 U.S. 468 & n.9 (2006.)

72. Nicholas Stephanopoulos and Eric McGhee, "Partisan Gerrymandering and the Efficiency Gap (June 21, 2014). *University of Chicago Law Review,* 2015, Forthcoming. Available at SSRN: http://papers.ssrn.com/sol3/papers.cfm?abstract_id=2457468, 14.

73. Ibid.

74. Ibid.

75. Madison Debates, June 12, 1787, The Avalon Project, Yale Law School. http://avalon .law.yale.edu/18th_century/debates_612.asp (accessed October 20, 2014).

76. Madison Debates; James L. Sundquist, *Constitutional Reform and Effective Government,* (Washington, D.C.: The Brookings Institution, 1992), 154–155.

77. Alan Renwich, "House of Lords Reform," *Political Studies Association*, p. 24. https://www.psa.ac.uk/sites/default/files/HL%20Reform%20briefing%20paper.pdf (accessed October 20, 2014).

78. James L. Sundquist, *Constitutional Reform*, 145; Harry McPherson, Jr., *A Political Education* (Austin: University of Texas Press, 1972).

79. James L. Sundquist, *Constitutional Reform*, 144; David Stockman Speech to the United States Chamber of Commerce, Washington, D.C., *The New York Times*, May 24, 1984.

80. Steven V. Roberts, "Republicans Cultivating Swing Votes," *The New York Times*, September 17, 1984.

81. James L. Sundquist, *Constitutional Reform*, 152; Paul C. Light, *The President's Agenda: Domestic Policy Choice from Kennedy to Carter*, (Baltimore: John Hopkins University Press, 1983), 36–38.

82. Lyndon B. Johnson, "Special Message to the Congress Proposing Constitutional Amendments Relating to Terms for House Members and the Electoral College System," The American Presidency Project. http://www.presidency.ucsb.edu/ws/?pid=27582 (accessed December 15, 2014); Dwight D. Eisenhower, *The White House Years: Mandate for Change 1953–1956* (New York: Doubleday, 1963).

83. Robert G. Kaiser, *Act of Congress: How America's Essential Institution Works, and How It Doesn't*, (New York: Alfred A. Knopf, 2013), 374.

84. Ryan Grim and Sabrina Siddiqui, "Call Time For Congress Shows How Fundraising Dominates Bleak Work Life," *Huffington Post*, January 8, 2013. http://www.huffingtonpost.com/2013/01/08/call-time-congressional-fundraising_n_2427291.html (accessed October 20, 2014).

85. Lyndon B. Johnson, "State of the Union, 1966," *American Experience*, PBS, http://www.pbs.org/wgbh/americanexperience/features/primary-resources/lbj-union66/ (accessed October 20, 2014).

86. Tom Harkin, "Sen. Harkin On Filibuster: 'We've Got To Change These Rules,'" *All Things Considered*, NPR, November 20, 2013. http://www.npr.org/templates/story/story.php?storyId=246409440 (accessed October 20, 2014).

87. Congressional Research Service, "Origin of the Senate: The Great Compromise," 2002. http://www.senate.gov/legislative/common/briefing/Senate_legislative_process.htm (accessed October 20, 2014).

88. Sarah A. Binder, "The History of the Filibuster," Brookings Institute, April 22, 2010. http://www.brookings.edu/research/testimony/2010/04/22-filibuster-binder (accessed October 20, 2014).

89. Senate Historical Office, "Senate History, Powers and Procedures: Filibuster and Cloture." http://www.senate.gov/artandhistory/history/common/briefing/Filibuster_Cloture.htm (accessed October 20, 2014).

90. Walter J. Oleszek, "Super-Majority Votes in the Senate," Congressional Research Service, April 12, 2010. http://www.senate.gov/CRSReports/crs-publish.cfm?pid=%26*2%3C4Q%3CG2%0A (accessed October 20, 2014).

91. Alexander Hamilton, "The Same Subject Continued: Other Defects of the Present Confederation," *Federalist 22*, December 14, 1787. http://thomas.loc.gov/home/histdox/fed_22.html (accessed October 20, 2014).

92. James Madison, "Objection That the Number of Members Will Not Be Augmented as the Progress of Population Demands Considered," *Federalist 58*, February 20, 1788. http://thomas.loc.gov/home/histdox/fed_58.html (accessed October 20, 2014).

93. Sanford Levinson, *Our Undemocratic Constitution*, (New York: Oxford University Press, Inc., 2006), 51–52.

94. Senate Historical Office, "Landmark Legislation: The Civil Rights Act of 1964." http://www.senate.gov/artandhistory/history/common/generic/CivilRightsAct1964.htm (accessed October 16, 2014).

95. Senate Historical Office, "Senate Action on Cloture Motions." http://www.senate.gov /pagelayout/reference/cloture_motions/clotureCounts.htm (accessed October 20, 2014).

96. Data from U.S. Senate, "Virtual Reference Desk, Cloture: Senate Action on Cloture Motions." http://www.senate.gov/pagelayout/reference/cloture_motions /clotureCounts.htm (accessed December 15, 2014).

97. Senate Historical Office, "Senate Action on Cloture Motions." http://www.senate .gov/pagelayout/reference/cloture_motions/clotureCounts.htm (accessed October 20, 2014).

98. Ezra Klein, "The History of the Filibuster, in One Graph," *The Washington Post,* May 15, 2012. http://www.washingtonpost.com/blogs/wonkblog/post/the-history-of -the-filibuster-in-one-graph/2012/05/15/gIQAVHfoRU_blog.html (accessed October 20, 2014).

99. Ibid.

CHAPTER SIX: THE POLICYMAKING

1. Olympia Snowe, *Fighting For Common Ground: How We Can Fix the Stalemate In Congress,* (New York: Weinstein Books, 2013), 3.

2. Patrick O'Connor, "WSJ/NBC News Poll: Obama's Approval Rating Hits New Low," *The Wall Street Journal,* March 12, 2014. http://m.us.wsj.com/articles/SB100014240527 02304250204579433533118580224?mg=reno64-wsj (accessed October 20, 2014).

3. Financial Crisis Inquiry Commission, *The Financial Crisis Inquiry Report,* January, 2011, (Washington D.C.: U.S. Government Printing Office, 2011), xviii–xxiv. http://www .gpo.gov/fdsys/pkg/GPO-FCIC/pdf/GPO-FCIC.pdf (accessed October 20, 2014).

4. Ibid., xxiv.

5. Ibid., xxiv, xxvii.

6. Ibid.

7. Henry Paulson, *Charlie Rose Show,* PBS, September 9, 2013.

8. Eduardo Porter, "Business Losing Clout in a GOP Moving Right," *The New York Times,* September 3, 2013. http://www.nytimes.com/2013/09/04/business/economy /business-losing-clout-in-a-gop-moving-right.html?pagewanted=all&_r=0 &pagewanted=print (accessed October 20, 2014).

9. Eric Lipton, "For Freshmen in the House, Seats of Plenty," *The New York Times,* August 10, 2013. http://www.nytimes.com/2013/08/11/us/politics/for-freshmen-in -the-house-seats-of-plenty.html (accessed October 20, 2014).

10. Financial Crisis Inquiry Commission, *Financial Crisis Inquiry Report,* xviii.

11. Adam Garfinkle, *Broken: American Political Dysfunction and What to Do About It,* (The American Interest EBooks, 2013). Kindle edition, Kindle locations 756–761. Garfinkle cites Nathaniel Popper, "In Search of a Market Speed Limit," *The New York Times,* September 9, 2012, p. B1, and Popper, "As U.S. Discusses Limits on High-Speed Trading, Other Nations Act," *The New York Times,* September 27, 2012.

12. Donna Borak, "Fed's Hoenig on the Failure to End Bailouts, and Why Another Crisis is Coming," *American Banker,* June 6, 2011. http://www.americanbanker.com /issues/176_108/hoenig-basel-tbtf-future-1038513-1.html (accessed December 10, 2014).

13. Kathleen Day, "Analysis: Credit Agencies Remain Unaccountable," *USA Today,* May 21, 2014. http://www.usatoday.com/story/money/business/2014/05/19/credit -rating-agencies-in-limbo/9290143/ (accessed October 20, 2014).

14. Tim Devaney, "Fed Rules Would End 'Too Big to Fail,' Lawmakers Say," *The Hill,* December 9, 2014. http://thehill.com/regulation/226528-fed-rules-would-end-too -big-to-fail-lawmakers-say (accessed December 10, 2014).

15. Steven Mufson and Tom Hamburger, "Jamie Dimon Himself Called to Urge Support for the Derivatives Rule in the Spending Bill," *The Washington Post,* December 11, 2014. http://www.washingtonpost.com/blogs/wonkblog/wp/2014/12/11/the-item -that-is-blowing-up-the-budget-deal/ (accessed December 12, 2014).

16. Lawrence Lessig, *Republic Lost: How Money Corrupts Congress—and a Plan to Stop It,* (New York: Hachette Books, 2011), 147; Simon Johnson and James Kwak, *13 Bankers: The Wall Street Takeover and the Next Financial Meltdown,* (New York: Vintage Books, 2010), 191–192.

17. Lawrence Lessig, *Republic Lost,* 44–47; Brian M. Riedl, "How Farm Subsidies Harm Taxpayers, Consumers and Farmers, Too," Backgrounder # 2043 Heritage Foundation (June 20, 2007), 8.

18. Lawrence Lessig, *Republic Lost,* 46; James Bovard, "Archer Daniels Midland: A Case Study in Corporate Welfare," Cato Policy Analysis, Cato Institute (1995), 1.

19. Lauren Servin, "How Our Government Incentivizes the Overproduction of Junk Food," Roosevelt Institute. http://www.rooseveltinstitute.org/new-roosevelt /how-our-government-incentivizes-overproduction-junk-food (accessed December 29, 2014); see also Union of Concerned Scientists, "Unhealthy Food Policy: How Government Subsidizes the Wrong Foods—and Creates Obstacles for Healthy Farms." http://www.ucsusa.org/our-work/food-agriculture/our-failing-food -system/unhealthy-food-policy#.VJCA6FfF_fA (accessed December 29, 2014).

20. "Farm Bill Legislation Fails to Embrace Reform," *Chicago Tribune,* February 8, 2014. http://cqrcengage.com/mncorn/app/document/1603471;jsessionid =34eI21agZxcoBWSqaYDoFpN1.undefined (accessed October 20, 2014).

21. Ibid.

22. Evan Bayh, *Fox News Sunday,* Fox News Channel, October 13, 2013. http://www .foxnews.com/transcript/2013/10/13/prospects-compromise-washington-rep -jim-jordan-tea-party-demands-deal/ (accessed November 17, 2014).

23. "Top Industries," Center for Responsive Politics. http://www.opensecrets.org/lobby /top.php?indexType=i (accessed October 20, 2014).

24. Lawrence Lessig, *Republic Lost,* (New York: Hachette Book Group, 2011), 181; Ethan Rome, "Big Pharma Pockets $711 Billion in Profits by Robbins Seniors, Taxpayers," *Huffington Post,* April 8, 2013. http://www.huffingtonpost.com/ethan-rome/big -pharma-pockets-711-bi_b_3034525.html (accessed October 20, 2014).

25. Paul Blumenthal, "The Legacy of Billy Tauzin: The White House-PhRMA Deal," Sunlight Foundation, February 12, 2010. https://sunlightfoundation.com /blog/2010/02/12/the-legacy-of-billy-tauzin-the-white-house-phrma-deal/ (accessed October 20, 2014).

26. Lee Drutman and Alexander Furnas, "How Revolving Door Lobbyists Are Taking Over K Street," Sunlight Foundation, January 22, 2014. http://sunlightfoundation.com /blog/2014/01/22/revolving-door-lobbyists-take-over-k-street/ (accessed October 20, 2014).

27. Adam Garfinkle, *Broken: American Political Dysfunction and What to Do About It,* (The American Interest EBooks, 2013). Kindle edition.

28. Paul Blumenthal, "Legacy of Billy Tauzin."

29. Alex Wayne and Drew Armstrong, "Tauzin's $11.6 Million Made Him Highest-Paid Health-Law Lobbyist," *Bloomberg,* November 28, 2011. http://www.bloomberg.com /news/2011-11-29/tauzin-s-11-6-million-made-him-highest-paid-health-law -lobbyist.html (accessed October 20, 2014).

30. Sanford Levinson, *Framed: America's 51 Constitutions and the Crisis of Governance,* (Oxford University Press, 2012). Kindle Edition.

31. Joe Manchin, *State of the Union,* CNN, May 4, 2014. http://transcripts.cnn.com /TRANSCRIPTS/1405/04/sotu.02.html (accessed October 20, 2014).

32. Jacob S. Hacker and Paul Pierson, *Winner-Take-All Politics: How Washington Made the Rich Richer—and Turned Its Back on the Middle Class,* (New York: Simon & Schuster, 2010), 53.
33. Ibid.
34. Eric Lipton, "Fight Over Minimum Wage Illustrates Web of Industry Ties," *The New York Times,* February 9, 2014. http://www.nytimes.com/2014/02/10/us/politics/fight-over-minimum-wage-illustrates-web-of-industry-ties.html?_r=0 (accessed October 20, 2014),
35. Ibid.
36. Olympia Snowe, *Fighting For Common Ground,* 265.
37. "Five Years after Market Crash, U.S. Economy Seen as 'No More Secure,'" Pew Research Center, September 12, 2013. http://www.people-press.org/2013/09/12/five-years-after-market-crash-u-s-economy-seen-as-no-more-secure/ (accessed October 20, 2014).
38. Scott Bronstein and Tom Cohen, VA Controversy: White House Aide Heading to Phoenix, *CNN Politics,* May 23, 2014. http://www.cnn.com/2014/05/20/politics/va-waiting-lists/ (accessed November 17, 2014).
39. American National Election Studies, "Is the Government Run for the Benefit of All 1964–2008," The ANES Guide to Public Opinion and Electoral Behavior. http://electionstudies.org/nesguide/toptable/tab5a_2.htm (accessed October 20, 2014).
40. President Bill Clinton, Clinton Lecture Series, Georgetown University, C-SPAN, April 30, 2014.
41. "The Dominance of Partisanship in Winner-Take-All Elections," FairVote, November, 2013. http://www.fairvote.org/assets/PowerofPartisanship2014.pdf (accessed October 20, 2014).
42. Nancy Cordes, "Why Isn't Congress Stressed Over Its Low Approval Rating?" *CBS News,* August 1, 2013. http://www.cbsnews.com/news/why-isnt-congress-stressed-over-its-low-approval-rating/ (accessed October 20, 2014).
43. Evan Osnos, "Embrace the Irony," *The New Yorker,* October 13, 2014. http://www.newyorker.com/magazine/2014/10/13/embrace-irony (accessed October 20, 2014).
44. Chuck Todd, Mark Murray and Domenico Montanaro, "Shutdown: Both Parties Avoid Action Until After Elections," *NBC News,* February 21, 2014. http://www.nbcnews.com/politics/first-read/shutdown-both-parties-avoid-action-until-after-elections-n35366 (accessed October 20, 2014).
45. Ibid.
46. David Brooks, *Meet The Press,* NBC News, February 23, 2014. http://www.nbcnews.com/meet-the-press/meet-press-transcript-feb-23-2014-n36721 (accessed October 20, 2014).
47. Cristina Marcos and Peter Schroeder, "House Approves Border Package," *The Hill,* August 1, 2014. http://thehill.com/homenews/house/214139-house-approves-border-funding (accessed October 20, 2014); Kristina Peterson, "House Passes $694 Million Border Bill," *The Wall Street Journal,* August 1, 2014. http://online.wsj.com/articles/house-republicans-confident-revised-migrant-bill-will-pass-friday-1406915143 (accessed October 20, 2014).
48. Kevin Bohn, "Key GOP Senator: Shame on Us As Republicans' for Immigration Bill Failure." *CNN Politics,* November 23, 2014. http://www.cnn.com/2014/11/23/politics/lindsey-graham-republicans-immigration/ (accessed November 24, 2014).
49. "Budget Compromise Championed by Just 38 Lawmakers," *USA Today,* April 3, 2012. http://usatoday30.usatoday.com/news/opinion/editorials/story/2012-04-03/budget-compromise-38-382/53981554/1 (accessed October 20, 2014).

50. David M. Walker, "Truth and Transformation," National Press Club, September 17, 2013. http://deficitranger.com/wp-content/themes/walker/images/091713 %20Truth%20and%20Transformation%20FINAL.pdf (accessed October 20, 2014).

51. James L. Sundquist, *Constitutional Reform and Effective Government,* (Washington, D.C.: The Brookings Institution, 1992, 154–155); Congressional Record, daily ed., March 26, 1992, p. S4306.

52. Mickey Edwards, *The Parties Versus the People,* (New Haven: Yale University Press, 2012), 168.

53. Bonnie Kavoussi, "Debt Ceiling Debate Cost Taxpayers $18.9 Billion, Study Finds," *Huffington Post,* November 28, 2012. http://www.huffingtonpost.com/2012/11/28 /debt-ceiling-cost-taxpayers_n_2204553.html (accessed December 17, 2014); Sarah Jones, "As Sequester Looms, the GOP Already Cost Us $18.9 Billion With Their Debt Ceiling Fiasco," February 10, 2013. http://www.politicususa.com/2013/02/10 /sequester-looms-gop-cost-18-9-billion-debt-ceiling-fiasco.html (accessed October 20, 2014); for updated details visit Bipartisan Policy Center, "Debt Limit Analysis," at http://bipartisanpolicy.org/library/staff-paper/debt-limit (accessed December 17, 2014).

54. As quoted in "Downgrading Our Politics," *The Economist,* August 6, 2011. http:// www.economist.com/blogs/freeexchange/2011/08/sps-credit-rating-cut (accessed October 20, 2014).

55. Mike Dorning, John Detrixhe, and Ian Katz, "Downgrade Anniversary Shows Investors Gained Buying U.S.," *Bloomberg,* July 16, 2012. http://www.bloomberg.com /news/2012-07-16/downgrade-anniversary-shows-investors-gained-buying -u-s-.html (accessed October 20, 2014).

56. Annie Lowry, "Budget Battles Keep Agencies Guessing," *The New York Times,* September 3, 2013. http://www.nytimes.com/2013/09/04/business/budget -breakdown-keeps-federal-agencies-guessing.html (accessed October 20, 2014).

57. Jonathan Martin, "G.O.P. Governors Warn Party Members in Congress Not to Shut Government," *The New York Times,* August 4, 2013. http://www.nytimes .com/2013/08/05/us/politics/gop-governors-warn-party-members-in-congress -not-to-shut-government.html (accessed October 20, 2014,).

58. David Wasserman, *The Rachel Maddow Show,* MSNBC, September 30, 2013, accessed October 20, 2014, http://video.msnbc.msn.com/rachel-maddow/53151884/#53151884

59. Mickey Edwards, *The Parties Versus the People,* 25–26.

60. Jonathan Weisman and Robert Pear, "Partisan Gridlock Thwarts Effort to Alter Health Care Law," *The New York Times,* May 26, 2013. http://www.nytimes.com /2013/05/27/us/politics/polarized-congress-thwarts-changes-to-health-care-law .html?pagewanted=all (accessed October 20, 2014).

61. Liz Hamel, Jamie Firth and MollyAnn Brodie, Kaiser Health Tracking Poll, March 2014," The Henry J. Kaiser Family Foundation, March 26, 2014. http://kff.org /health-reform/poll-finding/kaiser-health-tracking-poll-march-2014/ (accessed October 20, 2014).

62. Dennis Ross, "GOP Rep. Admits It's 'Absurd' to Rail on Obamacare without an Alternative," TPM, April 17, 2014. http://talkingpointsmemo.com/livewire /dennis-ross-no-alternative-absurd (accessed October 20, 2014).

63. Jonathan Weisman, Mark Landler and Jeremy W. Peters, *The New York Times,* September 8, 2014. http://www.nytimes.com/2014/09/09/us/as-obama-makes-case-con-gress-is-divided-on-campaign-against-militants.html?_r=0 (accessed October 20, 2014).

64. The MaddowBlog, "Congress Ducks Duty as U.S. Military Continues War on ISIS," *The Rachel Maddow Show,* MSNBC, September 19, 2014. http://www.msnbc.com /rachel-maddow-show/congress-ducks-duty-us-military-continues-war-isis (accessed October 20, 2014).

65. "Leadership Control Is Faulted for House Ills," Wilson Center. http://www .wilsoncenter.org/publication/leadership-control-faulted-for-house-ills (accessed October 20, 2014).

66. *Esquire Politics Blog.* "Thirteen Things That Define the New American Center," *Esquire,* October 5, 2013, http://www.esquire.com/blogs/politics/new-american-center-1113 (accessed October 20, 2014).

67. Norm Ornstein, "Why We Can't Stop Talking about Filibusters," *National Journal,* May 14, 2014. http://www.nationaljournal.com/washington-inside-out/why-we -can-t-stop-talking-about-filibusters-20140514 (accessed October 20, 2014); Paul Kane, "Senate Deadlocked on Energy Bill, Ending Chances of a Vote on Keystone," *The Washington Post,* May 12, 2014. http://www.washingtonpost.com/politics/senate -expected-to-deadlock-on-energy-bill-ending-chances-of-a-vote-on-keystone /2014/05/12/9018fd76-d9fb-11e3-8009-71de85b9c527_story.html (accessed October 20, 2014,).

68. Jessica Rettig, "Senate Republicans block DISCLOSE ACT," *U.S. News and World Report,* July 27, 2010. http://www.usnews.com/news/articles/2010/07/27/senate-republi-cans -block-disclose-act (accessed October 20, 2014); Rosalind S. Helderman, "DISCLOSE Act, new donor transparency law, blocked in Senate," *The Washington Post,* July 16, 2012. http://www.washingtonpost.com/blogs/2chambers/post/disclose-act-new -donor-transparency-law-blocked-in-senate/2012/07/16/gJQAbm7WpW_blog.html (accessed October 20, 2014).

69. Thomas E. Mann and Norman J. Ornstein, *It's Even Worse Than It Looks,* (New York: Basic Books, 2012), 98, 100.

70. Ibid.

71. "Alabama Sen. Shelby Releases Holds on Obama Nominees," *FoxNews.com,* February 9, 2010. http://www.foxnews.com/politics/2010/02/09/alabama-sen-shelby-releases -holds-obama-nominees/ (accessed October 20, 2014).

72. James Madison, "Objection That The Number of Members Will Not Be Augmented as the Progress of Population Demands Considered," *Federalist 58,* February 20, 1788. http://thomas.loc.gov/home/histdox/fed_58.html (accessed October 20, 2014).

73. Stephen Spaulding, "The New Nullification at Work," Common Cause, May, 2014. http://www.commoncause.org/research-reports/the-new-nullification.pdf (ac-cessed October 20, 2014); Executive Calendar, May 5, 2006 (109th Cong.); Executive Calendar, May 5, 1998 (105th Cong.)

74. Ibid.

75. Thomas E. Mann and Norman J. Ornstein, *It's Even Worse,* 97, 99, 100.

76. Michael C. Crittenden, "FDIC Chief Warns: Vacancies Pose Risk to Financial System," *The Wall Street Journal,* May 24, 2011. http://blogs.wsj.com/washwire/2011 /05/24/fdic-chief-warns-vacancies-pose-risk-to-financial-system/ (accessed October 20, 2014).

77. Stephen Spaulding, "The New Nullification at Work"; Stephen Spaulding, "Two Shameful Milestones," Common Cause, March 31, 2014. http://www.commoncause .org/democracy-wire/two-shameful-milestones.html (accessed October 20, 2014).

78. *District of Columbia v. Heller,* 554 U.S. 570 (2008).

79. Carolyn McCarthy, *Meet the Press,* NBC News, July 22, 2012. http://www.nationaljournal .com/whitehouse/gun-control-debate-heats-up-but-there-s-little-consensus -20120722 (accessed October 20, 2014).

80. Molly Moorhead, "A Summary of the Manchin-Toomey Gun Proposal," Politifact.com., April 30, 2013. http://www.politifact.com/truth-o-meter/article/2013/apr/30/summary-manchin-toomey-gun-proposal/ (accessed October 20, 2014).
81. Scott Clement, "Everything You Need to Know about Americans' Views on Guns—in Seven Easy Steps," *The Washington Post*, January 22, 2013. http://www.washingtonpost.com/blogs/the-fix/wp/2013/01/22/everything-you-need-to-know-about-americans-views-on-guns-in-7-easy-steps/ (accessed October 20, 2014).
82. Michael Cooper and Dalia Sussman, "Massacre at School Sways Public in Way Earlier Shootings Didn't," *The New York Times*, January 17, 2013. http://www.nytimes.com/2013/01/18/us/poll-shows-school-shooting-sways-views-on-guns.html (accessed October 20, 2014).
83. Emily Swanson, "Background Checks Beat Apple Pie, Baseball, Kittens In Americans' Hearts: Poll," *Huffington Post*, April 13, 2013. http://www.huffingtonpost.com/2013/04/13/background-checks-poll_n_3070954.html (accessed October 20, 2014,).
84. "Broad Support for Renewed Background Checks Bill, Skepticism about Its Chances," Pew Research Center, May 23, 2013. http://www.people-press.org/2013/05/23/broad-support-for-renewed-background-checks-bill-skepticism-about-its-chances/ (accessed October 20, 2014,).
85. Alan Berlow and Gordon Witkin, "Gun Lobby's Money and Power Still Holds Sway Over Congress," The Center for Public Integrity," May 1, 2013. http://www.publicintegrity.org/2013/05/01/12591/gun-lobbys-money-and-power-still-holds-sway-over-congress (accessed October 20, 2014).
86. Ibid.
87. Doris Kearns Goodwin, *Meet the Press*, NBC News, April 21, 2013. http://www.nbcnews.com/id/51611247/ns/meet_the_press-transcripts/t/april-deval-patrick-mike-rogers-dick-durbin-pete-williams-michael-leiter-michael-chertoff-tom-brokaw-doris-kearns-goodwin-peggy-noonan-jeffrey-goldberg/#.U302cV5wWqo (accessed October 20, 2014).
88. Joe Manchin, *State of the Union*, CNN, May 4, 2014. http://transcripts.cnn.com/TRANSCRIPTS/1405/04/sotu.02.html (accessed October 20, 2014).
89. Steve Schmidt, *Real Time With Bill Maher*, HBO, January 19, 2014.
90. Ezra Klein and Evan Soltas, "Wonkbook: 10 facts that explain the filibuster fight," *The Washington Post*, July 16, 2013. http://www.washingtonpost.com/blogs/wonkblog/wp/2013/07/16/wonkbook-10-facts-that-explain-the-filibuster-fight/ (accessed October 20, 2014,).
91. Letter to C.W.F. Dumas, September 19, 1787. The National Historical Publications and Records Commission "Founders Online" Database of the U.S. National Archives. http://founders.archives.gov/documents/Jefferson/01-12-02-0108 (accessed November 17, 2014).
92. Real Clear Politics, "Direction of Country (Poll Comparison)," November 23, 2014. http://www.realclearpolitics.com/epolls/other/direction_of_country-902.html#pollsa (accessed November 29, 2014).

CHAPTER SEVEN: THE PLATFORM

1. http://www.brainyquote.com/quotes/quotes/j/jiddukrish389324.html. (accessed December 17, 2014).
2. Leon Panetta, *Charlie Rose Show*, September 13, 2013.

3. Christopher Klein, "How Teddy Roosevelt Saved Football," History.com, September 6, 2012. http://www.history.com/news/how-teddy-roosevelt-saved-football (accessed October 20, 2014); Katie Zezima, "How Teddy Roosevelt Helped Save Football," *The Washington Post,* http://www.washingtonpost.com/blogs/the-fix/wp/2014/05/29/teddy-roosevelt-helped-save-football-with-a-white-house-meeting-in-1905/ (accessed October 20, 2014).
4. Ibid.
5. "Hears Football Men: Coaches in Conference with President Roosevelt, Would Put an End to Brutality." *The Washington Post,* October 10, 1905. Image reproduced by Matt DeLong, *Washington Post.* https://www.documentcloud.org/documents/1175005-144576144-1.html (accessed December 17, 2014).
6. Sanford Levinson, *Framed: America's 51 Constitutions and the Crisis of Governance* (Oxford University Press, 2012). Kindle edition. Kindle locations 348–353.
7. Andrea Seabrook, "House GOP Freshmen Face Pressure to Raise Cash," NPR, October 26, 2011, http://www.npr.org/2011/10/26/141729470/pressure-is-on-for-house-gop-freshman-to-fundraise (accessed October 20, 2014).
8. James L. Sundquist, *Constitutional Reform and Effective Government,* (Washington, D.C.: The Brookings Institution, 1992), 157.
9. Ernesto Dal Bó and Martín A. Rossi, "Term Length and the Effort of Politicians," *Review of Economic Studies* 78 no. 4 (2011): 1237–1263. Quotation here from abstract available at http://restud.oxfordjournals.org/content/78/4/1237.abstract (accessed December 18, 2014).
10. Ibid.
11. James L. Sundquist, *Constitutional Reform,* 157.
12. William A. Galston, "Four-Year House Terms Would End the Gridlock," *The Wall Street Journal,* February 25, 2014. http://online.wsj.com/news/articles/SB10001424052702303426304579404913687708426 (accessed October 20, 2014).
13. Lyndon B. Johnson, "Special Message to the Congress Proposing Constitutional Amendments Relating to Terms for House Members and the Electoral College System," The American Presidency Project, http://www.presidency.ucsb.edu/ws/?pid=27582 (accessed October 20, 2014).
14. "The Effects of a Term Limited Legislature in Michigan," Michigan Society of Association Executives, February, 2012, vi. http://michiganbusinessnetwork.com/docs/MI_Term_Limit_Effects.pdf (accessed October 20, 2014).
15. Ibid., vii.
16. Michael Lewis, "California and Bust," *Vanity Fair,* November, 2011, http://www.vanityfair.com/business/features/2011/11/michael-lewis-201111 (accessed October 20, 2014).
17. Charlie Mahtesian, "2012 Reelection Rate: 90 Percent," *Politico,* December 13, 2012, http://www.politico.com/blogs/charlie-mahtesian/2012/12/reelection-rate-percent-151898.html (accessed October 20, 2014).
18. Lyndon B. Johnson, "Special Message to the Congress."
19. "The Constitutional Amendment Process," National Archives, http://www.archives.gov/federal-register/constitution/ (accessed October 20, 2014).
20. Cristina Marcos, "Should House Members Serve Four-Year Terms," *The Hill,* April 16, 2014. https://thehill.com/blogs/floor-action/house/203660-should-house-members-serve-four-year-terms (accessed October 20, 2014).
21. Mickey Edwards, "Perverse Primaries," *The New York Times,* January 23, 2014. http://www.nytimes.com/2014/01/24/opinion/perverse-primaries.html?_r=0 (accessed October 20, 2014).
22. *Davis v. Bandemer,* 478 U.S. 109 (1986), 118–43.

23. John Paul Stevens, *Six Amendments: How and Why We Should Change the Constitution*, (Little, Brown and Company, 2014), 54–55. Kindle edition.

24. Bernard Grofman and Gary King. 2008. "The Future of Partisan Symmetry as a Judicial Test for Partisan Gerrymandering after *LULAC v. Perry*," *Election Law Journal* 6, no. 1: 2–35. http://gking.harvard.edu/files/abs/jp-abs.shtml (accessed December 17, 2014).

25. Nicholas Stephanopoulos and Eric McGhee, "Partisan Gerrymandering and the Efficiency Gap (June 21, 2014). *University of Chicago Law Review*, 2015, Forthcoming. Abstract at SSRN: http://papers.ssrn.com/sol3/papers.cfm?abstract_id=2457468, 14 (accessed September 3, 2014); LULAC v. Perry, 548 U.S. 399 (2006).

26. Ibid., 41, citing *Vieth v. Jubelirer*, 541 U.S. 267 (2004).

27. Mickey Edwards, *The Parties Versus the People*, (New Haven: Yale University Press, 2012), 67; Justin Levitt, "Who Draws the Lines?", All About Redistricting, http://redistricting.lls.edu/who.php#independent (accessed October 20, 2014).

28. Tracy Jan, "Iowa Keeping Partisanship Off the Map," *The Boston Globe*, December 8, 2013, http://www.bostonglobe.com/news/politics/2013/12/08/iowa-redistricting-takes-partisanship-out-mapmaking/efehCnJvNtLMIAFSQ8gp7I/story.html (accessed October 20, 2014).

29. Justin Levitt, "Essay: Weighing the Potential of Citizen Redistricting," 44 *Loyola Los Angeles Law Review* 513 (2011), 542–543. http://digitalcommons.lmu.edu/llr/vol44/iss2/4 (accessed December 17, 2014).

30. Mickey Edwards, interviewed by author, September 9, 2014.

31. Drew Spencer, "The Top Two System in Action—Washington State 2008–2012," FairVote, July 2013. http://www.fairvote.org/assets/WashingtonReport.pdf (accessed October 20, 2014).

32. Rob Richie, "Applying Ranked Choice Voting to Congressional Elections," FairVote. http://www.fairvote.org/assets/Applying-Ranked-Choice-Voting-to-Congressional-Elections.pdf (accessed October 20, 2014).

33. Ibid.

34. "Top Four Elections," FairVote. http://www.fairvote.org/reforms/instant-runoff-voting/top-four-elections/ (accessed October 20, 2014).

35. Ibid.

36. "Our View: Brennan, ranked-choice voting both winners," *Portland Press Herald*, November 12, 2011, http://www.pressherald.com/2011/11/12/brennan-ranked-choice-voting-both-winners_2011-11-12/ (accessed October 20, 2014).

37. Betsy Hodges, https://www.youtube.com/watch?v=vSGEcCqoR7o (accessed October 20, 2014).

38. Karl Kurtz, "Changes in Legislatures Using Multimember Districts after Redistricting," National Conference of State Legislatures, September 11, 2012, http://ncsl.typepad.com/the_thicket/2012/09/a-slight-decline-in-legislatures-using-multimember-districts-after-redistricting.html (accessed November 12, 2014).

39. *Reynolds v. Sims*, 377 U.S. 533 (1964).

40. FairVote, "Choice Voting: How Choice Voting Works," http://www.fairvote.org/reforms/fair-representation-voting/choice-voting/ (accessed December 29, 2014).

41. Rob Richie and Andrew Spencer, "The Right Choice for Elections: How Choice Voting Will End Gerrymandering and Expand Minority Voting Rights, from City Councils to Congress," *University of Richmond Law Review* 47, no. 3 (March 28, 2013): 966–967. http://lawreview.richmond.edu/wp/wp-content/uploads/2013/03/Richie-473.pdf (accessed October 20, 2014).

42. FairVote, "Extending the Sphere of Representation: The Impact of Fair Representation Voting on the Ideological Spectrum of Congress," November 2013. http://www.fairvote.org/assets/Fair-Voting-Impact-2014.pdf (accessed October 20, 2014).

43. Rob Richie and Steven Hill, "The Case for Proportional Representation," *Boston Review,* February/March, 1998. http://bostonreview.net/archives/BR23.1/richie.html (accessed October 20, 2014).

44. Rob Richie, "Applying Ranked Choice Voting to Congressional Elections: The Case for RCV with the Top Four Primary and Multi-Member Districts," FairVote. http://www.fairvote.org/assets/Applying-Ranked-Choice-Voting-to-Congressional -Elections.pdf (accessed October 20, 2014).

45. Rob Richie, interviewed by author, September 2, 2014.

46. Reihan Salam, "The Biggest Problem in American Politics," *Slate.com,* September 11, 2014. http://www.slate.com/articles/news_and_politics/politics/2014/09/abolish _the_single_member_district_that_s_the_best_way_to_ensure_truly_fair.2.html (accessed October 20, 2014).

47. FairVote, "Monopoly Politics 2014 and the Fair Voting Solution," November 6, 2013. http://www.fairvote.org/research-and-analysis/congressional-elections/monopoly -politics-2014-and-the-fair-voting-solution/ (accessed December 19, 2014).

48. Walter Scott, "Marmion," (Edinburgh: Archibald Constable and Company, and London: William Miller and John Murray, 1808). http://www.walterscott.lib.ed.ac.uk /works/poetry/marmion.html (accessed December 19, 2014).

49. Emmet Bondurant, interviewed by author, August 19, 2014.

50. *Common Cause v. Biden,* 909 F. Supp. 2d 9, Dist. Court, Dist. of Columbia, 2012.

51. Common Cause et al., "Complaint for a Declaratory Judgment," *Common Cause v. Biden,* 2012. Full text of complaint at: https://docs.google.com/document/d/1Icfvg-oCYp3e-tJOFWo7NnoxP1mQ3KXurjc2rFG36viA/edit?pli=1 p. 24 (accessed August 27, 2014.)

52. Ibid., 43–44.

53. Ibid., 44–45

54. Ibid., 45, citing *United States v. Ballin,* 144 U.S. 1, 6 (1892).

55. Sanford Levinson, *Our Undemocratic Constitution,* (New York: Oxford University Press, Inc., 2006), 51–52.

56. Common Cause, *Common Cause v. Biden,* 49–50. Text of the complaint reads "83 percent"; however, it's actually even more severe than that. Bondurant has since updated that figure to 89 percent. Interview with author.

57. Ibid., 51–52.

58. Emmet Bondurant, interviewed by author, August 23, 2014.

59. Russell Berman, "The Filibuster Survives a Supreme Court Challenge," *The Atlantic,* November 3, 2014. http://www.theatlantic.com/politics/archive/2014/11/the-filibuster -survives-a-supreme-court-challenge/382312/ (accessed November 6, 2014).

60. Burgess Everett, "How Going Nuclear Unclogged the Senate," *Politico,* August 22, 2014. http://www.politico.com/story/2014/08/how-going-nuclear-unclogged -the-senate-110238.html (accessed October 20, 2014).

61. Emmet Bondurant, interviewed by author, August 23, 2014.

62. Stephen Spaulding, interviewed by author, August 25, 2014.

63. Amanda Sakuma, "Poll: Public Support of Filibuster Reform Gathers Speed," MSNBC.com, September 13, 2013. http://www.msnbc.com/msnbc/poll-public -support-filibuster-reform-gat (accessed October 20, 2014); "National Survey of 1,000 Likely Voters [on filibusters]," Rasmussen Reports, July 13, 2013. http://www .rasmussenreports.com/public_content/politics/questions/pt_survey_questions /july_2013/questions_filibusters_july_12_13_2013 (accessed October 20, 2014).

64. Robert Barnes, "Supreme Court Strikes Down Limits on Federal Campaign Dona-tions," *The Washington Post,* April 2, 2014. http://www.washingtonpost.com/politics /supreme-court-strikes-down-limits-on-federal-campaign-donations/2014/04/02 /54e16c30-ba74-11e3-9a05-c739f29ccb08_story.html (accessed October 20, 2014).

65. Bill Mears and Tom Cohen, "Supreme Court allows more private money in election campaigns," *CNN Politics*, April 2, 2014, http://www.cnn.com/2014/04/02/politics /scotus-political-donor-limits/ (accessed October 20, 2014).

66. Robert Barnes, "Supreme Court Strikes Down Limits."

67. Jay Riestenberg, "Explanation of Campaign Finance Provision in Congressional Omnibus Spending Bill," December 10, 2014. http://www.commoncause.org /democracy-wire/explanation-of-campaign-provision-cromnibus.html (accessed December 29, 2014).

68. Martin Gilens, "Inequality and Democratic Responsiveness: Who Gets What They Want from Government?" (unpublished manuscript, August 2004), PDF file. http:// www.princeton.edu/~mgilens/idr.pdf (accessed October 20, 2014). Published as Gilens, Martin, 2005. "Inequality and Democratic Responsiveness." *Public Opinion Quarterly* 69 (5): 778–896.

69. Robert Barnes, "Supreme Court Strikes Down Limits."

70. Nancy Pelosi and John Sarbanes, "Reversing the Grievous Error of *Citizens United,*" *The Washington Post*, February 14, 2014. http://www.washingtonpost.com/opinions /nancy-pelosi-and-john-sarbanes-reversing-the-grievous-error-of-citizens -united/2014/02/04/0f197d0a-8dba-11e3-98ab-fe5228217bd1_story.html (accessed October 20, 2014,).

71. Lawrence Lessig, *Republic Lost: How Money Corrupts Congress—and a Plan to Stop It,* (New York: Hachette Books, 2011), 266.

72. Richard Painter, "A Tax Cut for Democracy/Taxation Only with Representation." *Legal Ethics Forum*, October 26, 2012. http://www.legalethicsforum.com/blog/2012/10 /a-tax-cut-for-democracy.html (accessed October 20, 2014).

73. Lawrence Lessig, *Republic Lost*, 271.

74. Federal Election Commission, "SpeechNOW.org v. FEC, Keating v. FEC: Case Summary," FEC Ongoing Litigation webpage. 2010. http://www.fec.gov/law/litigation/ speechnow.shtml#summary (accessed October 20, 2014).

75. Federal Election Commission, "*Buckley v. Valeo* [litigation summary]," FEC Court Case Abstracts webpage. http://www.fec.gov/law/litigation_CCA_B.shtml#buckley (accessed October 20, 2014).

76. Denver Nicks, "Poll: Support for Campaign Finance Reform Strong in Key Senate Races," *Time.com*, July 31, 2014, accessed October 20, 2014, http://time.com/3063942 /poll-support-for-campaign-finance-reform-strong-in-key-senate-races/

77. S.J. Res. 19, "A Joint Resolution Proposing an Amendment to the Constitution of the United States Relating to Contributions and Expenditures Intended to Affect Elections," 113th Cong. (2013–2014) June 18, 2013. https://www.congress.gov/bill /113th-congress/senate-joint-resolution/19/text/170198 (accessed October 20, 2014).

78. Nicholas Confessore, "Spending Big to Fight Big Donors in Campaigns," *The New York Times*, July 28, 2014. http://www.nytimes.com/2014/07/29/us/spending-big-to -fight-big-donors.html (accessed October 20, 2014).

CHAPTER EIGHT: THE POSSIBILITY

1. Pearl S. Buck, *A Bridge for Passing,* (New York: John Day, 1962).

2. Seabee Memorial, Arlington, Virginia. "Seabee History." http://www .seabeesmuseum.com/history.html (accessed December 29, 2014).

3. Gregory Watson, interviewed by author, August 4, 2014.

4. U.S. House of Representatives. "The Twenty-seventh Amendment," History, Art, and Archives webpage. http://history.house.gov/HistoricalHighlight/Detail/35665 (accessed October 20, 2014).

5. Melissa Bean, interviewed by author, November 12, 2014.

6. Blue Dog Coalition website, "About" page. http://bluedogdems.ngpvanhost.com
/content/about; http://newdemocratcoalition-kind.house.gov/about-me (accessed
August 1, 2014).

7. Becky Yerak, "Melissa Bean to Lead Executives Club of Chicago," *Chicago Tribune*,
March 1, 2011. http://articles.chicagotribune.com/2011-03-01/business/ct-biz-0302
-executive-club-20110301_1_kaarina-koskenalusta-melissa-bean-search
-committee (accessed November 20, 2014).

8. Chuck Todd, *Hardball*, MSNBC, June 6, 2014. http://www.nbcnews.com/id/55390544/
ns/msnbc-hardball_with_chris_matthews/t/hardball-chris-matthews-wednesday-
june-th/#.VExQob5wVQ8 (accessed October 20, 2014).

9. Stephen King (short story *Rita Hayworth and the Shawshank Redemption*) and Frank
Darabont (screenplay), *The Shawshank Redemption*, 1994. Quotation as cited at: http://
www.imdb.com/title/tt0111161/quotes (accessed December 19, 2014). Clip titled
"Andy's Escape" at: https://www.youtube.com/watch?v=SheaMMd8H5g (accessed
December 19, 2014).

POSTSCRIPT
1. National Conference on Citizenship, "Executive Summary," *America's Civic Health
Index*, August 27, 2009. http://ncoc.net/2gp56 (accessed October 15, 2014).

2. "Survey of Young Americans' Attitudes Toward Politics and Public Service," Institute
of Politics, Harvard University, April 30, 2013. http://www.iop.harvard.edu/sites
/default/files_new/spring_poll_13_Exec_Summary.pdf (accessed October 15, 2014).

3. Ron Fournier, "The Outsiders: How Can Millennials Change Washington If They
Hate It?", *The Atlantic*, August 26, 2013, http://www.theatlantic.com/politics
/archive/2013/08/the-outsiders-how-can-millennials-change-washington-if
-they-hate-it/278920/ (accessed October 15, 2014).

4. Jon Stewart, *The Daily Show*, Comedy Central, October 1, 2014.

Index

Page numbers followed by the letter *f* refer to figures